AN EVANGELICAL ON THE LEFT

AN EVANGELICAL ON THE LEFT

By Anna Waldherr

Tate Publishing & *Enterprises*

Published by Tate Publishing & Enterprises, LLC
127 E. Trade Center Terrace | Mustang, Oklahoma 73064 USA
1.888.361.9473 | www.tatepublishing.com

Tate Publishing is committed to excellence in the publishing industry. The company reflects the philosophy established by the founders, based on Psalms 68:11,
"The Lord gave the word and great was the company of those who published it."

Cover design by Kristen Polson
Interior design by Leah LeFlore

Published in the United States of America

ISBN: 978-1-5988694-1-5
07.06.12

In memory of two men of integrity—
each of whom loved his family, his country, and his God:

John P. Healy, Irish Catholic Democrat (1959–2003)
Simon, Jewish Republican (d. 2006)

For if you remain completely silent at this time, relief and deliverance will arise...from another place, but you and your father's house will perish. Yet who knows whether you have come to the kingdom for such a time as this? (Esther 4: 14)

The ultimate measure of a man is not where he
stands in moments of comfort, but where he stands
at times of challenge and controversy.
—Martin Luther King, Jr.

ACKNOWLEDGMENTS

My thanks extend, before all others, to Jesus Christ, my Lord and Savior.

Many people contributed to this book, both directly and indirectly. My sister, Margaret W. Smith, has supported me in all things. Without her, I would not be here at all.

An exceptional history teacher, John F. Corrigan, first introduced me to the law in high school. I remain grateful still. Raymond J. Furey, Esq. helped me to recognize that I have a voice. The list of talented legal professionals whose loyalty and devotion made possible whatever success I have had would fill volumes. My thanks go out to them all.

A good friend since law school, Sandra Meckler, Esq., not only encouraged me to write this book, but read and re-read draft upon draft. Even when she did not agree with me, Sandy patiently provided thoughtful insights and perspective.

Additional friends who read portions of the manuscript; contributed comments and suggestions, or generally cheered me on, included: Linda Levin; Tammy Schneider; Loren Haley, Esq.; Stephanie Kritikos, Esq.; Sarah Young, Esq.; Lilian Philiposian, Esq.; Jodi McCoy; the child of my heart, Retha Reid; and, of course, Stephen Farese, Esq.

My loving thanks go out to all of these and the many others (Marilyn Resnik, Karen Cullen, Esq., and Janet Darden, among them) whose belief in me—for reasons beyond my comprehension—has never wavered, and whose friendship has sustained me over the years.

There are friends whose lives may take them in a different direction from our own, but who remain part of us forever. Should this book ever find its way to any of those people from my own past—Patreece Thompson, MD, Anne Daubert, Esq., Michael Modansky, Esq., to name a few—it carries with it my sincere wishes for their happiness and success.

I am grateful to those who addressed controversial subject matter long before I attempted to do so, and graciously allowed me to incorporate portions of their material into my own. My particular thanks extend to my publishers for their courage and their faith in the project.

Last though hardly least, my gratitude extends to all those who gave their lives that, as Americans, we might have the rights so often taken for granted. It extends likewise to those who examine history in a careful and scholarly fashion, that the truth might be preserved for future generations.

The views expressed in this book are mine alone and should not, in any way, be held against any of the individuals mentioned or sources cited herein.

CONTENTS

INTRODUCTION

Stephen Farese and I met and became friends in a windowless room, measuring some 8'x 10.' It was in those humble surroundings (sometimes crammed with as many as 5 workstations) that I first became aware of the fear with which non-Christians in America have come to view Christians.

Despite a long and reasonably successful career, I had been driven by health, family issues, and financial concerns to what is known as "contract work," i.e. long-term temporary work in which free-lance attorneys assist established firms with large-scale, complex litigation. Stephen, because of prevailing economic conditions in the city of Philadelphia, found himself in the same predicament as my own.

I will never forget the look of horror on Stephen's face when he learned that I was an Evangelical (rather than a "normal" person, as he would have put it)—a fact, by the way, which I did *not* declare with a fanfare of trumpets, the first moment I stepped into the room.

Again and again, I found myself attempting to distinguish my political positions from those of the Bush Administration, notwithstanding its highly touted Christian base. Again and again, I found myself attempting to explain the true nature of Christianity (in the face of what, certainly to non-Christians, seemed glaring evidence to the contrary). And so the idea for this book was conceived.

God moves in mysterious ways. The book for more than a year remained a private joke between Stephen and myself (as in, "You should really write a book!"). It was a recurring tagline to our resounding—and thoroughly satisfying—arguments.

Meanwhile, national events moved on. The CIA scandal broke, reaching into the Vice President's Office. The nation watched in horror the appallingly slow federal and state response to Hurricane Katrina. The NSA monitoring of US citizens without judicial oversight was disclosed. The death toll in Iraq mounted without hint of an exit strategy or even an effective plan for long-term presence. Hope had long-since evaporated of any legitimate explanation for the invasion itself.

On January 10, 2006 my resolve to proceed with the book finally crystallized. When I called one of my oldest and closest friends to let her know, she began to weep. As it turned out, a friend of hers ("Simon" we can call him) had died the day prior. Though unknown to me, Simon had been deeply concerned over precisely the issues this book would address. "If you need a sign from God [to go forward]," my friend said, "this is it." (She is unnamed here to further protect the privacy of Simon's family in their grief.)

John Healy, the other individual to whom the book is dedicated, was a great friend who died three years earlier in New York's Staten Island Ferry disaster. John had a large heart, matchless political instincts, and a terrific sense of humor. John's help—like Simon's—extended to anyone in need, regardless of religion or political party.

Neither John nor Simon would agree with every opinion expressed in this book. That is exactly the point. Our marvelous country is expansive enough to allow for differing opinions. America has thrived on controversy from the outset, but will do so only as long as we continue to honor and defend our precious liberties. And remember that we are brothers.

PART I:

THE POLITICIZATION OF FAITH: ESAU'S TRADE

THE POWER OF THE CROSS V. WORLDLY POWER

If anyone desires to come after Me, let him deny himself, and take up his cross, and follow Me. (Matthew 16: 24)

One and God make a majority. —Frederick Douglass

There are many things I am not: a military strategist, a sociologist, an economist, a historian or an evangelist, let alone a politician. I have no training (or aspirations) along those lines. I write this rather as an American, a Christian, an attorney, and—not least—a woman deeply concerned over the perilous and turbulent times in which we live.

This nation we love is being torn in two—without genuine leadership from either Democrats or Republicans. There is fear in the eyes of our citizens—not fear of an external enemy, but of an internal one wielding immense power, and of inexorable forces over which individuals seem to have no control. The rule of law is increasingly abandoned and social justice a faded ideal. The Christian faith—or what purports to be the Christian faith—has morphed into a hammer for use against political opponents. How many have turned away from Christ because of this, we may never know. The revulsion among non-Christians is, however, palpable.

Some reading this book will view me as a Liberal—horns, tail, pitchfork, and all. Others may call me a Conservative in disguise, not nearly liberal enough by their standards. Some will see me as radical; others as more traditional than they would like.

Labels are just that. I seek to be moderate where I can. This puts me left of some, and right of others. I am—I hope—reform-minded; guided in all things by biblically-grounded faith.

I am most certainly left—socially and economically—of the political movement known as the Christian Right, the group responsible for having elected President George W. Bush to office. The rest you can assess for yourself.

I do not claim to have all the answers. I do know we have serious problems that urgently need to be addressed.

DEAL WITH THE DEVIL

How did we reach this point?

It should be made clear from the outset that what we term the "Christian Right" is not now, nor was it ever, a religion (or even a political movement derived from a single religious group).

Polls from the late 1980s suggest that the majority of the Christian Right were at that time Evangelical Protestants, i.e. those, like myself, holding that the Bible is authoritative and that eternal salvation requires a personal conversion with forgiveness through Jesus Christ (also, known as regeneration or being "born again") [162A].

Initially, many members of the Christian Right were not Evangelical Protestants, and many Evangelical Protestants were not members of the Christian Right. The political movement known as the Christian Right drew its support from politically conservative Jews, Catholics, and Mormons (actually considered a cult by the majority of mainstream Christians), as well as from a few religious skeptics [162B].

Other Evangelical Christians unaffiliated with the Christian Right at the time included:

> [C]onfessional Protestants (especially of Dutch and German extraction), Protestants from the generally apolitical peace churches like the Amish and Old Order Mennonites, fervently fundamentalist Protestants...and black and Latino Protestants who tended to be politically liberal though theologically and culturally evangelical. Evangelical

> outsiders also included millions of born-again Protestants who were generally sympathetic to the political aims of the Christian Right but, as a practical matter, remained more interested in the devotional aims or charitable work of the church than in winning elections [162C].

According to the later 1996 "Survey of American Political Culture" by Dr. James Davidson Hunter, white Evangelical Christians fell primarily in the demographic mainstream, with only somewhat less formal education and a slightly larger proportion of poor than the population as a whole. They were concentrated in the South, nearly 70% residing in small cities, towns, and rural areas [165A]. Their numbers (at least at the time of this survey) were growing in the suburbs of Sunbelt cities, where Conservative culture was being impacted by the influx of newcomers [165B].

Figures as to the exact size of the Christian Right are difficult to pin down. At the time of the Hunter survey, Evangelical Christians as a whole comprised 25% of all registered voters. This was comparable to mainline or non-Evangelical Protestants and to Roman Catholics. It was three times the number of African American Christians who were registered voters, an amazing four times the number of non-registered voters, and twelve times the number of Jewish voters [165E]. Arguably, as many as 35 million voters (counting the "hard-core" members of the Christian Right, along with more loosely-affiliated sympathizers) can be mobilized on key issues [162D].

The Christian Right may have developed in reaction to many factors: growing theological dispute in the seminaries; the teaching of evolutionary theory in the public schools; the threat of Communism; and the massive cultural changes in the 1960s [162E]. Some trace the roots of the movement back as far as the upheavals of the 1920s, the Great Depression, and World War II [164].

Gradually a packaged Christian response came to be articulated by Jerry Falwell, Pat Robertson, Phyllis Schlafly, and certain others. What distinguished this group was their emphasis on a simpler, small-town America of the past [162F]. The title changed as the leadership changed, and agenda matured. "Christian Conservatives" were thrilled by the election of a "born again" Christian in the person of

President Jimmy Carter (then disappointed that Carter was, in fact, the Democrat he proclaimed) [165C]. The "Moral Majority" was enamored of President Ronald Reagan [165D].

Over time, four basic tenets of the Christian Right emerged [162G]:

1. That objective standards of right and wrong exist, and are discernible by anyone honestly interested to know them [162H]. This is consistent with biblical teaching (and applied, both by Evangelicals and the Christian Right, to abortion and to the homosexual lifestyle) [163A]. Unfortunately—in contrast to biblical teaching—opposition to a homosexual lifestyle is often conveyed as bias against men and women who view themselves as gay. What is not biblically mandated at all (but was, nonetheless, incorporated by the Christian Right into its system of beliefs) is an emphasis on capitalism which has corrupted much of the underlying belief system.
2. That the public and private spheres of life are indistinguishable from one another. Influenced by the Enlightenment, mainline Protestants would allow for a distinction [162I].
3. That government's proper role is to "cultivate virtue," not interfere with the market or workplace [162J]. The cultivation of virtue may, in this view, justify interference by government in the most intimate of human affairs. There seems no comprehension on the part of the Christian Right of the irony in this. Here is where we see the emphasis on what have come loosely to be termed "traditional values" [162M] (and again on capitalism, rather than expressly on Christ's teachings). Here is, also, where the Christian Right runs into difficulty with the concept of "separation of church and state [163B]."
4. That only the Judeo-Christian societal tradition is at all legitimate [162K]. This is the "toleration" issue.

These four tenets were all set in the context of a siege mentality. Not only pornography [163C], but the media and public schools [162L] were identified as enemies of the traditional family. Internationally, the Christian Right has taken a pro-defense rather than pacifist stance, equating disarmament with the decline of America [163D]. Many Christians view such a stance at variance with the Gospel.

This brings us to former Richard Nixon mole, Karl Rove. Reams have been written about the role of Rove.

A few examples:

> ...Rove is masterminding the Bush administration's press strategy, but it's far more than a press strategy. It's the central strategy for how the American public understands what George W. Bush is doing to and for America. In an important sense, it *is* the Bush presidency. Rove's methodology largely explains why Bush's popularity remains strong despite the unremittingly awful economy (mounting job losses, weak profits and a three-year stock-market slide) and despite the shambles of the administration's foreign policy (Osama bin Laden still at large, al-Qaeda as dangerous as ever, North Korea more menacing than ever, Israelis and Palestinians as far away from the bargaining table as ever, anti-Americanism rising across the globe and a pending war in Iraq lacking clear justification).
>
> At midterm *USA Today*/CNN/Gallup Poll had Bush's job approval rating falling to 58 percent, dropping below 60 percent for the first time since the September 11 attacks. Under these circumstances, any other president would be in danger of losing his job. But Rove has convinced the press, and therefore the American public, that this presidency is nearly invincible. He has done it with an ingenious blend of chicanery and obfuscation, aided by the Democrats' utter incapability of devising a coherent message in response.
>
> *Use whatever excuse is available at the time to justify the administration's long-term ideological agenda.* Rove is adept at framing Bush's goals as responses to immediate problems, and orchestrating Republican and right-wing policy experts to give the policies enough patina of credibility to satisfy the media. A lousy economy? We need to eliminate taxes on dividends. Never mind that this supposed remedy has nothing to do with stimulating the economy; it's a "jobs

and growth plan for the long term," whatever that means. The continuing threat of terrorism? We need to invade Iraq. Forget that Saddam Hussein has for years been at odds with al-Qaeda or that North Korea is a more potent and dangerous supplier of nuclear components; we must eliminate Hussein's capacity to produce weapons of mass destruction before he uses them.

Count on the American public's (and the media's) inability to remember anything from one year to the next. The Rove machine gave Bush tough talking points on corporate fraud when the newspapers were full of Enron, Global Crossing, WorldCom and Tyco, and when reporters were asking uncomfortable questions about Bush's and Cheney's own corporate dealings. Rove played for time, assuming that warmongering about Iraq (carefully orchestrated to begin just a few months before the midterm elections) would bury the issue. He was right. The administration dragged its feet on reform, and a year out almost nothing has changed. Another example: Rove sold the administration's $1.35 trillion tax cut in 2001 as a way to spur the ailing economy. Obviously it had no such effect, but Rove assumed no one would remember. Right again. Now the White House is selling the administration's 2003 tax cut as a way to spur the ailing economy [253]...

—Reprinted with permission from Robert B. Reich, "The Rove Machine Rolls On," *The American Prospect*, Volume 14, No. 2, February 1, 2003. The American Prospect, 2000 L Street NW, Suite 717, Washington, DC 20036.

As the President's chief political advisor, Rove is involved in every decision coming out of the Oval Office... His relationship with the President is the most profound and complex of all of the White House advisors. And his role creates questions not addressed by our Constitution.

Rove is probably the most powerful unelected person in American history.

> The cause of the war in Iraq was not just about Saddam Hussein or weapons of mass destruction or Al Qaeda links to Iraq. Those may have been the stated causes, but every good lie should have a germ of truth. No, this was mostly a product of Rove's usual prescience. He looked around and saw that the economy was anemic and people were complaining about the President's inability to find Osama bin Laden. In another corner, the neoconservatives in the Cabinet were itching to launch ships and planes to the Mideast and take control of Iraq. Rove converged the dynamics of the times. He convinced the President to connect Hussein to Bin Laden, even if the CIA could not.
>
> This misdirection worked. A Pew survey taken during the war showed 61 percent of Americans believe that Hussein and Bin Laden were confederates in the 9/11 attacks [254].
>
> —Mark Karlin, "Bad Brains," *BuzzFlash*, June 5, 2003.

Presumably with the best of intentions, Christian leaders of the Conservative Right made a decision to support then candidate, George W. Bush in light of his professed opposition to abortion and same-sex marriage. It was, of course, Rove who formulated Bush's campaign of supposed "compassionate conservatism." Thus, naiveté made a bargain with naked ambition.

Following the 2004 election, Christian leaders made comments such as these:

> "Now that values voters have delivered for George Bush, he must deliver for their values. The defense of innocent unborn human life, the protection of marriage, and the nomination and confirmation of federal judges who will interpret the Constitution, not make law from the bench, must be first priorities come January [256]."
>
> —D. James Kennedy, Christian broadcast evangelist whose Sunday services are heard and watched by millions.

> "The President could have paused to thank all those good people who poured in and gave him power again. The GOP has been given four years to deliver on marriage and life and family, and if they fumble it...[we'll] stay home next time [255]."
>
> —James Dobson, founder of Focus on the Family, as reported by *US News & World Report.* Copyright 2004 *US News & World Report*, LP. Reprinted with permission.

Both Kennedy and Dobson are men whom I respect. Unfortunately, they do not seem to recognize that those who disagree with them politically can, nonetheless, be loyal Americans and devout Christians.

RENDER TO CAESAR

America was born in revolution. Protest, if we need to be reminded, is engrained in the American bone and sinew. It is, also, consistent with Christian beliefs. When Jesus was asked whether it was lawful for the conquered Jews to pay taxes to Rome, He requested to be shown a coin.

> *So they brought Him a denarius.*
> *And He said to them, "Whose image and inscription is this?"*
> *They said to Him, "Caesar's."*
> *And He said to them, "Render therefore to Caesar the things that are Caesar's, and to God the things that are God's"* (Matthew 22: 19–21).

Christians are, therefore, under an express obligation to be good citizens. Moral law, however, supersedes civil law. It is this principle which underlies peaceful civil disobedience. This is reflected, as far as back as 1660, in the Quaker "Declaration of Pacifism":

> We utterly deny all outward wars and strife, and fightings with outward weapons, for any and/or under any pretense

> whatever; this is our testimony to the whole world. The Spirit of Christ by which we are guided is not changeable, so as once to command us from a thing as evil, and again to move unto it; and we certainly know, and testify to the world, that the Spirit of Christ, which leads us into all truth, will never move us to fight and war against any man with outward weapons, neither for the kingdom of Christ, nor for the kingdoms of this world [242].

That an individual may view adherence to some civil law as a violation of conscience does not necessarily absolve that individual of the penalty for non-compliance. Moreover, individuals can and do differ on matters of conscience.

As an illustration, not all Christians are pacifists. Witness the Quakers, themselves. Isaac Penington maintained the virtue of the Quaker cause while upholding the right of governments to bear arms in a "just war" (a topic addressed at greater length at Part V, Chapter 2A):

> I speak not this against any magistrate's or people's defending themselves against foreign invasions, or making use of the sword to suppress the violent and evil-doers within their borders...but yet there is a better state which the Lord hath already brought some into, and which nations are to expect to travel towards [243A].
>
> —"Somewhat spoken to a Weighty Question, concerning the Magistrate's Protection of the Innocent" (1661), quoted in Peter Brock, *The Quaker Peace Testimony 1660 to 1914*, p. 27, published by Sessions Book Trust, York, England.

During the early 1700s a number of colonial governments drafted conscription laws exempting Quaker conscientious objectors (generally substituting a fine for service). Many Quakers believed they could not pay even this service fine in good conscience, consequently sustaining heavier penalties.

By the time of the French and Indian War, Pennsylvania Quakers were faced with the difficult choice of withdrawing from politics to preserve their pacifist position or voting for military expenditures. Weighed in the balance were the colony's cherished political and religious freedoms. After the Pennsylvania Assembly passed a supplies bill in 1755 (designating 60,000 pounds "for the king's use") Quakers confiscated the property of other Quakers, even sending objectors to prison. *See*, again, Brock, p. 95 [243B].

ESAU'S TRADE

Jesus said, "*My kingdom is not of this world*" (John 18: 36). Have we forgotten this? We were never promised triumph in this world; we were promised hardship.

As Christians, it is our privilege to follow in the footsteps of our Lord. Those lead us to Calvary, not the White House. "*For what profit is it to a man if he gains the whole world, and loses his own soul?*" (Matthew 16: 26).

For those who do not know the biblical story, two brothers, Jacob and Esau, vied for the inheritance from their father, Isaac. Returning ravenous from the hunt, the elder Esau, properly entitled to the inheritance, thoughtlessly gave up his right to it in exchange for a bowl of stew. Like Esau (Genesis 25: 29–34), the Christian Right traded its rich spiritual heritage for the mere "stew" of political power.

Whatever the motivation, this was a bad trade: the eternal for the ephemeral. A course correction urgently needs to be made before it is too late.

CHRISTIAN PERCEPTION OF AND BY THE NON-CHRISTIAN WORLD

Blessed are you when they revile and persecute you, and say all kinds of evil against you falsely for My sake. (Matthew 5: 11)

We build too many walls and not enough bridges. — Isaac Newton

There is a Bob Dylan song that explains the feelings experienced by persecuted Christians:

> Lord, they ask me how I feel,
> And if my love is real,
> And how I know I'll make it through.
> They look at me and frown.
> They'd like to drive me from this town.
> They don't want me around
> Because I believe in You.
>
> Lord, they show me to the door.
> They say, "Don't come back any more."
> Because I don't feel the way they'd like me to.
> I walk out on my own,
> A thousand miles from home,
> But I don't feel alone
> Because I believe in You.
>
> Don't let me change my heart.
> Keep me where You are,
> Where I will always be renewed.

Lord, what you've given me today
Is worth much more than I could pay,
And no matter what they say
I will believe in You.

I believe in You
When Winter time turns to Summer.
I believe in You
When white turns to black.
I believe in You
Even though we be outnumbered.
Oh, though the earth may shake me,
Though my friends forsake me,
Even that could not make me turn back.

Don't let me drift too far.
Keep me set apart
From the plans they do pursue.
I don't mind the pain.
I don't mind the driving rain.
I know I will sustain
Because I believe in You [244].

—Bob Dylan (COLUMBIA Records).

Scripture puts this concept in the language most familiar to Christians:

> *Beloved, do not think it strange concerning the fiery trial which is to try you, as though some strange thing had happened to you; but rejoice to the extent that you partake of Christ's suffering, that when His glory is revealed, you may also be glad with exceeding joy* (1 Peter 4: 12–13).

This is not masochism. It is the joy experienced despite, not because of, suffering. Pain, grief, and loss remain real.

> *But we have this treasure in earthen vessels, that the excellence of the power may be of God and not of us. We are hard-pressed on every side, yet not crushed; we are perplexed, but not in despair; persecuted, but not forsaken; struck down, but not destroyed—always carrying about in the body the dying of the Lord Jesus, that the life of Jesus also may be manifested in our body* (2 Corinthians 4: 7–10).

Significantly, what is perceived as persecution may actually be the result of earlier abuse, poor self-esteem, or errors in judgment. Discernment is necessary to determine the true sources of and motives for behavior at first viewed by the Christian as persecution.

There are many parts of the world where persecution is real. This is a sampling from *The Voice of the Martyrs* [110B] and *National Review Online* [110C]:

- In China, Christians suffer gravely since Bibles and church property are routinely confiscated. A 28 year old teacher and 34 year old female evangelist were among those beaten to death while in police custody in 2004.
- In Iraq, the Christian minority suffered a wave of persecution in the run up to elections—nearly one million indigenous Chaldo-Assyrians (who speak Aramaic) fleeing into exile. This has historic precedent, since Iraqi Jews constituted a third of the country's population until their persecution last century. Ransom demands for Christians currently average $100,000. A 29 year old who had been kidnapped, was found beheaded in December 2005. Both Sunni and Shiite extremists are harsh toward Christians, throwing acid in the faces of women not wearing the hijab (veil). Unlike the Kurds, the ChaldoAssyrians, thus far, have received no US funding.
- In Afghanistan, public persecution vanished with the Taliban, but the open practice of Christianity is still not permitted without risk of harm from radical Muslims.
- In Indonesia, militant Muslims have initiated a jihad against Christians, killing thousands and destroying hundreds of churches. Areas such as Central Sulawesi and the Maluku Islands where

Christians are in the majority, have been subjected to outright military attacks. For the first time in 50 years, Aceh province was opened to Christian missionaries in early 2005, in connection with tsunami relief efforts. Nonetheless, in May 2005 Muslim radicals detonated two bombs in a marketplace in the Christian city of Tentena killing 23 and injuring 50.

- In Colombia, Marxist guerrilla groups like FARC (Armed Revolutionary Forces of Colombia) demand "war tax" from churches, kidnap individuals for ransom, threaten missionaries, and force Christian school and church closures.
- In India, radical Hindus have become increasingly violent toward Christians. In 2005 several pastors and evangelists were killed. Hindus who convert face ostracism and poverty.
- In the Sudan, a jihad was waged by the Muslim government of the north against the primarily Christian south. In 2005 a peace treaty was signed which ended armed hostilities, but not before a deliberate attempt was made to eliminate the Christian population entirely. This involved the killing of church leaders; destruction of schools, hospitals, churches, and entire Christian villages; torture or death of men, women, and children who refused to convert to Islam.
- In Algeria, Christians have suffered violence from the Islamic Salvation Front, which is known to slit the throats of those not responding to the call for Islamic fundamentalism.
- In Bangladesh, Muslim extremists are reported often to deny Christians access to public wells; force Christians from their homes and beat them.
- In Egypt, Christians are denied political representation and discriminated against in employment.
- In Bhutan, both public worship and evangelism by non-Buddhists are illegal. Christians are denied government benefits there (including public education).
- In Brunei, the celebration of Christmas was outlawed in 1992, and constitutional guarantees of the free practice of religion have been eroding.

This is in sharp contrast to the situation in the United States. Which begs the question, is the persecution which the Conservative Right perceives as present in the United States, genuine or not? I would argue that it is not. Christian Conservative leaders might be shocked to learn that they are, themselves, perceived as smug, arrogant, and insensitive to the rights of others.

Admittedly, there are misconceptions about Christians and Christianity. The politicization of faith has not, however, served to clarify matters. Admittedly, there is bias on the part of some individuals against Christians. Hatred in some form will exist as long as this earth does. Admittedly, there have been (and will be) wrongs inflicted against Christians—as well as against non-Christians. Having been a litigator for over 20 years, I wholeheartedly support the pursuit by Christians—and non-Christians—of their rights in court. [1]

By contrast, the "persecution" in question here arises from a combination of the following:

a) Appropriate criticisms,
b) Differences of opinion over lifestyle, and (pardon my bluntness)
c) Widespread ignorance—by Christians and non-Christians—as to the role of the courts, and the law applicable to freedom of religion and freedom of speech.

Recall that Christ's blessing on the persecuted requires that they be *falsely* reviled for His sake. If your adversaries call you a scoundrel, and you are a scoundrel, you have not been reviled. Consequently, you are not being persecuted. Put another way, truth is an absolute defense to claims of libel and slander.

Nor does the fact your adversaries' opinions differ from your own demonstrate that you are being persecuted. Consider carefully. You may simply be wrong. Before the Civil War, Christian masters instructed their slaves in obedience from the Bible.

Let me digress sufficiently to state that a given lifestyle can certainly be sinful. This does not necessarily mean that criminal penalties should attach. Adultery is both a biblical and civil ground for divorce; nonetheless, we do not criminalize it (unless it rises to the level of bigamy). In other words, the moral analysis may be correct, yet opinions still differ over the practical application.

Freedom of religion and of speech will be addressed at greater length further on. A short civics lesson, however, seems in order on the role of the Courts.

Our Founding Fathers in their wisdom provided in the Constitution for three branches of government: executive, legislative and judicial. The three branches were intended to work with (and, to some degree, against) one another so that a balance might be achieved. The purpose of this dynamic arrangement was to avoid concentrating power in any single branch. Based on the Massachusetts State Constitution drafted by John Adams, this is the system of "checks and balances" with which we are familiar—an attempt to reign in the natural passions and ambitions that drive men and women.

The Judiciary from the outset served an active role. We *want* a Judiciary that is active and involved or the system does not function properly. Chief Justice John Marshall in the landmark case of *Marbury v. Madison* (1803) stated the matter this way:

> It is emphatically the province and duty of the judicial department to say what the law is. Those who apply the rule to particular cases, must of necessity expound and interpret that rule. If two laws conflict with each other, the courts must decide on the operation of each.

At the Supreme Court level, in particular, this has always involved "making law"—a term with which lawyers are entirely familiar and comfortable. A new law is applied to an old situation. An old law is applied in a novel manner. A new concept or new understanding is developed as circumstances change.

The law evolves slowly, to ensure predictability; however, it does evolve as society changes.

That judges may not be elected at certain levels or in certain jurisdictions does not make this a sinister process. For the Christian Right (or any other group) to represent the court system as undemocratic for that reason is entirely incorrect, as well as highly misleading. The French Revolution was mob-driven with a mock Judiciary replacing qualified jurists. We all know the bloody outcome. The Judiciary—recognized for its central role in the administration of justice—was the first institution stripped of its independence and undermined in Nazi Germany. Stripped of its authority, the German Judiciary became a mere rubber stamp for the Nazis.

Is this the path we recommend be followed? Surely not.

It was Supreme Court Justice Learned Hand who said, "Liberty lies in the hearts of men and women; when it dies there, no constitution, no law, no court can save it."

THE END DOES NOT JUSTIFY THE MEANS

While they promise them liberty, they themselves are slaves of corruption... (2 Peter 2:19)

No man is justified in doing evil on the ground of expedience.
—Theodore Roosevelt, Republican President

We Christians are convinced beyond doubt of the truth of our beliefs. The urgency of conveying that truth and the size of the stakes, i.e. eternal life, have made us into zealots. The Christian Right has translated this into the righteousness of its political cause. The two are not, however, identical.

Nowhere in the New Testament does Jesus speak of conversion by force. Any question of pre-destination aside[2], we each of us must make a free will choice whether to accept the offer of salvation or not. That decision may be rationally based. We wrestle over it; we consider all our options. At heart, however, it is as visceral and personal as falling in love. No one can make the critical decision for us. Certainly no one can mandate it.

The Christian Right would argue that it is not attempting to make Christian beliefs mandatory—"merely" the behavior consistent with such those beliefs, as if that were less offensive. This is an attempt to institutionalize so called traditional values.

While it is primarily the responsibility of parents to instill values in their children, in the present climate the above approach is somewhat understandable. We are assaulted by images which a generation ago would have been considered pornographic. These reflect radical changes in society's mores. Reality shows document "sweet 16" parties costing thousands of parent dollars, at which strippers are the entertainment. Jeans are sold by barely clad 14 year olds. Video games depict graphic violence against police officers and prostitutes alike.

How are we to protect our children? So the Christian Right, thinking to be pro-active, sought to align itself with a candidate that would guarantee the restoration of traditional values. There was not so much a plan to impose those values on others (bulldozing civil rights in the process), as there was to defend against what seemed an onslaught of hedonism.

Regrettably, an alliance was made with the wrong individual.

> Everyone admits how praiseworthy it is in a prince to keep faith, and to live with integrity and not with craft. Nevertheless our experience has been that those princes who have done great things have held good faith of little account, and have known how to circumvent the intellect of men by craft, and in the end have overcome those who have relied on their word [226].
>
> —Niccolo Machiavelli, *The Prince*, Chapter XVIII "Concerning the Way in Which Princes Should Keep Faith."

The Bible speaks of the deceptions of false prophets and false teachers this way:

> *Beware of false prophets, who come to you in sheep's clothing, but inwardly they are ravenous wolves. You will know them by their fruits. Do men gather grapes from thorn bushes or figs from thistles?* (Matthew 7: 14–16)
>
> *For when they speak great swelling words of emptiness, they allure through the lusts of the flesh, through lewdness, the ones who have actually escaped from those who live in error...For if, after they have escaped the pollutions of the world through the knowledge of the Lord and Savior Jesus Christ, they are again*

entangled in them and overcome, the latter end is worse for them than the beginning (2 Peter 2: 18, 20).

You will know them by their fruits, the Bible tells us. Consider carefully. What fruit have we seen from the Bush Administration?

These are excerpts from recent headlines:

- President [George W.] Bush took a ride on the Laffer Curve yesterday and espoused a tax-cut theory his father once derided as "Voodoo Economics"..."Well we have a deficit because tax revenues are down," he [the President] said. "Make no mistake about it, the tax relief package that we passed—that should be permanent, by the way—has helped the economy, and that the deficit would have been bigger without the tax-relief package." Most economists since then [the Reagan era] have reached a consensus that while tax cuts have an "economic effect" that partially offsets the lost revenue from tax cuts, the overall result is still lost revenue [69]..."

  —Dana Milbank, "This Time a Bush Embraces 'Voodoo Economics' Theory," *Washington Post*, November 14, 2002 © The Washington Post. Reproduced with permission of the copyright owner.

- *The President's [2006] budget sets a new, record-setting deficit of $427 billion.*[3] It wipes out the $5.6 trillion surplus President Bush inherited...omits the cost of the war in Iraq and Afghanistan ($80 billion), the true cost of making the Bush tax cuts permanent ($1.6 trillion), modifying the Alternative Minimum Tax which is hitting increasing numbers of middle class taxpayers ($774 billion), or the $4.5 trillion cost of his Social Security plan [70]...

  Now, instead of being eliminated, debt held by the public—real debt—is on track to reach $6.5 trillion by 2011 [84].

  —"Soaring Ceilings," Editorial Board, *Washington Post*, November

17, 2004 © The Washington Post Company. Reproduced with permission of the copyright owner.

- *Bush Rewards Wealthiest One Percent with More Tax Cuts Than Bottom 60 Percent Combined* [4]

  Bush wants to make his massive tax cuts permanent, at an estimated price tag of $1.7 trillion over the next ten years. According to the Center for Budget Policy and Priorities (CBPP), when all of the enacted tax cuts are in effect the 1.3 million tax filers who make up the most affluent 1% will receive about twice as much in tax cuts as the 78 million low- and moderate-income filers who comprise the bottom 60% of filers [66].

  —Source: Center on Budget and Policy Priorities, "The Administration's Proposal to Make the Tax Cut Permanent," Joel Friedman, Robert Greenstein, and Richard Kogan, February 4, 2002.

- President Bush yesterday signed into law his third tax cut in as many years...The tax cut that Bush signed...was made possible in part by legislation he quietly signed a day earlier that increased the federal government's debt ceiling by nearly $1 trillion...[T]he White House and Democrats continued to squabble over who would benefit...Democrats said Bush's dividend tax cut would affect only 22 percent of those with incomes below $100,000 [67]...

  —Dana Milbank, "Bush Signs $350 Billion Tax Cut Measure," *Washington Post,* May 29, 2003 © The Washington Post Company. Reproduced with permission of the copyright owner.

- Analysis by the Urban Institute-Brookings Institution Tax Policy Center shows that when fully in effect, the tax cuts enacted in 2001 and 2003 (including AMT relief) will provide an average tax cut of *$650 for the middle* fifth of households, but of *$136,000 for people who make over $1 million a year.* (These figures are in 2004 dollars.) The tax cuts, if made permanent, would provide an estimated $900 billion in tax cuts over the next ten years to the top one percent of households, with more than $600 billion of this amount going to the 0.2 percent of households that make over $1 million a year [241C]. [Emphasis added.]

—The President's Budget: A Preliminary Analysis, *Center on Budget and Policy Priorities,* February 10, 2006.

- *The President's budget calls for drastic cuts in many federal programs and services which will harm millions of children, seniors, and working adults…*[5] Given expected inflation, this would mean a cut, in real terms, of 14 percent by 2010. The budget also reduces or eliminates 150 programs…The cuts are especially harmful for job training, community development programs, social services, veterans' health care, law enforcement, housing, election reform assistance to the states, and child care[73]…
- *Bush's '06 Budget Would Scrap or Reduce 154 Programs.* From $4 million for an agriculture biotechnology program to $18 million for foreign-language assistance for small elementary and secondary schools and $489 million for congressionally earmarked Environmental Protection Agency projects, President Bush's fiscal 2006 budget plan calls for the elimination of or drastic cuts in 154 programs…The president's entire fiscal 2006 budget, not including a supplemental request for military costs related to Iraq and Afghanistan, amounts to $2.57 trillion [247]…

—Judy Sarasohn, "Bush's '06 Budget Would Scrap or Reduce 154 Programs," *Washington Post,* February 22, 2005 © The Washington Post Company. Reproduced with permission of the copyright owner.

Only God can know what is in a man's heart. "…*Man looks at the outward appearance, but the Lord looks at the heart*" (1 Samuel 16: 7).

Whether George W. Bush is a sincere man misled, the slave of corruption, or a wolf in sheep's clothing, the impact on our nation has been equally detrimental.

PART II:

SEPARATION OF CHURCH AND STATE: THEOCRACY AND HUMAN FALLIBILITY

RELIGIOUS FREEDOM HISTORICALLY

I am the Lord your God, who brought you out of the land of Egypt, out of the house of bondage. (Exodus 20: 1)

Everyone ought to worship God according to his own inclinations, and not to be constrained by force. —Flavius Josephus (37 AD - 100 AD), *Life*

Our country was founded by those seeking, among other things, religious freedom—for themselves, at least, if not for their neighbors. This is reflected in the country's earliest writings and enshrined in the First Amendment to the Constitution.

> Congress shall make no law respecting an establishment of religion, or prohibiting the free exercise thereof; or abridging the freedom of speech, or of the press; or the right of the people peaceably to assemble, and to petition the Government for a redress of grievances.
>
> —First Amendment, US Constitution, Adopted December 15, 1791.

All fifty state constitutions (1776–1959) make reference to God (using terms such as Almighty God, the Author of Existence, the Creator, Divine Providence, Great Legislator of the Universe, Supreme Being, Sovereign Ruler of the Nations, and Supreme Ruler of the Universe). *See*, **Appendix I**.

Religion was, thus, a matter of importance and the Creator viewed as the ultimate source of moral values (themselves, seen as the basis of civil laws).

> Those people who will not be governed by God will be ruled by tyrants.
>
> —William Penn.

We assume from our vantage some 385 years later—and with the limited knowledge of history for which Americans are notorious—that religious freedom was a foregone conclusion. This was hardly the case.

A brief review of events may put this in better perspective.

SPAIN

As of 1381 half the world's Jews lived in Spain, serving in essential but secondary scientific and economic positions. The Spanish Inquisition was introduced the same year. A century of forced conversions began in 1391, with most Spanish Jews converting (at least publicly) to Catholicism [1A].

Early in 1492, the remaining Spanish Jews were given a choice to convert or leave the country. Under duress, the majority converted. Most of those who did not, emigrated to Portugal. They were permitted to take what they could carry, but forced to abandon theirs lands [1B]. The same year, Columbus left Spain for the New World. Among his crew of 87 was a Jewish sailor named, Luis de Torres [1C]. Columbus' second voyage, in 1493, was actually funded by property left behind by the Jews whom Spain had expelled. Some idea of the scope of the abandoned lands can be garnered from the fact they funded a crew of 1,500 [2].

By the 1600s no one was allowed to leave Spain for the colonies, or obtain a government job there, without establishing "*limpieza de sangre*"—blood purity—for four generations (listing parents, grandparents and great-grandparents without known Jewish ancestry) [3]. The Inquisition, also, crossed over to the New World. According to Mathias de Bocanegra, once Conquistadors had left their bloody mark, New World Inquisitors did not trouble themselves over vestigial Aztec or Inca practices. Technically ferreting out covert Protestants and Muslims, the Inquisitors' concentration remained focused on Jews [3A].

ENGLAND

The majority of English Jews came over from France with William the Conqueror in 1066. At the coronation of Richard the Lionhearted in 1189, they were refused entry, despite bringing lavish gifts. Many were killed in mob riots. King John in 1210 imprisoned and tortured the wealthy Jews in his realm, extorting ransom for their release [43E and 43I]. In 1218, Jews were required to wear a cloth "badge of shame" [43A] of yellow felt or taffeta, in the shape of the tablets of Moses [43F].

Jewish communities throughout Europe suffered from "blood libels" (false tales of Christian children being ritually murdered) [43D and 43H]. Edward I finally expelled Jews from England altogether in 1290. The penalty for any remaining behind was death [43C]. At least 16,000 left for France and Belgium [43G]. The following year, however, Philip the Fair expelled from France all English Jews not profitable to the Crown. Yet more poignant, the French expulsion was announced on "*Tisha BaAv*," the anniversary of the destruction of the first and second Temples [43B].

In England, Catholic Mary Tudor, the daughter of King Henry VIII and Catherine of Aragon, so vigorously persecuted Protestants when she assumed the throne that she earned the nickname "Bloody Mary." A popular volume by Anglican bishop, George Carleton, described unsuccessful Catholic conspiracies against her Protestant successors Queen Elizabeth I (1558–1603) and King James I (1603–1625) [2A].

Until overshadowed by Guy Fawkes' scheme to blow up the King in Parliament in 1605, the most famous of these plots was the attempt to assassinate Queen Elizabeth "by the means of Doctor Lopez, a Jew, the Queen's physician, for fifty thousand crowns promised him [2C]." An engraving of Roderigo Lopez (a Portuguese forced convert and refugee, described as "compounding to poyson the Queene") portrays him as asking, "How much will you give?"—the question directed to a double agent for Spain and the Earl of Essex, in the sting operation that resulted in Lopez' execution [2D].

Shakespeare preserved the resulting anti-Semitism for us in "*The Merchant of Venice*" [2B] where Shylock asks:

> If you prick us do we not bleed?
> If you tickle us do we not laugh?
> If you poison us do we not die?
> And if you wrong us shall we not revenge [2E]?

A tenuous compromise in the form of the Elizabethan Settlement of 1559 was ultimately reached between Catholics and Reformed Church supporters [22]. Though Elizabeth I opposed Catholicism, she did not favor Protestant extremism either. Her solution was to create a middle way ("*via media*"). Under the Elizabethan Settlement, a new edition of the *Book of Common Prayer* was created which allowed as many different interpretations as possible. Maximum inclusiveness continues to be an important goal for the Anglican Church [22A].

Nonetheless, dissent was fanatically monitored. Moreover, remnants of Catholicism remained of which radical Protestants wished to "purify" the church. For this they became known as Puritans. John Udall, an early Puritan known for his humanitarianism and humor, was sent by the Archbishop of Canterbury to the White Lion prison for "wicked, scandalous and seditious libel," i.e. Puritanism. Udall died there in 1593, the first Puritan martyr [11A].

Henry Jessey—himself, a strict observer of Jewish law as well as founder of the Baptist Church in England—and John Dury, a non-sectarian, were the key activists in the Ecumenical Millenarian Movement which gave rise to the modern concept of toleration. It was through their lobbying efforts in 1656 that Jews were again tolerated in England after a 366-year hiatus [24A].

This was the same year Dury's *A Case of Conscience, Whether it be Lawful to Admit Jews into a Christian Common-wealth?* was published. Dury based "Civill Liberty" on 1 Corinthians 10:32: "*Give no offense, either to the Jews or to the Greeks or to the church of God...*" concluding that it "may be a sin to refuse them [Jews] admittance..."

He, nonetheless, proposed the following restrictions on Jews:

> ...Not to blaspheme the person of Jesus Christ...Not to seduce any, or go about to make proselytes...Not to profane the Christian Sabbath. . [E]xpedient that they live by themselves and that their worship be performed in their own tongue [24B]...
>
> —John Dury, *A Case of Conscience, Whether it be Lawful to Admit Jews into a Christian Common-wealth?* (London: Printed for Richard Wodenothe, 1656). Rare Books Division, The New York Public Library, Astor, Lenox and Tilden Foundations.

THE NEW WORLD

By 1620, pressure from the dominant Church of England had driven Puritans and Pilgrims to American shores [11B].

The leading Puritan figures, William Bradford of Plymouth, John Cotton of Massachusetts, and John Davenport of New Haven, were all "Hebraists," committed to the concept that the Law of Moses was as binding on Christians as on Jews.

In 1636, John Cotton and others were invited to contribute to the codification of Massachusetts law. Cotton's goal was to recreate a pure Israelite theocracy, purged of any trace of English common law. With that in mind, he submitted a code entitled "Moses, his Judicials," i.e. Moses' judicial (as opposed to ritual) laws [12].

This code called for the *death penalty* in cases of:

> ...blasphemy; idolatry; witchcraft; perjury; seducing others to heresy; profaning the Lord's day; betraying the country; reviling governor and council; sedition; rebellious children, whether they continue in riot or drunkennesse (sic) after due correction from their parents; murder; adultery; incest; unnaturall filthinesse (sic), man with man or woman with woman; buggery; pollution of a woman known to be in her flowers; whoredom of a maiden in her father's house; man stealing; and false witness bearing [13].

—John Cotton, *An abstract of the Lawes of New England As They are Now Established* (London: Printed for F. Coules and W. Ley, 1641). Rare Books Division, The New York Public Library, Astor, Lenox and Tilden Foundations.

Thankfully, it was rejected.

Instead, in 1641, the "*Body of Liberties*" was adopted by Massachusetts. Drafted by Nathaniel Ward, another Hebraist, this drew both on common and Mosaic law [14]. In Plymouth, however, Mosaic law was accorded the status of principal authority [15]. In the colony of New Haven (Connecticut) a majority of all statutes ever enacted derived from biblical authority [16].

The first direct attack on New England theocracy came from Roger Williams, the Salem minister who decided it was not the province of Massachusetts courts to enforce conformity of belief on behalf of the colony's religious establishment [17A]. Williams defined freedom of conscience (which he called "soul liberty") as the freedom of each person to follow his or her own heart, in matters of faith [206D]. Though Thomas Jefferson is often credited, it was Williams who first introduced the concept of separation of church and state, coining the phrase "wall of separation" [17B].

For his "new and dangerous opinions against the authority of magistrates," Williams was banished from the colony by the Massachusetts General Court in 1635 [18]. He, thereafter, founded Rhode Island, the first colony with no established church. Jews, Quakers, and others not welcome elsewhere found a home there [206E]. Some historians, also, argue that Williams' writings influenced the Enlightenment philosopher, John Locke, an important source for Jefferson's views on religious liberty [206F].

Around 1609, Dutch explorers first encountered the Iroquois in the eastern woodlands. According to Lewis H. Morgan and Ely S. Parker, the religion of the Iroquois Nation (*"Gai'wiio"*) was proclaimed by their prophet, Handsome Lake [8B]. Replacing older beliefs, it was monotheistic, characterized by belief in an all-powerful, caring Creator (*"Hadio"yâ?'geono""*) a/k/a the "Great Spirit." Worship and gratitude were extended for the Great Spirit's protection. Evil was personified as the brother of the Great Spirit or "the Evil-minded." Diverse other Native American religions existed, as well.

> ...the sacred hoop of my people was one of the many hoops that made one circle, wide as daylight and as starlight, and in the center grew one mighty flowering tree to shelter all the children of one mother and one father [8A].
>
> —Black Elk, Oglala Sioux Medicine Man.

In the fall of 1654 the first group of Jews arrived—via Portugal—in the Dutch city of New Amsterdam (later to become New York) [4]. This is not meant to imply that Portugal was a safe haven for the Jews. According to Amsterdam's Chief Rabbi Mortera, the Portuguese were the Jews' worst enemy, "a people accustomed to take intense pleasure in making human sacrifices" of Jews [5].

The Minutes of the New Amsterdam Burgomasters and Schepens already by 1655 indicate that a Jewish shopkeeper named Abram de la Sina was deprived of his trade and fined six hundred florins, for having kept his store open during the Sunday sermon [6]. Peter Stuyvesant the same year wrote: "Jewish liberty here is very detrimental, because the Christians cannot compete against them; and if they receive liberty, the Lutherans and papists cannot be refused [7]."

Matters, however, improved. A report made on July 23, 1658 to the West India Company Directors by the New Netherlands Council reads, in part:

> We desire not to judge lest we be judged, neither to condemn lest we be condemned, but rather let every man stand and fall to his own Master. The law of love, peace and liberty in the states extending to Jews, Turks, and Egyptians, as they are considered the sons of Adam, which is the glory of the outward state of Holland, so our desire is not to offend one of his little ones, in whatsoever form, name or title he appears in, whether Presbyterian, Independent, Baptist or Quaker, but shall be glad to see anything of God in any of them, desiring to do unto all men as we desire all men

> should do unto us, which is the true law both of Church and State [10].
>
> —New Netherland Council Report to West India Company Directors, 1657–8, July 23, 1658. New Netherland Papers, The New York Public Library, Astor, Lenox and Tilden Foundations.

Membership in the Dutch Reformed Church was a prerequisite for membership in the self-governing corporation of New Amsterdam [8]. The prohibition against public worship by other than the Dutch Reformed Church remained in place throughout the life of New Amsterdam. However, restrictions on Jewish trade were ultimately lifted [9]. The Minutes of the New Amsterdam Burgomasters and Schepens reflect that by 1660 one, Levy, was a respected town elder; a founder of the butchers' guild, as well as "granted special exemption from slaughtering hogs and allowed to take oath in Jews' manner." The owner of a butcher shop on Wall Street and tavern, Levy in 1672 supported religious diversity by way of a large loan toward erection of the first Lutheran church in New York City [7A].

William Penn in the charter he drafted for the original Quaker colonists of New Jersey, described a place where no one would have:

> ...power or authority to rule over men's consciences in religious matters [26A].
>
> —William Penn, *The Frame of the Government of the Province of Pennsilvania in America* (London, 1682). Rare Books Division, The New York Public Library, Astor, Lenox and Tilden Foundations.

Unfortunately, the early Quakers were as hostile to Jews as the majority of other radical English Protestants were [19].

In 1681, Penn obtained a massive land grant as repayment of a debt owed to his father by King Charles II. He wrote the constitution for this "holy experiment" in planting "the seed of a nation." According to Article 35:

> [A]11 persons living in this province who confess and acknowledge the one almighty and eternal God to be the

> creator, upholder and ruler of the world and that hold themselves obliged in conscience to live peaceably and justly in *civil society*, shall in no wayes (sic) be molested or prejudiced for their religious perswasion (sic) or practice in matters of faith and worship; nor shall they be compelled at any time to frequent or maintain any religious worship, place or ministry whatever [26C].
>
> —William Penn, *The Frame of the Government of the Province of Pennsilvania in America* (London, 1682). Rare Books Division, The New York Public Library, Astor, Lenox and Tilden Foundations.

Penn's *Frame of Government of the Province of Pennsilvania (sic) in America* provides for an elective legislature, the vote limited by a small property qualification. Despite Article 35's rejection of religious prejudice, however, Article 34 required that:

> ...all who have the right [through property ownership] to elect such members shall be such as profess faith in Jesus Christ and that are not convicted of ill fame [26B].
>
> —William Penn, *The Frame of the Government of the Province of Pennsilvania in America* (London, 1682). Rare Books Division, The New York Public Library, Astor, Lenox and Tilden Foundations.

The first important Quaker theologian to settle in America was George Keith (in New Jersey from 1685, then Philadelphia from 1689). In the City of Brotherly Love, Keith wound up in the dock. The Philadelphia establishment maintained that Quakerism allowed its members complete freedom in matters of belief. When Keith disagreed, he was tried for sedition [20].

Jewish atheist Benedict de Spinoza in *Tractatus Theologico-Politicus* (circa 1700), a critical review of the Hebrew Bible and the institutions of ancient Israel, concluded that "in a free commonwealth, every man may think as he pleases and say what he thinks [21]."

By the late 17th century, Jews could count on toleration as resident aliens in England or in colonies such as New York. They could not, however, become citizens. Among the disadvantages (or "disabilities") entailed in this status, they were required (like other aliens) to pay a much higher rate of import duty [25].

It was in the American colonies, where the English government was eager to encourage settlement (especially of entrepreneurs), that it attempted to address this problem first [32A]. The Colonial Naturalization Act of 1740 allowed colonial authorities to waive the Sacramental Test for "persons professing the Jewish religion who have inhabited or resided, or shall inhabit or reside for the space of seven years or more in any of His Majesty's colonies in America [32B]." In 1753, the American experiment was deemed successful and—through enactment of the so-called "Jew Bill"—it was extended to the mother country [32C].

The Jew Bill continued for only a few months, having been received by England "with horror and execration," historians tell us [33]. The legislators who had voted for it were vilified [29]. Though citizenship was ultimately granted those of Jewish extraction, it was not until 1858 (after 10 legislative attempts by the House of Commons) that England's House of Lords finally agreed to allow Jews elected to municipal office to omit the words "on the true faith of a Christian" from the oath of office, thereby permitting them to take their duly won seats [36].

REVOLUTIONARY WAR

This brings us to the Revolutionary War period.

Between 1728 and 1790 a series of religious revivals took place known as the "Great Awakening [206M]." The message of the Great Awakening was salvation through Christ alone. This produced a deeply personal and emotional reaction on the part of thousands of Americans.

Similar to our own today in spirit, Evangelical ardor in the 18th Century apparently had the opposite political effect. Cutting across denominational lines, it undermined support for established churches, and created a groundswell in favor (rather than against) the "separation of church and state" by Baptists, Presbyterians, Quakers and others [206N].

Patriot, Patrick Henry (renowned for his statement, "As for me, give me liberty or give me death!" [99]) made this lesser known assertion from the gallows:

> It cannot be emphasized too strongly or too often that this great nation was founded, not by religionists, but by Christians; not on religions, but on the Gospel of Jesus Christ. For this very reason peoples of other faiths have been afforded asylum, prosperity, and freedom of worship here.
>
> —Patrick Henry, upon his hanging March 23, 1775.

Fifty-six men from the original thirteen colonies participated in the Second Continental Congress and signed the Declaration of Independence. Pennsylvania sent nine delegates to the congress, followed by Virginia with seven and Massachusetts and New Jersey with five. Connecticut, Maryland, New York, and South Carolina each sent four delegates. Delaware, Georgia, New Hampshire, and North Carolina each sent three. Rhode Island, the smallest colony, sent only two delegates to Philadelphia [27A].

Nine of the signers were immigrants. The average age of a signer was 45. The oldest delegate was Benjamin Franklin of Pennsylvania, who was 70 when he signed the Declaration. The youngest was Thomas Lynch, Jr., of South Carolina, who was 27 years of age [27B].

Eighteen of the signers were merchants or businessmen, fourteen were farmers, and four were doctors. Forty-two signers had served in their colonial legislatures. Twenty-two were lawyers—although William Hooper of North Carolina was "disbarred" when he spoke out against the Crown—and nine were judges. Stephen Hopkins had been Governor of Rhode Island [27C].

Although two others had been clergymen previously, John Witherspoon of New Jersey was the only active clergyman to attend. Almost all were Protestant Christians. Charles Carroll of Maryland was the only Roman Catholic signer [27D] (someone forgotten in the rhetoric of the anti-Catholic "Know-Nothing" Party by mid-19th Century) [206O].

There was, nonetheless, a Jewish presence in the colonies. Revolutionary Charleston was the largest American Jewish community of the Federal Era. The South Carolina General Assembly was the first legislative body in America in which a Jewish individual held elected office. Francis Salvador was a member of the Provincial Congress and its successor, the General Assembly, until his death (and scalping), in a battle with Tories and Indians, in 1776 [23].

Fifteen of the signers of the Declaration of Independence later participated in their states' constitutional conventions [27E]. Six—Roger Sherman, Robert Morris, Benjamin Franklin, George Clymer, James Wilson, and George Reed—signed the United States Constitution. Elbridge Gerry of Massachusetts attended the federal convention, but refused to sign the Constitution. He did later support it [27F].

After the Revolution, thirteen of the signers of the Declaration went on to become governors; eighteen served in their state legislatures. Sixteen became state or federal judges. Seven became members of the United States House of Representatives, and six became United States Senators. James Wilson and Samuel Chase became Justices of the United States Supreme Court [27G].

Thomas Jefferson, John Adams, and Elbridge Gerry each became Vice President. John Adams and Thomas Jefferson became President, as well [27H].

When the Declaration of Independence declared it "self-evident" that all men are created equal, that they are endowed by their Creator with certain inalienable Rights, it anticipated an equality that no nation had ever acknowledged or implemented [205]. Ten of the states proceeded rapidly to adopt constitutions that denied civil rights to non-Christians. Two others simply retained the laws of their colonial past that excluded non-Christians from political participation [28A].

New York, however, was different [28G].

The New York State Constitution was drafted in 1776 by then 30-year-old John Jay who, according to Jefferson, wielded "the finest pen in America." It was adopted on April 20, 1777. Article 38 read:

> And whereas we are required by the benevolent principles of rational liberty, not only to expel civil tyranny, but also to guard against that spiritual oppression and intolerance, wherewith the bigotry and ambition of weak and wicked

> priests and princes have scourged mankind: This Convention doth further, in the name and by the authority of the good people of this State, Ordain, Determine and Declare, that the free exercise and enjoyment of religious profession and worship, without discrimination or preference, shall for ever hereafter be allowed within this State to all mankind. Provided that the liberty of conscience hereby granted, shall not be so construed as to excuse acts of licentiousness or justify practices inconsistent with the peace or safety of this State [28B].[6]
>
> —*The Constitution of the State of New York* (Fishkill, NY: Printed by Samuel Loudon, 1777). Rare Books Division, The New York Public Library, Astor, Lenox and Tilden Foundations.

Virginia enacted religious equality in 1785 and others followed suit, the process being expedited in 1787 by Article Six of the United States Constitution, which provided that "no religious Test shall ever be required as a Qualification to any Office or public Trust under the United States," and in 1791 by the first provision of the Bill of Rights: "Congress shall make no law respecting an establishment of religion, or prohibiting the free exercise thereof." The only holdouts were Rhode Island, North Carolina and New Hampshire [28C and 28E].

For the first time in history, a nation had abolished one of the most powerful tools of the state for oppressing religious minorities [206G].

Meanwhile, Founding Father, James Monroe, in a draft memorandum on the proposed French Constitution, stressed that American style nation-building required a Bill of Rights. Monroe noted that among "the most important objects of such an instrument…it should more especially comprise a doctrine in favor of the equality of human rights; of liberty of conscience in matters of religious faith, of speech and of the press [37A]." Monroe had argued successfully in Virginia—at the tender age of 25—that religious liberty was not a concession by the state (or the established church), but a natural right of every citizen [206L].

Some twenty years after the Declaration of Independence—in

what was not his finest hour—Monroe as President James Madison's Secretary of State wrote to Mordecai Noah, the first American Jew to achieve national stature:

> At the time of your appointment as Consul at Tunis, it was not known that the religion which you profess would form any obstacle to the exercise of your Consular functions. Recent information...proves that it would produce a very unfavourable effect. In consequence of which, the President has deemed it expedient to revoke your commission [37B].
>
> —James Monroe, "Notes on a Constitution for France" (Paris, 1795). James Monroe Papers, Manuscripts and Archives Division, The New York Public Library, Astor, Lenox and Tilden Foundations.

Monroe, in this context, made the statement: "...the government of the United States of America is *not*, in any sense, founded on the Christian religion [37C]..." [Emphasis added.]

CIVIL WAR

Though we revere their names, none of the Founding Fathers was African American. The countless Africans enslaved to build the economic foundations of this country slipped anonymously into history. The religions they had practiced included Akan, Ifa, La Reglas de Congo, Mami Wata, Orisha, and Vodoun ("Voodo") [40A]. A small percentage were African Muslims, having adopted ancestor worship and family deities into Islamic rituals [40B].

By the 1780s, Methodists and other Christian denominations had taken strong stands against slavery which was considered "contrary to the laws of God, man and nature, and hurtful to society, contrary to the dictates of conscience and pure religion." In or around 1784 Methodists "promised to excommunicate all Methodists not freeing their slaves within two years." In less than 40 years, however, the Methodist Church had been co-opted by Southern culture on the question of race and was urging, in place of emancipation, a "mission" to the slaves [41A].

With a very few exceptions, the purpose of this mission was *not* the welfare of the slaves. Large slaveholders (like Rev. Charles Colcock Jones who compiled a religious primer for slaves) worked to indoctrinate slaves in a blighted version of Christianity as a means of forestalling insurrection [41C]. As concern for preservation of the South's way of life increased, whites demanded their legislatures pass laws restricting the rights of African Americans to literacy, free assembly, and worship [41B].

Among the most staunch advocates of the Southern cause was Judah Benjamin, another Jew to play a significant role in American public life. A senator for Louisiana from 1852 (and termed by Jefferson Davis, "the brains of the Confederacy"), Benjamin was in March 1861 appointed Attorney General for the Confederacy, then Secretary of War for the South. Rather than admit the futility of the Southern cause, Benjamin resigned in March 1862 in response to groundless charges of unfitness to conduct the war by reason of his religion [38].

The first attempt by the Jewish community in the US to lobby for the advancement of Jewish rights at the federal level, involved an act of Congress passed in July 1861. This authorized the officers of any Union regiment to elect their own chaplain, with the proviso that he be "a regularly ordained minister of some Christian denomination [35A]."

Despite the measure's obvious discrimination against Jews, the opposition of controversial Ohio congressman, Clement Vallandigham to its constitutionality had been fruitless. Nonetheless, the officers of the largely Jewish 5th Pennsylvania Cavalry ("Cameron's Dragoons") commanded by Colonel Max Friedman, elected a Jewish chaplain. Word reached the Secretary of War who called for the resignation of the chaplain (neither a Christian nor an ordained minister, instead operating a Philadelphia liquor store) [35B].

To minimize the grounds for objection, Cameron's Dragoons then elected Arnold Fischel, and the Board of Delegates of American Israelites sent him to Washington. Lincoln was readily persuaded. Through Fischel's efforts and with Lincoln's support, Congress in

July 1862 amended the language of the act to read "some religious denomination" instead of "some Christian denomination" [35C].

Rhode Island in 1843, and finally after the Civil War the last two states, North Carolina in 1868 and New Hampshire in 1877, acquiesced to religious equality [28D].

With all this as background, we turn now to examine the future of religion and religious freedom in a country of diverse faiths.

RELIGIOUS FREEDOM IN A COUNTRY OF DIVERSE FAITHS

Many nations shall be joined to the Lord in that day, and they shall become My people.' (Zechariah 2: 11)

Each one prays to God according to his own light. —Mahatma Gandhi

It has become politically correct on the Left to take the position that ours is a nation in whose history religion played no role, and in whose future religion has no part. The former is obviously incorrect. The latter has yet to be decided.

While religion was a source of conflict, it, also, inspired and strengthened our forebears.

> When you rise in the morning, give thanks for the light, for your life, for your strength. Give thanks for your food and for the joy of living. If you see no reason to give thanks, the fault lies in yourself.
>
> —Tecumseh, Shawnee War Chief (1768–1813).

> Whereas it is the duty of all nations to acknowledge the providence of Almighty God, to obey His will, to be grateful for His benefits, and humbly implore His protection, and favors...Now, therefore, I do recommend and assign Thursday the 26th day of November next, to be devoted by the

> people of these states to the service of that great and glorious Being, who is the Beneficent Author of all the good that was, that is, or that will be that we may all unite in rendering unto Him our sincere and humble thanks for His kind care and protection of the people of this country, and for all the great and various favors which He has been pleased to confer upon us.
>
> —First Thanksgiving Proclamation, George Washington, 1789.

The "Second Great Awakening" in the 19th Century led to urban social work, schooling for poor children, and the Abolitionist Movement [206I]. African American churches provided much of the moral and political leadership of the Civil Rights Movement [206J]. Unitarians, Quakers, and Reform Jews have been involved with the peace movement and advocacy for social justice [206K].

Along with Orthodox, Reform, Conservative, and Hasidic Jewish sects and numerous Christian denominations (including Baptist, Lutheran, Catholic, Methodist, Presbyterian, Pentecostal, Episcopalian/Anglican, Eastern Orthodox, Mennonite, Reformed/Dutch Reformed, Quaker, Jewish Christian/Messianic Jewish and more), the American population today includes Muslim, Hindu, Buddhist, Wiccan, Unitarian, Scientology, Deist, Tao, and New Age believers—not to mention those who doubt or deny the existence of God, altogether. There are today, in fact, some 3,000 religious groups in this country [206A].

These men and women are all searching for meaning in their lives; for answers to the ultimate questions with which human beings have grappled since the beginning of time. How did we get here? What is our place in the universe? Is there purpose to our lives? How do we respond to suffering and injustice? Do we have an obligation toward others? Is there a life beyond this one?

Each individual's search is unique. My own—for reasons I will not dwell on here—led from Catholicism, through atheism, to non-denominational Christianity and (by God's grace alone) the "born again" experience, which restored my faith and changed my life forever.

Moreover, each individual has an inherent God-given right (protected by the Constitution and Bill of Rights) to pursue that search.

> Government must permit the expression of beliefs and faith—even those offensive to others—while remaining neutral on the appropriateness of those beliefs.
>
> —Charles "Chuck" Colson (former Watergate Conspirator) and Pat Nolan of Prison Fellowship.

This is far different from any statement that truth is relative or that each of us has his or her own truth. Jesus said, "'*I am the way, the truth, and the life. No one comes to the Father, but through Me*'" (John 14: 6). We know, too, that "...*God has dealt to each one a measure of faith*" (Romans 12: 3).

Though Christians (like Jews) are instructed to serve as light to the world—*"For you were once darkness, but now you are light in the Lord. Walk as children of light...in all goodness, righteousness, and truth..."* (Ephesians 5: 8–9)—we have often failed at this task. Best estimates, for instance, place the total number killed in the Crusades around 1.5 million [45A]. Some place it as high as 5 million [45B].

From Northern Ireland to Bosnia, religious differences add to the daily toll of death and destruction around the globe [206H]. The use of faith as a sword, rather than a shield has been a grievous error on Christians' part—one we should not repeat in our day.

The "free exercise" of religion (meaning the freedom of every citizen to "reach, hold, practice and change beliefs according to the dictates of conscience" [206C]) allows individuals and groups to speak out on issues of moral concern in the public interest [206Q]. Attacks on those whose faith or values differ from our own as unfit to hold office may be constitutionally protected, but are not in accord with the spirit of religious freedom [206D].

Despite or because of our diverse culture, some today seek to establish *by law* (or in revisionist terms to "re-establish") a Christian nation. Others—equally revisionist—seek to exclude religion from public life entirely, ignoring the enormous contribution by Judeo-

Christian concepts of morality to American ideals. Neither of these views is consistent with religious freedom [206P].

Nor are Christians to sit in judgment of others.

> *"I did not come to judge the world but to save the world"* (John 12: 47).
>
> *"Judge not, that you be not judged. For with what judgment you judge, you will be judged; and with the measure you use, it will be measured back to you. And why do you look at the speck in your brother's eye, but do not consider the plank in you own eye?...Hypocrite! First remove the plank from your own eye, and then you will see clearly to remove the speck from your brother's eye"* (Matthew 7: 1–3, 5).

The Williamsburg Charter (drafted by members of America's leading faiths, in conjunction with political, academic, and educational leaders) was signed in 1988 by former Presidents Gerald Ford and Jimmy Carter, as well as nearly 200 national figures [206R]. It reads, in relevant part:

> We affirm that a right for one is a right for another and a responsibility for all. A right for a Protestant...is a right for a Jew is a right for a Humanist...is a right for a Muslim is a right for a Buddhist—and for the followers of any other faith within the wide bounds of the republic.
>
> That rights are universal and responsibilities mutual is both the premise and the promise of democratic pluralism. The First Amendment in this sense, is the epitome of public justice and serves as the golden rule for civic life. Rights are best guarded and responsibilities best exercised when each person and group guards for all others those rights they wish guarded for themselves [206S].

When Christianity first came into being, a handful of men and women faced a world of skeptical unbelievers with nothing more than their knowledge of the risen Lord and their faith. In some respects, the situation now is similar to that in the First Century.

The Apostle John explained:

> *Now by this we know that we know Him, if we keep His commandments...For this is the love of God, that we keep His commandments* (1 John 2: 3; and 5: 3).
>
> *...everyone who loves is born of God and knows God. He who does not love does not know God, for God is love. In this the love of God was manifested toward us, that God has sent His only begotten Son into the world, that we might live through Him. In this is love, not that we loved God, but that He loved us and sent His Son to be the propitiation for our sins. Beloved, if God so loved us, we also ought to love one another* (1 John 4: 7–11).

Our imperative remains the same:

> *"'You shall love the Lord your God with all your heart, with all your soul, and with all your mind.' This is the first and great commandment. And the second is like it: 'You shall love your neighbor as yourself.' On these two commandments hang all the Law and the Prophets"* (Matthew 22: 37–40).
>
> *A new commandment I give to you, that you love one another; as I have loved you...By this all will know that you are My disciples...*(John 13: 34).

THE TEMPTATION TO PRIDE

By pride comes nothing but strife… (Proverbs 13: 10)

Nearly all men can stand adversity, but if you want to test a man's character, give him power. —Abraham Lincoln

The Christian Right made the tactical decision to pursue a number of goals impacted by and impacting on the First Amendment to the Constitution. Those goals have distorted the image of Christians everywhere. Whether that decision was the result of poor judgment, bad advice, or desire on the part of a few individuals for public acclaim, the goals taken together reflect a sense of false pride and self-righteousness inconsistent with Christ's teachings.

As a result, many non-Christians see Christian Conservatives as determined to abandon the First Amendment or irretrievably alter it.

> *…[Jesus] spoke this parable to some who trusted in themselves that they were righteous, and despised others:*
>
> *"Two men went up to the temple to pray, one a Pharisee and the other a tax collector [a collaborator with the Roman occupiers]. The Pharisee stood and prayed thus with himself, 'God I thank You that I am not like other men—extortioners, unjust, adulterers, or even as this tax collector. I fast twice a week; I give tithes of all that I possess.' And the tax collector, standing afar off, would not so much as raise his eyes to heaven, but beat his breast, saying, 'God, be merciful to me a sinner!' I tell you, this man went down to his house justified rather than the other;*

for everyone who exalts himself will be humbled, and he who humbles himself will be exalted" (Luke 18: 9–14).

PUBLIC REFERENCES TO GOD

The majority of devout Christians find political claims about God—along the lines of, "He is on *our* side" (whichever side that might be)—presumptuous, even blasphemous. The God who existed before time began, who made the stars in the heavens and uses the earth for a footstool, need hardly be limited to a single political party.

That having been said, I believe discussions of God and references to Him have a place in the public forum.

Nonetheless—as welcome and reassuring as public references to God may be, to those of us who know and trust in Him—such references do not, in and of themselves, make a nation more godly. They can easily be empty phrases used by politicians for the purpose of garnering votes. We get from government what we demand. Unscrupulous politicians referring to the Lord in their speeches remain unscrupulous.

The concern underlying the First Amendment is that government not be seen as establishing a state religion or endorsing one religion above others. The Hindu pantheon, for instance, has numerous deities. As Christians, we would be distressed in the extreme were an American president to invoke Brahma or Vishnu during a Presidential Address without, at a bare minimum, identifying his beliefs as personal.

This does not require that we worship at a secular altar.

> The Supreme Court in its 1983 decision Marsh v. Chambers[7]...abandoned modern establishment-clause tests when it found the practice of legislative prayer constitutional based on historical usage. Chief Justice Warren Burger wrote that as early as 1774 the Continental Congress opened its sessions with prayer by a paid chaplain. He also noted, "Clearly the men who wrote the First Amendment Religion Clause

> did not view paid legislative chaplains and opening prayers as a violation of that Amendment, for the practice of opening sessions with prayer has continued without interruption ever since that early session of Congress"...Although the Supreme Court declined to review a 1991 case involving a North Carolina judge's practice of beginning court sessions with a prayer, the 4th US Circuit Court of Appeals found the practice unconstitutional in *North Carolina Civil Liberties Union Legal Foundation v. Constangy*...[T]he 4th Circuit distinguished this practice from legislative prayer...saying, "The opinion in *Marsh* clearly focuses on legislative prayer and its 'unique history' and that 'there is no similar longstanding tradition of opening courts with prayer [112H].'"

It may be worth remarking here that Lawrence M. Friedman in *American Law in the 20th Century* concluded, "Prayers were chased out of the schools because pluralism made them less and less practical. It became harder and harder to find any religious common denominator. Ultimately, it became so difficult to package religion without offending someone that the schools (and courts) totally gave up [112I]."[8]

TEN COMMANDMENTS DISPLAYS

In the two centuries and more since adoption of the First Amendment, courts and legal scholars have articulated (and argued over) many different interpretations of the establishment clause.

> Thomas Jefferson is often quoted for his view that the establishment clause should be considered "a wall of separation between Church and State." [However, t]he Supreme Court itself seemed uneasy with that principle in some early cases when it declared that the United States is a "Christian country" in *Vidal* [*v. Girard's Executors*, in 1844], and a "Christian nation" in the 1892 decision *Church of Holy Trinity v. United States* [112A].

Some scholars...believe modern interpretations of the clause are significantly attenuated from its original meaning. As Philip Hamburger wrote in his 2002 book, *Separation of Church and State,* Thomas Jefferson's belief that the First Amendment erected a wall between church and state did not reflect the popular sentiment at the time the Constitution's framers drafted the First Amendment...Hamburger argues that the framers did not contemplate true separation of church and state when they drafted the establishment clause because the religious dissenters of the 18th century "did not ordinarily demand a separation between church and state" and only wanted to forbid an established national church. Nonetheless, separation has become a substantial part of American society and varied interpretations of the establishment clause are sure to continue [112B].

The Supreme Court did not review a direct establishment-clause challenge until its 1899 decision in *Bradfield v. Roberts* (upholding federal funds given to the Roman Catholic Church to maintain and operate a hospital in Washington, D.C.). The number of establishment-clause challenges began to increase after the Supreme Court made the clause applicable to the states through the 14th Amendment in the first modern establishment-clause case: *Everson v. Board of Education* (1947), which upheld a New Jersey statute authorizing tax money to be used to reimburse parents for providing transportation for public and parochial students. Consequently, federal courts after *Everson* exercised their powers to review state and federal aid to religion [112C].

Each federal court decision involving an establishment-clause challenge reflects a fact-sensitive examination and application of one of the modern tests used to resolve perceived government involvement with religion. Because of the number, structure, ambiguity and varied interpretations of the modern tests among courts and among Supreme Court Justices, attempting to predict the outcome of a particular case is an uncertain exercise...[This is not necessarily a negative, since] a rigid application would detract from the critical thinking and historical perspective required in constitutional analysis [112D]. *See*, Justice Stephen Breyer's comments, *below*.

There has been much litigation on the issue of Ten Commandments[9] displays, in this connection. The *Lemon* Test, the Endorsement Test, and the Coercion Test are the three applicable to religious displays.

- The *Lemon* Test is a three-pronged inquiry formulated in the 1971 case of *Lemon v. Kurtzman*. To withstand this test, the government activity in question must: 1) have a secular purpose, 2) have a primary effect that neither advances nor inhibits religion, and 3) avoid excessive entanglement with religion or religious institutions [112E].
- The Endorsement Test focuses on government treatment of adherents of the preferred religion as "favored members of the political community," in former Justice Sandra Day O'Connor's words. "Disapproval sends the opposite message." In the 1995 decision *Capitol Square Review and Advisory Board v. Pinette*, Justice O'Connor clarified how the endorsement test should be applied when she said it must be applied according to the "reasonable observer" standard. "[T]he applicable observer is similar to the 'reasonable person' in tort law, who 'is not to be identified with any ordinary individual, who might occasionally do unreasonable things' but is 'rather a personification of a community ideal of reasonable behavior, determined by the [collective] social judgment [112F].'"
- The Coercion Test was enunciated in the 1992 case of *Lee v. Weisman*. The Supreme Court there said that, "[A]t a minimum, the Constitution guarantees that government may not coerce anyone to support or participate in religion or its exercise, or otherwise act in a way which establishes a state religion or religious faith, or tends to do so [112G]."

As Justice Breyer said in the 2005 case of *Van Orden v. Perry*:

> The Court has found no single mechanical formula that can accurately draw the constitutional line in every case...[In borderline] cases, I see no test-related substitute for the exercise of legal judgment...That judgment is not a personal judgment. Rather, as in all constitutional cases, it must reflect and remain faithful to the underlying purposes of the Clauses, and it must take account of context and consequences measured in light of those purposes [112J].

It remains our responsibility as parents to convey the law of God to our children. Were displays of the Ten Commandments mandated on every street corner, they would remain as ineffective as loyalty oaths, if not written in our hearts.

> *I will speak of Your testimonies...before kings,*
> *And will not be ashamed.*
> *And I will delight myself in Your commandments,*
> *Which I love.*
> *My hands also I will lift up to Your commandments,*
> *Which I love,*
> *And I will meditate on Your statutes* (Psalm 119: 46–48).

INTELLIGENT DESIGN

Respected physicist, mathematician, and philosopher, Blaise Pascal (1623–1662) remarked, "Faith certainly tells us what the senses do not, but not the contrary of what they see; it is above, not against them [114]."

Catholic theologian and philosopher, Thomas Aquinas (1225–1274) was even more forceful on this topic. "The truth of our faith becomes a matter of ridicule among the infidels if any Catholic, not gifted with the necessary scientific learning, presents as dogma what scientific scrutiny shows to be false [115]."

This statement by Aquinas does *not suggest* that the Bible may occasionally be incorrect, and science true. As Christians, we know that the Bible is true and accurate—historically, scientifically, spiritually, and in every other way—by reason, among other things, of Christ's claims for it; its textual unity despite forty authors (using three different languages, spanning three continents, and 1600 years of composition); its textual preservation (14,000 consistent manuscripts compared with, say, twenty of Livy's *History of Rome*); its prophetic accuracy;[10] and its social and personal impact [239A].

What the statement by Aquinas does mean is that—if we seek to contest, in the scientific realm, what is consistent with scientific knowledge at the time—we must be able to make our case in terms based solely on observation and testing, i.e. in terms that do not require faith on the part of non-Christians. It, also, means that Christians cannot transpose religious belief and science (expecting our public schools to teach as science, what we understand on the basis of faith).

We cannot impose our faith. To do so—other important concerns aside—damages our witness.

Numerous renowned scientists have been Christian. These have included friar and philosopher, Roger Bacon (1220–1292), a proponent of empiricism [119]; Johannes Kepler (1571–1630), discoverer of the laws of planetary motion [120]; Robert Boyle (1627–1691), founder of modern chemistry [121]; Carolus Linnaeus (1707–1778), inventor of the classification system now used for all living things; Michael Faraday (1791–1867), a giant in electrical research; George Boole (1815–1864), the discoverer of "pure" mathematics; biologist, botanist, and monk, Gregor Mendel (1822–1884), often referred to as the Father of Genetics [113]; mathematical physicist and engineer, Lord William Kelvin (1824–1907), credited as discoverer of the atom [118]; James Maxwell (1831–1879), the Father of Modern Physics, developer of the equations describing the basic laws of electricity and magnetism [117]; botanist, George Washington Carver (1864–1943) developer of over 300 uses for the peanut to increase the profitability of farming [122]; and Catholic priest and astronomer, Georges Lemaitre (1894–1966), author of the "big bang" theory [123]. Physicist and mathematician, Sir Isaac Newton (1642–1727), recognized as a founder of modern physical science and one of the foremost scientific intellects of all time [116] can be added to the list, if it is recognized that he denied the Trinity, yet had a profound sense of Providence at work in history [127A].

This brings us to perhaps the most infamous dispute between scientific and religious truth, that between Galileo Galilei and the Catholic Church. The telescope played a central role in this controversy [124] between the traditional geocentric (or earth-centered) astronomy of Ptolemy—which viewed the earth as the center of the universe, with the sun revolving around the earth [125]—and the newer heliocentric (or sun-centered) astronomy advocated by Copernicus.

> The Inquisition was a permanent institution in the Catholic Church charged with the eradication of heresies. A committee of consultants declared to the Inquisition that the Copernican proposition that the Sun is the center of the universe was a heresy. Because Galileo supported the Copernican system, he was warned by Cardinal Bellarmine, under order of Pope Paul V, that he should not discuss or defend Copernican theories. In 1624, Galileo was assured by Pope Urban VIII that he could write about Copernican theory as long as he treated it as a mathematical proposition. However, with the printing of Galileo's book, *Dialogue Concerning the Two Chief World Systems*, Galileo was called to Rome in 1633 to face the Inquisition again. Galileo was found guilty of heresy for his *Dialogue*, and was sent to his home near Florence where he was to be under house rest for the remainder of his life [126].

Andreas Idreos Professor Emeritus of Science & Religion at Oxford University, John Brooke speaks eloquently to the perceived conflict between science and religion:

> A lesson that history emphatically teaches is that scientific theories are not born with implications but have implications thrust upon them. Debates so often construed in terms of an essential "conflict between religion and science" usually turn out to be something else...The real issue is the cultural meaning of scientific conclusions, which need

not be identified with the views of scientific or religious extremists.

Take the famous example of the displacement of the Earth from the center of the cosmos by Copernicus and Galileo. Commentators still write as though there was but a single implication of that dislocation. Like Freud they see a dethroning of the human race, no longer the special darling of God's creation. But contemporaries of Copernicus and Galileo saw things quite differently. Given the entrenched Aristotelian distinction between an imperfect Earth and the incorruptible heavens, to be projected among the planets was a form of exaltation...

The mathematical laws governing planetary motion, formulated by Kepler and later embraced by Newton, have often been seen to imply the exclusion of a deity from the clockwork universe. But this was not how Kepler or Newton saw them. *On recognizing* an elegant *correlation between* the period of a *planet's orbit and* its mean *distance from the sun, Kepler confessed to being "carried away by unutterable rapture at the* divine spectacle of *heavenly harmony*"...Nor have the so-called implications of science always favored the secularists. *With his successful rebuttal of* claims for *spontaneous generation, Louis Pasteur* was able to *launch a public attack on materialism and atheism...*

The reaction to the Darwinian theory was also diverse when it first exploded onto the Victorian scene. This was not the simple polarization that we assume today. There were Anglican clergymen who, after the initial shock, claimed that Darwin had given them new theological insight: For Charles Kingsley, a deity who could make all things make themselves was far wiser than one who simply made all things; for Frederick Temple, a future Archbishop of Canterbury, the unity of the evolutionary process bore more eloquent testimony to the unity of a Creator than a series of separate creations. Other Christians, including the American botanist Asa Gray, claimed that Darwin had illuminated the classic problem of theology: the problem

> of pain. If competition and struggle were preconditions of the very possibility of evolutionary change, then pain and suffering were the price levied for the production of beings who could reflect on their origins. Even Darwin's "bulldog," Thomas Henry Huxley, conceded that there was no reason, in principle, why the evolutionary process should not have been incorporated into an initial design of the universe [127B]. [Emphasis added.]
>
> —From Brooke, SCIENCE: 282: 1985–86 (1998). Reprinted with permission from AAAS.

Against this background, it is unclear why Creation Science (or, by another name, Intelligent Design) has been so heavily promoted by the Christian Right. A close examination of the recent case of *Kitzmiller, et al. v. Dover Area School District* [128A], is highly instructive, in this regard.

Creation Science came on the scene when in 1968 the Supreme Court in *Epperson v. Arkansas* struck down Arkansas' statutory prohibition against the teaching of evolution. In essence, Creation Science was an attempt by Fundamentalist opponents of evolution to use scientific-sounding language to describe their religious beliefs, then demand that those beliefs be taught as science.

In *Edwards v. Arkansas*, the Supreme Court in 1987 held that a requirement that public schools teach Creation Science along with evolution violated the establishment clause of the First Amendment. Intelligent Design came into existence, thereafter.

In the *Kitzmiller* case, the Dover Area School Board passed a resolution that students be made aware of gaps/problems in Darwin's theory and of other theories of origin including, but not limited to, Intelligent Design. It then announced by Press Release that teachers would be required to read the following statement to students in 9th grade biology at Dover High School:

> Because Darwin's Theory is a theory, it continues to be tested as new evidence is discovered. The Theory is not a fact. Gaps in the Theory exist for which there is no evidence.

> A theory is defined as a well-tested explanation that unifies a broad range of observations.
>
> Intelligent Design is an explanation of the origin of life that differs from Darwin's view. The reference book, *Of Pandas and People*, is available for students who might be interested in gaining an understanding of what Intelligent Design actually involves.
>
> With respect to any theory, students are encouraged to keep an open mind. The school leaves the discussion of the Origins of Life to individual students and their families. As a Standards-driven district, class instruction focuses upon preparing students to achieve proficiency on Standards-based assessments [128B].

A number of parents residing in the school district brought suit, arguing that Intelligent Design was not science at all. The District Court applied both the *Lemon* and Endorsement Tests discussed earlier [128C].

John Haught, a theologian who testified on behalf of the plaintiff-parents, traced the concept of Intelligent Design at least as far back as Thomas Aquinas. Intelligent Design was not, therefore, a new scientific argument, but an old religious argument for the existence of God, with a new label. Wherever complex design exists, there must have been a designer; nature is complex; therefore nature must have had an intelligent designer [128D]. Dr. Haught testified that Aquinas was explicit that this intelligent designer "everyone understands to be God [128E]."

Defense experts, Michael Behe and Scott Minnich, admitted their argument for Intelligent Design ("purposeful arrangement of parts") was the same one made by Rev. Paley in the 19th Century for the existence of God. It was this—not any misunderstanding on Judge Jones' part about whether Behe and Minnich were Fundamentalists—that led to his decision. The defense experts acknowledged personally viewing the Designer as God—Professor Minnich testifying that many leading supporters of Intelligent Design do, also. Moreover, the recommended text was based almost word for word on a Creation Science text.

The *Wedge Document*, developed by the Discovery Institute's Center for Renewal of Science and Culture, explains the strategy behind Intelligent Design, i.e. replacement of the "materialistic explanations with the theistic understanding that nature and human beings are created by God [128F]." Professor Steven William Fuller actually testified that it is the purpose of Intelligent Design *to change the ground rules of science to include the supernatural* [128G].

Add the following:

1. The definition of "theory" as commonly understood by the lay public was—deliberately or not—confused with "theory" as understood by the scientific community, suggesting far more uncertainty over evolution than exists;
2. Mention of gaps and problems was made only in respect to the theory of evolution;
3. Unlike the theory of evolution, Intelligent Design has undergone no stringent peer review; and
4. Sad to say, there are strong indications from the trial transcript a number of Christian defense witnesses may have perjured themselves, outright.

Has our God ever asked that we lie for Him? Do we believe Him so small that lying should be necessary...even were it something He would tolerate?

Despite all the above, the Press Release by ID Net about the *Kitzmiller* case was titled "Dover Court Establishes State Materialism." It read, in part, "*[O]utlawing* the inference of design that arises from observation and analysis...Judge Jones...*omits any discussion of the religious implications of evolution* and the acknowledged naturalistic/materialistic which has protected it from scientific criticism [129]..." [Emphasis added.]

The extreme nature of this statement confirms the misguided intentions of ID Net. This was not a criminal trial, so as to "outlaw" anything. It was entirely proper that the religious implications of evolution not be discussed. The purpose of the trial was *not* to debate these. It was to determine whether Intelligent Design was a scientific theory.

Admittedly, evolutionary theory may serve as the basis for a materialistic view of life; may be as much a philosophy as the product of science to some [130]. Christian parents, however, have the Bible as a powerful tool to counter this.

It is not critical to my personal faith whether God made the world in what we understand to be seven 24-hour days or not. He most certainly made the world, and most certainly was capable of doing so in seven 24-hour days. On the other hand, He made the natural laws. They are His will in place for the ordinary.

From a human perspective, I see no reason why God could not have incorporated the evolutionary process as a mechanism to create one or more Adams, i.e. the first being(s) with a conscience. *That is not, however, the issue.* The issue is how the Scriptural text was intended to be interpreted. In that regard, I am content to defer to biblical scholars.

Either way, I am awed by the beauty and complexity of creation. I see the work of God's hand everywhere. The breeze in my hair is His gentle touch; the wild geese flying low are His signature.

When the Bible speaks of the sun setting, or the "four corners" of the earth, these statements are not meant to be taken literally [239C]. That some aspects of the Bible use poetic language or metaphor does not contravene the fact that the Bible remains *absolutely and in every way true and accurate.*

The Bible is not, however, a science text book [239B]. When the Bible is interpreted correctly, and science reaches proven conclusions, they are in perfect accord [239D]. For example, the Bible at Job 26: 7 speaks of God stretching out the north over empty space; and hanging the earth on nothing. By contrast, worldly knowledge (rudimentary at the time) held that the earth was a flat disc surrounded by water.

Since science is necessarily a "trial and error" approach, it errs on occasion while the Bible does not. This is not intended as a criticism of science. Scientific techniques constantly change and improve. Scientific theories are (and should be) assessed and reassessed, which is the very purpose of peer review.

A few illustrations:

- There is, of course, the infamous Piltdown Hoax, a contrived archaeological find accepted for forty years by the scientific community as legitimate [275].
- Our concept of Neanderthals in much different today than when their bones were first discovered.
- A fortress at Hisarlik in Turkey is now believed to be the legendary city described in Homer's epic poem, *The Iliad* [240A]. However, Heinrich Schleimann's excavation of that Bronze Age fortress has been criticized for methods that today seem crude [240B]. As a result of those methods, much information was permanently lost.
- "String Theory" is currently being debated among physicists.

Flawed though science may be, it is the most reliable method human beings have for understanding the world around them within the ordinary realm of the senses, i.e. *without resort to the Divine.* We must guard the integrity of scientific thought or risk returning to alchemy and the Dark Ages.

Pastor Phil Bloom in "The Moral Law: A Response to Carl Sagan" relates the Moral Law to science on a profound level:

> Jesus summed up the basic precepts of the moral law when a rich young man asked Him, "Master, what must I do to have eternal life?" He replied simply: "You know the commandments. Do not kill, do not commit adultery, do no lie, do not steal. Honor your father and mother."...They are readily acknowledged by all peoples, all cultures, all times. Some people attempt to brush off a universal moral law. They point to widely differing practices in various cultures, especially regarding sexuality. For example, Mark Twain humorously describes how the New Englanders tried to impose their standards on South Sea Islanders...[who] in actuality knew the moral law even before the Christian missionaries arrived...
>
> That point was made dramatically—and humorously—in a movie called "Thief." The opening scene shows [the main character] in the slow and dangerous process of breaking

open a huge vault...But at a certain point someone steals money from him. He howls, "You can't rob me. I worked hard for this money."...A thief cannot afford to say robbery is OK. A liar survives only if truthfulness is generally valued. Even if we rail against the moral law in the end we will always acknowledge its demands...Because we have a law written in our inner being, we make statements like, "It is not fair." "You must not do that." Or as President Clinton declared after the bombing in Atlanta, "It was an evil act..."

In his book, *The Abolition of Man*, CS Lewis lines up expressions of [the moral law] from a wide range of cultures (ancient Chinese, Egyptian, Norse, etc.)...The moral law is simply too deep in our being to attribute it to culture or evolutionary development...

Pope John Paul II makes a similar case in what many... consider his greatest encyclical: *"Veritatis Splendor."* He starts by arguing that man is free...But he says, and this is the most difficult point for modern men, we are *not so free that we can invent our own moral law*. The moral law is "given." To try to escape it brings our own destruction. But if we obey that law we discover the true meaning of our freedom.... I can allow others to suffer or even cause their suffering for my own fulfillment, but in the end my reason rebels against doing so...Does not this common experience of self-transcendence imply a source and a goal? Can the depth and universality of the moral law really be explained apart from a Law Giver?...We are in fact back where the Bible itself brought us. The ground and purpose of our very acts of going beyond has a name: Yahweh ("I AM"), Jesus...

[A scientist] contemplates the universe and concludes how insignificant man is when compared to such immensity. A believer considers that vastness as nothing in comparison with the destiny of one human being...

That unlimited desire to know, which...really all human beings share, is in fact directed to Something. Something

> really substantial. All this discovery, all the exploration does have a genuine goal. As St. Paul said to the Athenians, "*What therefore you worship as unknown, this I proclaim to you*" (Acts 17:23). The unlimited desire to know, as well as the moral law each one of us discovers in his own heart, does have an Origin and a final Goal. In fact, from Revelation we know it actually has a name and we can enter into a personal relation with Him [131]. [Emphasis added.]

HARRY POTTER

Christians have made a great point of banning or boycotting the Harry Potter books by J.K. Rowling, so popular with children around the world. This stems from the fact the books deal in magic, which the Bible prohibits in all forms. *See*, for example:

> *There shall not be found among you anyone who...practices witchcraft, or a soothsayer* [who receives magical power through incantations], *or one who interprets omens, or a sorcerer* [who brews herbs to make magical potions to control people and circumstance], *or one who conjures spells, or a medium, or a spiritist* [who contacts spirits], *or one who calls up the dead. For all who do these things are an abomination to the Lord...* (Deuteronomy 18: 10–12).
>
> *"Thus says the Lord God: 'Woe to the women who sew magic charms on their sleeves... Will you profane Me among My people for handfuls of barley...by your lying to My people who listen to lies?...[Y]ou have strengthened the hands of the wicked, so that he does not turn from his wicked way to save his life'"* (Ezekiel 13: 18–19, 22).
>
> *For the king of Babylon stands at the parting of the road, at the fork of the two roads, to use divination: he shakes the arrows, he consults the images, he looks at the liver* (Ezekiel 21: 21).

Those who practice so called white magic argue it is used for the good of others. For Christians, there is no distinction made between white and black magic. These practices were often associated with pagan cults, and are considered demonic in origin by Christians.

We Christians did a very poor job of conveying that biblical truth—particularly against the shameful backdrop of the Salem witch trials. The public was left with a series of engaging children's stories, whose principal characters are loyal friends who seem to step into fairy tales. That these same characters from time to time use improper means to accomplish good ends was lost in the uproar (addressed only by those perceptive parents—Christian and non-Christian—who noticed, and brought the fact to the attention of their children).

And that is my point. We missed the forest for the trees. We missed an opportunity to explain *why* there are some things we as Christians can do, and some things we cannot. And we overlooked the positive in the Harry Potter novels—the fact that thousands of children were excited by reading and that the books contain nuggets of truth.

> Numbing the pain for a while will make it worse when you finally feel it.
>
> —J.K. Rowling, *Harry Potter and the Goblet of Fire*
>
> Dark and difficult times lie ahead. Soon we must all face the choice between what is right and what is easy.
>
> —J. K. Rowling, *Harry Potter and the Goblet of Fire* (*movie adaptation*)
>
> It is our choices…that show what we truly are, far more than our abilities.
>
> —J.K. Rowling, *Harry Potter and The Chamber of Secrets*

Instead, we began collecting wood for our bonfires.

Pope Gregory issued a papal edict or bull in 1239, encouraging the burning of the Talmud, the collection of Jewish civil and ceremonial law, wherever found [135A].

The first American trial on issues of freedom of the press took place in 1692, in connection with a pamphlet entitled, "Truth

Advanced in the Correction of Many Gross & Hurtful Errors." First Philadelphia printer, William Bradford, had published this pamphlet by Quaker (later Anglican) George Keith criticizing the Quaker government. Bradford later published Keith's account of the trial as "New-England's Spirit of Persecution Transmitted to Pennsilvania (sic) [31A, B and C]."

By the 18th Century, the Spanish Inquisition specialized in destroying books it saw as dangerous to the faith. The now classic *Robinson Crusoe* was an example[30]. The Portuguese Inquisition—which destroyed not only the social and economic fabric of Portugal, but Brazil—was not abolished until 1821[34].

I mention none of this to pillory other Christians (or to suggest that we assimilate into the general culture), merely to urge that we choose with great care the means we, ourselves, utilize in achieving our ends.

One way the Nazis "cleansed" Germany of supposedly "un-German" ideas was censorship [134]. On May 10, 1933, just months after the Nazis gained power, a book-burning with scripted ceremonies took place, as 70,000 people watched. The SA cordoned off the main courtyard of Berlin's Humboldt University, piling high stacks of books by Jews, Communists, and so called "degenerate" or homosexual authors. Some 20,000 books were destroyed [133A and 135B].

One horrified witness to the event, 93 year old Elfrieda Bruenning, was a member of the banned writer's union. She recounts, "[Heinrich] Heine said: if you burn books today, you burn people tomorrow. But we never imagined what was to come [133B]."

These are associations we Christians should deeply regret.

A statement to the effect that no idea is so dangerous it cannot be talked about is attributed to Stephen Hopkins, one of the signers of the Declaration of Independence. Whether accurately attributed or not, the sentiment is uniquely American in spirit. As President Franklin Delano Roosevelt put it, "We all know that books burn—yet we have the greater knowledge that books cannot be killed by fire. People die, but books never die."

We Christians should be extremely leery of censorship; we should never be afraid to engage in debate.

PART III:

THE VALUE OF LIFE

ABORTION: MOTHERS, CHILDREN, AND THE CHURCH

For You formed my inward parts; You covered me in my mother's womb. (Psalm 139: 13)

Somebody who should have been born is gone. —Anne Sexton, *The Abortion*

Christian opposition to abortion is by now well-known, though not always well-understood.

Ours is the God Who shaped a thousand, thousand hills yet knows when every leaf will fall. Ours is the God for Whom a single life is of infinite value—so much so that He gave the life of His only begotten Son, Jesus, to pay for our sins.

The titanic forces of the earth are under His control, as are the seasons...even the seasons of our lives. His is the life force in a fawn, and to Him it returns. He cherishes the heartbeats of an infant in the womb, and knows beforehand all the days of that child's life even into old age.

Ours is the God Who filled this world with astounding beauty. Not by accident or from some sterile aesthetic sense, but as the reflection of His deepest heart, His desire to surround His children daily with love.

Why He should love us to such an extent is incomprehensible. His love, however, should make every life immeasurably precious to us.

> It is not a question of "moral" people on one side and the immoral on the other. As a "pro-lifer" I am sometimes inclined to take that viewpoint, but it won't work. I may think that pro-abortionists are totally immoral because they refuse to defend the life of an unborn child. But none will say, "The life of an unborn child does not matter to me." They will either deny that the fetus in fact is a tiny child or they will say, "It is you who do not care about the life and health of the mother. You only seem to think about the child before birth; what about the misery he has to live in. And furthermore you probably think capital punishment is OK, so don't talk to me about being pro-life."
>
> What we have is not one person acknowledging the moral law and the other rejecting it. No, both acknowledge it. Both argue from it. And not just to win debating points; in fact, we both sincerely feel its demands. As St. Paul says, "*That law is written in your hearts*" (Romans 2:15) [132A].

Where we, as Christians, too often fail when addressing abortion is:

a) in ignoring the desperate conditions contributing to abortion; [11]
b) in treating the women seeking abortion as criminals; and
c) in overlooking the plight of children already living in poverty.

God poured His love into these women and children, as well. He saw their substance when they were yet unformed. Yet women are beaten, left abandoned. Little ones are conceived at least as frequently in a reckless search for love, as out of ignorance over birth control; born with AIDS; abused; shuffled from one parent to another, assuming a father is present at all.

True, affluent women seek abortions, as well. However, 60% of the women who had abortions in 2000, had incomes less than twice the poverty level (the same women who routinely have less access to health care and family planning services) [173A]. True, some women use abortion in place of birth control (a fact most women find reprehensible). True, many Christian charities do serve the poor. Their resources are, however, severely limited.

None of this gives anyone—let alone anyone claiming to be Christian—the right to throw blood or shout insults at pregnant women entering an abortion clinic. Nor is violent protest (even if by a limited few) in justified defense of the innocent, as it asserts.

Is there a better approach? The extreme Left would have us believe that a woman's right to control her own body is sacrosanct. The argument is made that government involvement in the reproductive process should be kept to an absolute minimum.

There is some appeal to this argument. The difficulty lies in the fact that there are competing interests here: the woman's and the child's. The child has no choice, but to grow in the womb. He or she cannot relocate to neutral real estate. And the child has no voice. He or she must rely on us to remember that he or she is human—no matter how else we may choose to define him or her.

I am reminded of a line from Dr. Seuss' *Horton Hears A Who!*: "A person's a person. No matter how small. A person's a person after all." Perhaps even the ACLU would agree.

Indeed, the alternative utilitarian argument is an extremely dangerous—not to mention illogical—one. The child in the womb is a child only if he or she is "wanted." The moment he or she is no longer "wanted," he or she becomes an "it," a clump of cells, detritus. If the woman should change her mind before the abortion takes place, the clump of cells magically becomes a child again. This demonstrates nothing more than the power of words, for the science stays the same—as does the spiritual reality. Those disposable cells, if cultured in a jar, would remain human. They would certainly not grow into an asparagus.

Based on this approach, the value of life depends entirely upon the assessment of someone else—in this instance, the mother at the very moment she may be most discouraged. How can she know—how can any of us predict—the future of that child? And do a child's future "achievements" determine his or her worth? Does the social standing of a child make a life of less value?

From the perspective of those protesting abortion, photos of loving mothers and smiling babies would be much effective than photos of dead fetuses. Better yet, we should be standing ready with maternity clothes and baby blankets, with formula and diapers, with offers of genuine assistance (childcare, job training, etc.).[12] We should be lining up in droves to adopt these children into loving homes, if the mothers are willing.

This does *not* require that we force women to carry their unborn children to term, or "give men control" over women's bodies.

If we want to reach these women and win them for Christ, we need to identify the root causes of their own pain. That will require much more than placards and a bullhorn. The woman who has serial abortions performed has a seared conscience, has been deeply wounded, or both.

A few more points:

- The fact that abortions are permitted by law allows women to make the moral choice of whether to have them or not. Some will choose not. It is offensive in the extreme that neither the political far Left nor far Right seems to think women capable of making that moral decision. The Left views women who select not to have abortions as relics of the Stone Age, rather than agents of conscience. The Right seeks to instruct us on the moral implications of pregnancy, as if it we were not sentient. Women are the ones who for nine months carry children under their hearts. At times the thought of bringing another child into this sad world may seem overwhelming. But we know what is growing in our wombs is life.
- We have so convinced men they have no say in the lives they created that a significant portion now consider it in bad taste even to express an opinion. The decision is "entirely the woman's," as if the child had sprung into being via parthenogenesis. Too many men see themselves as having no responsibility toward the life they had a part in creating (other than perhaps providing sufficient funds for an abortion). Neither approach is remotely satisfactory from the perspective of the child—the most vulnerable party to the transaction.
- Medical professionals who serve the women seeking abortions must act as their consciences direct. A physician may see the

medical procedure as morally neutral, something to which the woman is perfectly entitled under law; or—wishing to spare a woman the back-alley abortion she would otherwise pursue—as the lesser of two evils. A nurse lovingly seeing to the needs of a dying child—aborted but alive, despite the procedure—is extending the only mercy that child will experience on this earth. That same nurse may earlier have laid a caring hand on the brow of the mother.

A Harris Poll conducted in March 2005 demonstrated that between overturning *Roe v. Wade* (52% against v. 42% supporting *Roe*) and abortion without restriction (26% favoring no restrictions whatever v. 76% favoring some/all restrictions), there was room for compromise among the electorate [173B]. Consequently, the 95–10 Empower Act was put forward. This series of measures, if ultimately enforced, should reduce the number of abortions by 95% in ten years [173C].

The provisions of the Empower Act, as of this writing, included the following:

- Increased funding for domestic violence programs.
- Ban on pregnancy as a "pre-existing condition" in health care insurance.
- Full funding of the federal WIC program.
- State Children's Health Insurance Program coverage of pregnant women.
- Support for a "woman's right to know" (full, informed consent including factual information on how the abortion procedure is performed, possible risks and complications, and alternatives to abortion).
- Support for parental notification measures [173E].

EXTREMELY LOW BIRTH WEIGHT (ELBW) INFANTS

Ironically, while some women have been seeking abortions, others (including older mothers and those undergoing fertility treatments) have been entreating science to save the lives of their premature infants. Neonatal Intensive Care Units (NICUs) are on the front-line of this battle to save children's lives. "Here, it is common practice to have to weigh one baby's life against another's or the life of a mother against her child's. And even to decide that an infant's life will be so filled with illness, disability and pain that it isn't worth saving at all [152]."

The minimum viability of infants has been reduced as low as 23 weeks of gestation (pregnancy). Infants at or under the age of 27 weeks and with a birth weight of 1000 grams (2 lbs. 3 oz.) or less, are classified as Extremely Low Birth Weight (ELBW) [149A].

African American births constitute 15.5% of those taking place in the United States annually, but make up 36% of ELBW infants [149B]. Three major risk factors account for a large proportion of all low weight births: cigarette smoking during pregnancy, low maternal weight gain, and low pre-pregnancy weight [153A]. The disparity is commonly attributed to adverse economic and social conditions. However, adjustment for these does not eliminate ethnic differences [153B].

Generally, the survival rate of ELBW infants correlates with gestational age, but increases with weight. It is, for example, 50% at 500–749 grams [149C]. Overall, survival of these infants has been improved by the widespread use of surfactants (wetting agents which reduce the surface tension of the lungs and stabilize the alveoli), and maternal steroids (which accelerate infant growth in the womb) [149D].

Unfortunately, these medications do not equally well reduce the rate of developmental difficulties such as cerebral palsy, deafness, and mental retardation [149E]. Long-term difficulties occur in a substantial percentage of premature infants [150G and 150H], with one study reporting rates of low achievement or special school needs as high as 61% for preterm children (compared with 23% of full-term children) after ten years [150A]. The growth rate of ELBW infants, also, lags because of complications such as hypoxia and sepsis. Numerous other complications can occur, many fatal [149F].

These circumstances raise multiple legal, ethical, and moral dilemmas (not to mention financial difficulties) for the families involved. Bioethics consultants and multi-disciplinary committees discuss such issues and make recommendations [149G]. These are excruciating decisions for the parents.

In Holland, doctors do not routinely administer intensive care to infants born before 25 weeks of gestation [151A]. As of June 2005, the Nuffield Council on Bioethics was considering a 24 week limit for Britain, with the exception of infants demonstrating a strong chance for a healthy life [151B].

By contrast, a study funded jointly by grants from the Canadian Institutes of Health Research and the U.S. National Institute of Child Health and Development followed 166 infants born weighing as little as 1.1 to 2.2 lbs. with normal birth weight infants until 22 years of age [150F]. The hypothesis of these researchers was that children of lower birth weight would have lower levels of educational achievement, employment, and independence. Instead, they found no significant differences in educational achievement. In fact, 82% of these low birth weight children graduated high school. There were no major differences between the two groups as far as independent living or marriage [150B].

A larger proportion of extremely low birth weight participants in the study were not employed due to chronic illness or permanent disability (compared to normal birth weight subjects). However, 48% were employed (compared with 57% of normal birth weight young adults) [150D].

According to study leader, neonatologist, Dr Saroj Saigal, a significant majority of young adults who were originally low birth weight infants managed to overcome their earlier difficulties and become functional members of society [150C].

Survivors of the early NICU era are only now reaching adulthood, so there are few such studies beyond ten years available [150E].

ADOPTION/FOSTER CARE

> *Child Welfare*: President Bush has once again proposed his risky, untested option for states to convert their foster care entitlement programs into fixed-funded block grants. This would leave the states financially responsible for any

> surge in foster care cases due to severe economic downturns, spikes in drug use, or other societal changes. The budget cuts federal funding support for the foster care program by $252.5 million [80B].
>
> —*LEGISLATIVE ACTION, Homepage of* American Federation of State, County and Municipal Employees (AFSCME), February 8, 2005.

The number of children worldwide without loving families is staggering. There are 5.5 million orphans in Africa; 3.5 million orphans in Asia; 1.5 million orphans in Eastern Europe; 400,000 orphans in Latin America [136A].

If we Christians support life, why are there children waiting for adoption, even through their teens? Why are disabled children passed over? Why must "adoption parties" be held, with children paraded before potential parents like show dogs? Why are there 135,000 children available for adoption in the US Foster Care System alone [136B]?

FamilyLife's "Hope for Orphans" Ministry at http://www.familylife.com/hopefororphans provides resources to assist churches across the country in establishing their own orphans ministries. The purpose of these is to encourage church members—whatever their circumstances or stage in life—prayerfully to consider adoption.

Many of us have been greatly blessed with worldly goods. We have spacious homes, two-car garages. We are members of the local country club. Our 2.5 children attend fine schools. We never ask ourselves why we were chosen to be so fortunate. We accept elevated status as our due. Oh, we may have worked hard to attain financial success. But it never occurs to us that our talents—our very molecules—are on loan. We were blessed for a reason: to share our blessings with others.

It does not, of course, require a trust fund to create a good home.

Could you make room in your heart and your home for a child? It is an enormous responsibility, but a gift beyond measure to both the adoptive child and parent. For those interested, a number of adoption websites are listed in **Appendix II**, along with information from FamilyLife on financial assistance with adoption (as well as on single parent adoption).

MENTORING

If we wish to reduce the number of abortions, we can start by teaching women and girls that there are other ways of achieving meaning in life than becoming pregnant. If we hope to educate on abstinence or model a different lifestyle, we cannot simply go home at 5PM.

Mentoring, i.e. the establishment of one-on-one caring relationships, is an effective method of reaching out. A strong emphasis must be placed on trust, with the focus the younger individual's well-being. Mentoring cannot be viewed as a pet project. The younger individual is not a captive audience anxiously awaiting lectures.

With time, a bond of friendship and respect is formed. This can open worlds for both parties to the mentoring relationship. The mentor will be made sharply aware of the hardships to which the younger individual is exposed on a daily basis. The younger individual may seize opportunities that seemed out of reach before.

I am *by no means* suggesting that mentoring be used as an indoctrination vehicle, whether by pro-life or pro-choice proponents. What I am saying is that Christians, if we are committed to life, cannot isolate the single issue of abortion and feel that we have "done our duty."

If we reach out in love, we will be blessed with joy. The young woman I have mentored since she was in her mid-teens is now hoping to attend college. Raised in the inner city, she has faced every obstacle imaginable yet (like every child) is a miracle in progress. The boy I currently mentor has a special sense of peace about him, despite medical challenges.

If you take on mentoring, be prepared to have your heart broken. These children will matter to you. You will be stunned at what they have missed out on. It may as simple as a sight of the ocean. You will wince to hear stories of the rejection and deprivation they take for granted. You will become conscious that theirs are the only black or brown faces in a sea of white at some upscale mall or theatre you would not otherwise have thought of as elitist. If you have not grown up there, you will learn firsthand what the housing projects look—and smell—like.

And you will not always see the impact you have had. Families will move or drop out of the program. You may hear second-hand that the child you mentored has taken up drugs, gotten pregnant, or been arrested.

But know that you will have an impact. These children, somewhere down the road—maybe when it matters most—will remember that you encouraged them, that you laughed at their jokes, that you cared to spend time with them. That may be enough.

Not surprisingly, for those of us unable to have children of our own, the chance to give back can be transmuted by God into an extraordinary opportunity to receive:

> *"Sing, O barren, you who have not borne! Break forth into singing, and cry aloud, you who have not labored with child! For more are the children of the desolate, than the children of the married woman," says the Lord* (Isaiah 54: 1).

For further information on mentoring, contact the Children's Aid Society in your area or Big Brothers/Big Sisters at www.bbbsa.org.

POVERTY

[F]or I was hungry and you gave Me food; I was thirsty and You gave Me drink; I was a stranger and you took Me in; I was naked and you clothed Me; I was sick and you visited Me; I was in prison and you came to Me. (Matthew 25: 35)

The test of our progress is not whether we add more abundance to those who have much; it is whether we provide enough for those who have too little. —Franklin Delano Roosevelt

We would like to believe that we are a classless society—a society in which even the poorest of the poor may attain fame, fortune, and the highest office in the land. We would prefer to believe that those who are poor are somehow poor by choice, less motivated than we, less deserving.

That would relieve us of guilt, as well as eliminate any obligation on our part to remedy the situation.

Hopefully, Hurricane Katrina changed some of those misconceptions. It is difficult to look into the face of a hungry child and turn away. Yet, that is what we as a society have done.

According to the latest US Census Bureau, fully 12.7% of the population or 37 million Americans live in poverty [224E].

> Whereas before 1996 welfare reform, younger children were more likely than their school-age counterparts to receive monetary assistance, this situation reversed under the 1996 [Temporary Assistance for Needy Families] TANF bill. Coverage for older children in extreme poverty fell from 57% to 33% between 1996 and 2000, at the same time as coverage for younger children in extreme poverty fell from 61% to 26%. Now, the youngest and poorest children (those who are less than six years old and in extreme

poverty) are less likely than older children to receive TANF assistance.

Furthermore, between 1996 and 2000, the proportion of children in single-parent families who received no food stamps increased from 36% to 47% for quite poor children (family income is between 50% and 100% of the poverty line) and from 27% to 37% for extremely poor children. By 2000, the percentage of children living in extreme poverty and not receiving food stamps had increased by 32% for school-aged children and by a staggering 44% for young children [63].

Nonetheless, under the "compassionate conservatism" of the Bush Administration's 2001 Tax Proposal:

Women and Children Left Behind Under Bush's 2001 Tax Plan According to The National Women's Law Center, 17 million women would receive no tax cut under Bush's plan. Three million families headed by women with children have an income below the federal poverty rate. This large group would receive no benefit from the tax plan. Thirty-six percent of all single mothers would receive no tax benefit, and nearly half of all African American and Hispanic single mothers would not benefit from Bush's tax cut [65].

—Original Source: National Women's Law Center, "Women and Children Last: The Bush Tax Cut Plan," March 5, 2001.

Moreover:

Food Stamps: The budget proposes $1 billion in food stamp cuts over 10 years, which means that 200,000–300,000 fewer low-income individuals will receive nutrition assistance. Under the plan, welfare recipients who receive child care, education, training and other services but no welfare cash assistance would no longer be automatically eligible for food stamps…Meals on Wheels, and other nutrition pro-

> grams vulnerable to program cuts in the years beyond FY 2006 [72A].

According to the Center on Budget and Policy Priorities, the Bush Administration's 2007 Budget proposals would terminate completely the *Commodity Supplemental Food Program*, which supplies food packages to more than 400,000 low-income elderly at a cost of less than $20/month each [241D].

> "*Community Services Block Grant (CSBG)*: Bush [again] proposes to end the CSBG, a $637 million program that helps pay for community action agencies that have been fighting poverty for more than 35 years [76 and 241G]."

The problems with TANF run deeper even than budgetary cuts.

> Avis Jones DeWeever, Ph.D, Study Director at the Institute for Women's Policy Research, presented research from studies conducted by the [Institute for Women's Policy Research] that highlighted some of the problems with the current TANF bill for single-parent families. For instance, between 1996 and 2000, work participation of single-parent families in extreme poverty increased by 50%, yet income for these families decreased by 9%. Despite the jobs that workers in these families acquired, this additional income still could not compensate for the huge drop in cash assistance from government programs that these families experienced between 1996 and 2000. In addition, these types of families also lost access to health care during the same time period; the proportion of extremely poor children (family income is below 50% of the poverty line) without health insurance increased from 15% to 25% [64].
>
> *Shortchanges Uninsured Children:* Rather than invest more money in the State Children's Health Insurance Program (SCHIP) to cover uninsured children and adults, Bush chose instead to devote $89 billion over 10 years for health-related tax credits which many experts have said will pri-

> marily benefit higher-income and healthy workers; and in the case of one tax credit, could potentially be used as a tax shelter [68].
>
> —Original Sources: Center on Budget and Policy Priorities, "Administration Budget Includes Additional Health Tax Cuts That Primarily Benefit Higher-Income Individuals," and "Health Proposals in Administration's Budget Could Weaken the Employer-Based Health Insurance System," Edwin Park, February 5, 2002.

The Center on Budget and Policy Priorities indicates the Administration's 2007 Budget would reduce Federal funding for Medicaid, the health insurance for low-income children, parents, seniors, and people with disabilities, by $1.5 billion over 5 years ($5.1 billion over 10 years). Regulatory changes are additionally proposed which would reduce Medicaid spending a further $12.2 billion over 5 years—principally by shifting costs to the states.

This is hardly an achievement for a president who claims to be Christian [241I].[13]

> Vicky Lovell, Ph.D, Study Director at the Institute for Women's Policy Research...[i]n a June 2003 report entitled, "40-Hour Work Proposal Significantly Raises Mothers' Employment Standard." . .found that a 40-hour-a-week, year-round work requirement, which [the President favors [74] and] Congress is considering making a requirement for TANF recipients, would be significantly higher than the current level of mothers' employment activity. Although most mothers do work for pay, half of those are employed either part-time or part of the year, or both.
>
> Analysts have suggested that low-income mothers cannot afford the child care they would need in order to work full-time, as well as that many low-wage jobs available to women with few job-related skills are available either as part-time or part-year opportunities, or both. In addition, Dr. Lovell pointed out that many jobs that low-income women are able to get are structured in such a way that they

> are almost impossible to hold on a permanent basis. These low-wage jobs often lack health benefits, paid sick leave, or a living wage that pays enough to keep a woman financially self-sufficient. Given that employment is not steady for low-income people and that most low-income mothers are unable to work for pay full-time and full-year, it would be illogical and irresponsible for lawmakers to demand that mothers who are TANF recipients nearly double their current average level of paid work [62A].
>
> Dr. Lovell also noted the special difficulties that women with disabilities face. They are more likely to have a lower family income, a lower level of education, a child with a disability, and are more likely to be single. Lawmakers need to take all of these factors into consideration in order to effectively revise TANF [62B].

Originally, the Bush Administration proposed a five-year freeze on child care funding. This would have cut the number of low-income children receiving such assistance by 300,000 in 2009 though only one in seven eligible children actually receives child care subsidies [72B].

The Center on Budget and Policy Priorities confirms that the Bush Administration's 2007 Budget proposals, instead of freezing child-care funding, cut deeply into discretionary child care funding for low- and moderate-income families, totaling $1 billion over the next five years [241E]. The number of needy children receiving child care assistance in 2011 would drop by more than 400,000 as compared with 2005 [241F].

Add to this, cut-backs to subsidized housing, and so called reform to the Bankruptcy Act.

> *Housing and Community Development*: The Department of Housing and Urban Development's budget would shrink by 11.5 percent under the President's budget. It would cut $252 million from the public housing capital fund, zero-out the program funding revitalization of severely distressed public housing (HOPE VI), cut $118 million from hous-

ing for persons with disabilities, cut five percent from the Housing Opportunities for Persons with AIDS (HOPWA), cut more than $1 billion from community development programs, and consolidate and eliminate the Community Development Block Grant (CDBG) and 17 other programs [77 and 241H]...

Bankruptcy Reform Hurts Struggling Families. For a president who has spoken eloquently about America as "the land of the second chance," George W. Bush is grimly committed to stripping second chances from millions of families. (Op Ed) [146B].

—Robert Gordon, *Baltimore Sun,* March 4, 2005.

We are professors of bankruptcy and commercial law. We are writing with regard to The Bankruptcy Abuse Prevention and Consumer Protection Act of 2005 (S. 256)...We have been watching the bankruptcy reform process for the last eight years with keen interest. *The 90 undersigned professors come from every region of the country and from all major political parties. We are not members of a partisan, organized group. Our exclusive interest is to seek the enactment of a fair, just and efficient bankruptcy law.* Many of us have written before to express our concerns...[W]e write again as yet another version of the bill comes before you. The *bill is deeply flawed and will harm small businesses, the elderly, and families with children*...It is a stark fact that the bankruptcy filing rate has slightly more than doubled during the last decade, and that last year approximately 1.6 million households filed for bankruptcy...Bankruptcy, the bill's sponsor says, has become a system "where deadbeats can get out of paying their debt scot-free while honest Americans who play by the rules have to foot the bill." We disagree...In our view, the fundamental change over the last ten years has been the way that credit is marketed to consumers. *Credit card lenders have become more aggressive in marketing* their products, and a large, *very profitable, market has emerged in sub-prime lend-*

> *ing. Increased risk is part of the business model*...[I]t should not come as a surprise that *as credit is extended to riskier and riskier borrowers, a greater number default when faced with a financial reversal.* Nonetheless, consumer lending remains highly profitable, even under current law. The ability to file for bankruptcy and to receive a fresh start provides crucial aid to families overwhelmed by financial problems...[T]his bill would cripple an already overburdened system [146A]. [Emphasis added.]

This is so shocking as to be incomprehensible. It is certainly a pattern, not an aberration.

Is government excess to be balanced on the backs of the poor? Who gave any of us the right to condemn an entire class of people to remain destitute? Clearly in any group of people some will have made bad choices. So have we. For most of us, however, the weight of generations has not reduced the odds of recovery from a bad choice or series of bad choices to infinitesimal levels.

The question is whether we will reach out a helping hand.

Justice for the poor should matter to us. Both the Old and New Testaments make that clear. The Scripture verses on the subject are too numerous to cite. These are just a few:

> *Defend the poor and fatherless; do justice to the afflicted and needy...free them from the hand of the wicked* (Psalm 82: 3–4).
>
> *Whoever shuts his ears to the cry of the poor will also cry himself and not be heard* (Proverb 21: 13).
>
> *The righteous considers the cause of the poor, but the wicked does not understand such knowledge* (Proverb 29: 7).
>
> *Open your mouth for the speechless... Open you mouth, judge righteously, and plead the cause of the poor and needy* (Proverb 31: 8–9).
>
> *"He judged the cause of the poor and needy; then it was well. Was not this knowing Me?" says the Lord* (Jeremiah 22: 16).
>
> *And He looked up and saw the rich putting their gifts into the treasury, and He saw also a certain poor widow putting in two*

> *mites. So He said, "Truly I say to you that this poor widow has put in more than all; for all these out of their abundance have put in offerings for God, but she out of her poverty put in all the livelihood that she had."* (Luke 21: 1–4).

Whether we realize it or not, the test is for us. Not for the poor. How are we going to respond?

It is easy to make excuses. We have no time. Surely someone else will take up the cause. On and on…

Whatever our religion or politics, we as Americans face a growing crisis. Adequate Federal assistance to the underprivileged has not been forthcoming. Pressure must be brought to bear on our elected representatives to bring that about. We cannot afford to abandon another generation.

More than government assistance, community safety nets must be re-established by all of us. Families and communities must be reconstructed as the primary building blocks and support systems of society.[14] Though this cannot be mandated, neither can it be accomplished without individual and business commitment.

There is no one single solution to poverty, just as there is no single cause. The causes include lack of opportunity, as well as a breakdown in family. Conversely, the solutions include adequate employment, quality education, safe communities in which to live and work, access to affordable health care, strengthened families, addiction rehabilitation, and renewed personal and community responsibility.

How then can we assist the poor?

Churches, faith-based initiatives, and secular agencies serving the poor and disadvantaged are on the "front lines" of the war on poverty, and intimately familiar with the difficulties and frustrations, in a particular geographic area. All can be useful sources of information regarding specific community needs. Roundtable discussions involving church, business, law enforcement, and/or political leaders can be a means of exchanging such information, and exploring possible solutions.

Benjamin Hess in "Measuring Poverty" in the *Peace & Conflict Monitor* of the University of Peace adds these perceptive remarks:

To understand poverty, one must understand its relationship to the Four A's: access, assets, abilities, and accountability.

1. Access: It has been shown that access to clean water, food, social support, education, health care, and a variety of other factors all influence poverty levels. For example, a person living on $1 a day in a Bangladeshi slum with access to water, basic health care, and a social support structure might be better off than someone living on $3 a day in a shantytown in Buenos Aires, Argentina, without access to these services.
2. Assets: The Peruvian economist Hernando de Soto emphasizes the importance of assets in the determination of poverty. This includes physical capital, such as land, housing, cars, or livestock, and human capital, including labor potential, education, health, and training. (Deepa Narayan affirms that two other types of assets are social, as in social networks, and environmental, which refers to water, trees, soil, and so on.) De Soto also maintains that access to formal financial and legal institutions that provide credit and protect property rights and human rights is a key issue related to assets.
3. Abilities: Abilities are related to human capital assets. Nobel laureate, Amartya Sen writes that poverty should be viewed as the "deprivation of basic capabilities" rather than the result of low incomes. He argues that a strong link exists between income and capability due to a person's age, gender, location, education, and additional aspects that he or she may be unable to control, such as illness or disability.
4. Accountability: Often, when analysts examine poverty, they focus on the poor themselves rather than the state's role. However, the state's accountability to the poor is a decisive factor that must be contained within any definition of poverty. The state's level of responsiveness to its poorest sectors and poor people's access to the political process are critical elements in the eradication or deepening of poverty...

> The best way to fight poverty is on an individual level, taking into account each person's access to basic needs, human rights, and services; assets, both physical and human; physical and mental abilities; and the state's accountability to the poorest sectors in a particular area. Placing a focus on the individual rather than a nation or region is much more time-consuming and costly, but in the long run our understanding of poverty's causes and effects and how we can eradicate it will be far more advanced. Poverty affects real people; it is important that we treat it as more than a set of statistics [95]...

We can support parenting classes and fatherhood initiative programs. We can lobby for, support, and/or become active in education; tutoring, and mentoring programs; job creation and training programs; drug treatment programs; ex-offender programs; neighborhood watch programs, and mediated gang truces. We may serve as counselors, mediators, or otherwise as our abilities dictate.

The options are virtually endless. Any would be worthwhile. What we must *not* do is sit safely on the sidelines, in our "ring cities" or gated suburban communities, and watch as the decaying cores of our older urban centers (and the lives of those condemned to inhabit them) deteriorate yet further.

PUBLIC WORKS PROGRAM AND WELFARE REFORM

With so many uneducated, unskilled, and unemployed; with the inner cities in disrepair, held hostage by crime and drugs, we need a viable public works program that would restore human dignity and create a livable environment.

I do not propose to convert Americans from capitalists to socialists. The meritocracy that capitalism under ideal circumstances fosters has served this country well.

Unfortunately, the circumstances of many are far from ideal. For them, it has not been a level playing field. Large segments of society have consequently been ignored—to their detriment and the country's, as a whole. A few brilliant minds have always persevered. The talents of many others are simply lost. The programs we have put in place to assist them have often been half-hearted (in the long-run, even counter-productive).

Fearful of failing means testing and losing government benefits (yet still finding themselves not sufficiently well-off financially to be self-supporting), the disadvantaged have at times altered, distorted, or lied about their family situations to receive needed benefits.

A solid works program (linked to mentoring, childcare, education, jobs training with a *real* future, and permanent job placement) could combine the best of Conservative and Liberal philosophies, and restore credibility to both. Not only would single parent families be provided a way out of poverty, but the family structure itself might be strengthened, and the tax base ultimately enlarged.

CHRISTIAN LEGAL AID

Our great nation—with the highest concentration of lawyers in the world—has one of the least accessible systems of justice. A leading expert on legal ethics, Deborah L. Rhode comments in *Access to Justice* that approximately 80% of the civil needs of low-income Americans go unmet. The poor—the group "least likely to have the education, skills and self-confidence to handle problems effectively without assistance"—go unassisted [259].

There is a special role that Christian attorneys can play, on behalf of the poor.

Bound as they are by both biblical standards and the Canons of Ethics governing attorney behavior, Christian attorneys are required to provide legal advice of the highest quality.[15] This does not violate American Bar Association (ABA) Guidelines. In fact, it conforms specifically with Rule 2.1 (adopted 2002) encouraging attorneys to bring moral and ethical consideration to bear on the clients' legal problems:

> Advice couched in narrowly legal terms may be of little value to a client, especially where practical considerations,

> such as cost or effects on other people are predominant. Purely tactical legal advice, therefore, can sometimes be inadequate. It is proper for a lawyer to refer to relevant moral and ethical consideration in giving advice. Although a lawyer is not a moral advisor as such, moral and ethical considerations impinge upon most legal questions and may decisively influence how the law will be applied [261].

For many Christian attorneys this means addressing legal problems with advice and intervention that is consistent with compassion, as well as with the doctrines and traditions of Christian Scriptures.

By establishing volunteer legal aid clinics for the poor, Christian attorneys attempt not only to resolve the immediate legal problems of that underserved population, but hope to attack the underlying causes of poverty, and begin to rehabilitate the whole person.

> *And behold, there was a woman who had a spirit of infirmity eighteen years, and was bent over and could in no way raise herself up. But when Jesus saw her, He called her to Him...and she immediately was made straight and glorified God* (Luke 13: 11–13).

The attorneys involved with legal aid (Christian or secular) hope to drive home the enormity of this crisis to other attorneys, law students, and paralegals—in the process, creating informed and vocal advocates for the poor. Jesus was, after all, born in a manger.

Not all attorneys are in a position to practice poverty law for a living. However, the ABA recommends that attorneys donate 50 hours or the equivalent to *pro bono* work annually. Volunteering several hours per month at a community legal clinic (Christian or non-Christian), accepting one or more referrals from such a legal clinic, or donating funds comparable to 50 hours at the attorney's normal rate, can readily fulfill that obligation, as well as giving back to the community in a positive way.

Christian legal aid is offered to all those in need (regardless of religious affiliation or lack thereof). Muslims, atheists, Christians of whatever denomination (as well as those long fallen away) may all apply. Clients are not required to become Christian to qualify, and are not treated with any less respect if they are not Christian. Nor are they required to listen to the Gospel after legal advice has been given, if they do not wish to do so.

While the Lord is capable of effectuating healing in the lives of clients and legal professional alike, Christian attorneys do not attempt to act as pseudo-psychiatrists, psychologists, or social workers. In fact, they are strongly discouraged from doing so. Rather, they address the legal issue; to the extent possible, attempt to connect the client to a network of social resources; then—if and only if the client is willing—pray with him or her and share the Gospel.

Frequently, this approach will prompt clients to speak movingly of their lives.

I have had the privilege of counseling a father of four young sons. He had returned home from work to find his entire family on the porch, evicted. The client described having been abandoned as a boy by his father, leaving home not long afterwards, and fathering his first son at 14 years of age. He was determined not to abandon his own family, despite the temptation to do so.

I met with a mother who struggles daily to feed her children. We sat together in what was once a beautiful Victorian home—a gingerbread porch, high tin ceilings, and hand-carved stair railing (now badly water-damaged). A few pieces of broken furniture lay scattered around. Despite her problems, I could not help but be impressed by the woman's valor. Such homes lean wearily against one another, row on row, in West Philadelphia—each representing another forgotten life.

Attorneys, law students, and paralegals are not always in a position to solve all the underlying problems presented which may include drug addiction or mental illness. Some clients will present as broken by life.

Such clients are perhaps the greatest challenge to those of us desiring to see justice done in the world. There may be no earthly way to improve their situation, but to share their pain and grieve with them. Ultimately the work of healing in such cases must be left to God. *"He heals the brokenhearted and binds up their wounds"* (Psalm 147: 3).

At a minimum, sharing their problems allows clients the opportunity to unburden to a receptive audience, and examine their options. Whatever the nature or magnitude of their problems, the Gospel provides clients the assurance that they are not alone.

Those of us who, through the grace of God, have been "born again" can attest to the essential changes a personal relationship with Jesus Christ has effected in our own lives. It is the precious knowledge that God gave His only Son for our sins that we hope to share with willing clients. *"For God so loved the world that He gave His only begotten Son, that whoever believes in Him should not perish but have everlasting life"* (John 3: 16).

Those interested in obtaining more information about Christian legal aid may contact the Christian Legal Aid Society directly at www.clsnet.org.

PRISON MINISTRIES

- *The United States has the highest incarceration rate on earth* [109A].
- One out of every 37 Americans is incarcerated [109B].
- 49% of those incarcerated nationally are African American, compared with their 13% share of the overall population [204A].
- Nearly 1 in 3 (32%) African American men in the age group 20–29 is under some type of criminal supervision on any given day (prison, jail, probation or parole) [204B].
- 5.6 million Americans are or have been in prison [109C].

We cannot overlook these facts. There are too many lives being wasted.

> Six hundred thirty thousand inmates in the United States will complete the serving of their sentences and be released into society this year. Under the best of circumstances this massive re-entry into the communities of America would tax our resources and pose problems of re-adjustment for the returning inmate, his or her family and the neighborhoods into which they will relocate. The

> repair of tattered family relationships, the quest for gainful employment, overcoming lingering suspicions and dealing with addictions that led to imprisonment in the first place must all be managed with skill and courage...
>
> The country is woefully unprepared for the challenge. Many of the returning inmates will be without a dwelling place, unable to find work remunerative enough to meet their basic needs, in need of substance abuse treatment and, most critical, without a support group of any kind to help them with the adjustment. Unless immediate attention is given to the problem, it is estimated that something like 70% of these inmates will be re-arrested within two years of their release [109E]...
>
> —Reprinted with permission of Prison Fellowship, www.prison-fellowship.org.

Prison Fellowship, a Christian ministry with the goal of reforming the criminal justice system in accord with biblical principles, cites the following as essential for a successful return to society by the offender: a changed heart (genuine repentance); a concerned mentor; a welcoming church; a safe place to live; a good job; freedom from addiction; access to medical and mental health services; healed relationships with family and friends; healthy relationships, going forward; insofar as possible, repair for the harm done to the offender's victims; concrete steps to earn the community's trust; and restored citizenship rights [109D].

Most of these things require that the community at large—individuals, churches and private organizations—be more receptive, caring, and forgiving to the offender while not forgetting the victim. We may view some crimes, e.g. child abuse, as so heinous that that the offender, by his own actions in committing them, has waived certain rights for life. This is not inconsistent with forgiveness. Sin has consequences.

A list of ex-offender resources can be found at **Appendix V**. A study by the University of Pennsylvania's Center for Research on Religion and Urban Civil Society on InnerChange Freedom Initiative,[16] a faith-based pre-release program between Prison Fellowship and the Texas Department of Criminal Justice, can be found at http://www.manhattan-institute.org/pdf/crrucs_innerchange.pdf. For additional information, Prison Fellowship can be contacted directly at www.prisonfellowship.org.

Supporters of the bipartisan Second Chance Act of 2004: Community Safety Through Recidivism Prevention [144A and 144B] include the American Bar Association, American, American Center for Law and Justice, American Probation and Parole Association, Children's Defense Fund, Family Research Council, Human Rights Watch, National AIDs Housing Coalition, and National Black Church Taskforce Initiative on Crime and Criminal Justice [145].

President George W. Bush speaks of America as the "land of the second chance" and commended Representatives Rob Portman (R-OH) and Danny Davis (D-IL) who introduced the Second Chance Act, for their efforts [147]. However, the Administration's 2005 Budget proposed cuts to Juvenile Justice and Delinquency Prevention funding which, if implemented, would have amounted to a 40% reduction from 2004 levels (more than a 2/3 reduction over the prior 3 years) [143]...a striking disconnect.

Ex-slave, orator, and reformer, Frederick Douglass, warned us, well over a century ago:

> Where justice is denied, where poverty is enforced, where ignorance prevails, and where any one class is made to feel that society is an organized conspiracy to oppress, rob and degrade them, neither persons nor property will be safe.

RACISM

If someone says, "I love God," and hates his brother, he is a liar; for he who does not love his brother whom he has seen, how can he love God whom he has not seen? (1 John 4: 20)

There's not an American in this country free until every one of us is free. —Jackie Robinson

Both the Bible and science support the fact that we are all brothers under the skin. Population genetics has traced the divergent branches of the human family tree back to a common ancestor in Africa [184]. Even the most disparate groups of people share some 99.9% of DNA [207]. Latest genetic studies show that African Americans adults average 17–18% white ancestry [208A]. Approximately 10% of African Americans are over 50% white [208B]. More than 50 million white Americans have at least one African ancestor [208C].

SLAVERY

Slavery is the bitter root from which racism in America derives. To this day, there is substantial overlap between poverty and race.

> The first Africans in America arrived as Indentured Servants via Jamestown, Virginia in 1619. From 1619 to about 1640, Africans could earn their freedom working as laborers and artisans for the European settlers. Africans could become free people and enjoy some of the liberties like other new settlers. By 1640, Maryland became the first colony to institutionalize slavery. In 1641, Massachusetts, in its written legislative "Body of Liberties," stated that "bondage was legal" servitude, at that moment changing the conditions of

> the African workers—they became chattel slaves who could be bought and solely owned by their masters [39A].

Not only Africans but Native Americans were held as slaves in New England [215A]. That the regular slave trade included Native Americans can be seen from various Connecticut General Court documents [215B].

In 1660 the General Court authorized a company of men to demand four of the Narragansetts in exchange for a raid against settlers [215C]. The four were to be sent to Barbados as slaves [215D]. An enactment dated 1711 refers to "all negro, mulatto, or Spanish Indians [215E]." The account book of Major John Talcott (1674–1688), treasurer of the colony, reflects the sale by a Captain John Stanton of Stonington of Indian captives taken in battle, from which sale he "gained much." In 1677 it confirms the gift of a 7 year old Native American girl by Stanton to one Captain Joseph Gorham, for services rendered the crown [215F]. A deed dated 1722 then reflects the sale by Gorham of what seems to have been the same girl (now referred to as an "Indian woman named Dinah, of about 26 years of age…my own property…free and clear of all incumbrances…") [215G].

The estimates as to slave mortality vary greatly, but are enormous figures even at their most conservative:

> In *American Holocaust* (1992), David Stannard estimates that some 30 to 60 million Africans died being enslaved. He claims a 50% mortality rate among new slaves while being gathered and stored in Africa, a 10% mortality among the survivors while crossing the ocean, and another 50% mortality rate in the first "seasoning" phase of slave labor. Overall, he estimates a 75–80% mortality rate in transit.
>
> In *Slavery, A World History*, Milton Meltzer estimates that 10 million slaves arrived in the Americas. This would be the residue after 12.5% of those shipped out from Africa died on the ocean, 4–5% died while waiting in harbor, and 33% died during the first year of seasoning.
>
> In "The Atlantic Slave Trade and the Holocaust" (*Is the Holocaust Unique*, A. Greebaum, ed., 1996), Seymour

Drescher estimates that 21M were enslaved, 1700–1850, of which 7M remained in slavery inside Africa. 4M died "as a direct result of enslavement." Of the 12M shipped to America, 15%, or 2M more, died in the Middle Passage and seasoning year.

Jan Rogozinski, *A Brief History of the Caribbean* (1994): "[A]s many as eight million Africans may have died in order to bring four million slaves to the Caribbean islands."

In *The Slave Trade*, Hugh Thomas estimates that 13M left African ports, and 11,328,000 arrived...Fredric Wertham claims that 150,000,000 Africans died of the slave trade. [Matthew White estimates]...at the very least, 35% of those enslaved in Africa died before they were ever put to work in America.

On the other hand, at least 20% of them survived. Between these extreme possibilities (35–80%), the most likely mortality rate is 62%. In terms of absolute numbers, the lowest possible (and only barely possible at that) death toll we can put on the trans-Atlantic slave trade is 6 million. If we assume the absolute worst, a death toll as high as 60 million is at the very edge of possibility; however, the likeliest number of deaths would fall somewhere from 15 to 20 million...

Keep in mind that these numbers only count the dead among the first generation of slaves brought from Africa. Subsequent generations would contribute additional premature or unnatural deaths [45A]. [Emphasis added.]

—Matthew White, "Selected Death Tolls for Wars, Massacres and Atrocities Before the 20th Century," *Twentieth Century Atlas—Historical Body Count*, Slavery—African American Slavery.

Intellectual dishonesty supported the practice of slavery:

The deep involvement of the champion of absolute liberty, the Founding Fathers' intellectual hero, [John Locke] in the Royal Africa Company and other transatlantic slaving concerns, such as the Bahama Adventurers, is well-known. In 1669, Locke was invited by another colonial corporation, the Lords Proprietors of Carolina, to collaborate in formulating language, particularly on religious toleration, for the *Fundamental Constitutions* it was drafting (Carolina was one of several proprietary—privately- or shareholder-owned—colonies, like Pennsylvania and New Jersey). Locke's contribution enacts that "no person whatsoever shall disturb, violate or persecute another for his speculative opinions in religion or his way of worship." Locke's wording calls for toleration in the colony, so "that Jews, heathens and other dissenters from the purity of the Christian religion may not be scared and kept at a distance from it, but by having an opportunity of acquainting themselves with the truth and reasonableness of its doctrines...may be won over to embrace and unfeignedly receive the truth." This is not Locke sugarcoating toleration to commend it to the Lords Proprietors. Although ranked second only to Spinoza among the founding philosophers of modernity, there is extraordinary difference between the two. Locke is a particularist; it does not seem to require examination for him that whiteness and Christianity, say, are better than blackness and Judaism [80A].

—Original Source: John Locke, *The Fundamental Constitutions of Carolina* (London, 1682). Rare Books Division, The New York Public Library, Astor, Lenox and Tilden Foundations.

This form of hypocrisy was not limited to secular thought:

Slavery was a form of persecution which, in the eyes of colonial America, had to be justified. The black slave, easily identifiable, was targeted as being inferior, subhuman, and destined for servitude. The early Christian churches did not take up the cause of eliminating slavery until much later. The famous Boston theologian, Cotton Mather, in 1693 included in his *Rules for the Society of the Negroes* the explanation that, "Negroes were enslaved because they had sinned

> against God."[17] He later included a heavenly plan that "God would prepare a mansion in Heaven," but little or no way for the end of forced slavery on earth was undertaken by most religious groups [39B].

Contrast this with what Ben Patterson writes on the biblical slave, Hagar, in his excellent book, *Waiting: Finding Hope When God Seems Silent*:

> For a slave girl who had no rights of her own, who was no more than a piece of property to her master, who was the victim of the arbitrary choice of another, there could be no better name for a God who had shown himself to her as a God of grace. He cared for her. He *saw* her...To God, she was not a slave, she was Hagar!...and...what happened to her mattered to him...
>
> Old Puritan homes often had hanging on their walls an embroidered sampler with the words, "Thou seest me." It was an adaptation of the name Hagar gave God [after she had fled from Sarai into the desert. The phrase was intended by Puritans]...as a warning to those who read it, something to sober them up as they pondered God's unblinking gaze, His unceasing watchfulness of them...[B]ut this was not the intent of Hagar's name for God...He keeps His eyes on us because He wants to care for us, not because He wants to catch us in some sin...
>
> "I have now seen the One who sees me," Hagar said as she left the spring...Because she has seen the one who sees her, she is now free to go back to a very difficult situation at home and do the will of God there, even though it was not something she would have chosen for herself. She cannot know how things will turn out for her, but she knows she is seen by a God who sees what is ahead [260].

The earliest formal American protest against slavery was the Germantown Petition of 1688. Four German Quakers and Mennonites signed the Petition, referring to Matthew 7: 12 (the "Golden Rule") [258A].

"The Selling of Joseph," by former Salem judge, Samuel Sewall, in 1701, was one of the first American anti-slavery tracts published [257]. Sewell based his opposition to slavery on the Puritan guide for society, i.e. the Bible, concluding that "God hath given the Earth [and all its commodities] unto the Sons of Adam, and hath made of One Blood all Nations of Men [258B]."

Had there been a more "activist"—or perhaps more courageous—bench, the *Dred Scott*[18] decision might have been decided differently and the Civil War (with its 600,000 dead) avoided. Instead, Chief Justice Roger Taney wrote in 1857:

> ...We think they [people of African ancestry] are...not included, and were not intended to be included, under the word "citizens" in the Constitution, and can therefore claim none of the rights and privileges which that instrument provides for and secures to citizens of the United States....

Compare the language of *Plessy v. Ferguson* with that of *Brown v. Board of Education*, some 58 years later:

> The object of the [Fourteenth] Amendment was undoubtedly to enforce the absolute equality of the two races before the law, but in the nature of things it could not have been intended to abolish distinctions based upon color, or to enforce social, as distinguished from political, equality, or a commingling of the two races upon terms unsatisfactory to either.
>
> —Justice Henry Billings Brown (1896).

> We conclude that the doctrine of "separate but equal" has no place. Separate educational facilities are inherently unequal.
>
> —Chief Justice Earl Warren (1954).

It was not the law which had changed, but society which had advanced (albeit, not swiftly enough for those Americans who had suffered injustice and discrimination during the intervening half century simply because of the color of their skin).

Abraham Lincoln said, "Those who deny freedom to others deserve it not for themselves." Today the shackles imposed are economic.

> *Cuts Education*: Almost one-third of the domestic programs the President targets for cuts are in education, with funding reductions totaling $1.3 billion. He has proposed total elimination of 48 programs, including Drug-Free Schools State Grants, Educational Technology State Grants, the Perkins Loan program for students with exceptional financial need and the Even Start family literacy program [78].
>
> *Employment and Training Programs*: Funding for Workforce Investment Act (WIA) programs and the Employment Service (ES) would decline by $559 million, adjusted for inflation.... The popular Job Corps program is cut by $30 million in real terms, and the Migrant and Seasonal Farmworker program is eliminated. State unemployment insurance (UI) administrative grants would decline by $41 million [79B]...

Slavery contributed greatly not only to the economy of the Antebellum South, but the economic success of our nation as a whole:

> ...Of the 6.5 million immigrants who survived the crossing of the Atlantic and settled in the Western Hemisphere between 1492 and 1776, only 1 million were Europeans. The remaining 5.5 million were African. An average of 80 percent of these enslaved Africans—men, women, and children—were employed, mostly as field-workers. Women as well as children worked in some capacity...Even on plantations, however, they worked in other capacities. Some were domestics and worked as butlers, waiters, maids, seam-

stresses, and launderers. Others were assigned as carriage drivers, hostlers, and stable boys. Artisans—carpenters, stonemasons, blacksmiths, millers, coopers, spinners, and weavers—were also employed as part of plantation labor forces.

Enslaved Africans also worked in urban areas. Upward of ten percent of the enslaved African population in the United States lived in cities. Charleston, Richmond, Savannah, Mobile, New York, Philadelphia, and New Orleans all had sizable slave populations. In the southern cities they totaled approximately a third of the population.

The range of slave occupations in cities was vast. Domestic servants dominated, but there were carpenters, fishermen, coopers, draymen, sailors, masons, bricklayers, blacksmiths, bakers, tailors, peddlers, painters, and porters. Although most worked directly for their owners, others were hired out to work as skilled laborers on plantations, on public works projects, and in industrial enterprises. A small percentage hired themselves out and paid their owners a percentage of their earnings.

Each plantation economy was part of a larger national and international political economy. The cotton plantation economy, for instance, is generally seen as part of the regional economy of the American South. By the 1830s, "cotton was king" indeed in the South. It was also king in the United States, which was competing for economic leadership in the global political economy.

But the American financial and shipping industries were also dependent on slave-produced cotton. So was the British textile industry. Cotton was not shipped directly to Europe from the South. Rather, it was shipped to New York and then transshipped to England and other centers of cotton manufacturing in the United States and Europe. As the cotton plantation economy expanded throughout the southern region, banks and financial houses in New York supplied the loan capital and/or investment capital to purchase land and slaves.

> Recruited as an inexpensive source of labor, enslaved Africans in the United States also became important economic and political capital...The value of the investments slaveholders held in their slaves was often used to secure loans to purchase additional land or slaves. Slaves were also used to pay off outstanding debts. When calculating the value of estates, the estimated value of each slave was included. This became the source of tax revenue for local and state governments. Taxes were also levied on slave transactions.
>
> Politically, the US Constitution incorporated a feature that made enslaved Africans political capital—to the benefit of southern states. The so-called three-fifths compromise allowed the southern states to count their slaves as three-fifths of a person for purposes of calculating states' representation in the US Congress. Thus the balance of power between slaveholding and non-slaveholding states turned, in part, on the three-fifths presence of enslaved Africans in the census [100].

This does not even begin to take into account the contribution by individuals of color since the Civil War period [101]. There have been a great many success stories...as well as a great many tragedies, recorded and unrecorded.

> During the 1930s, after thousands of African Americans had been put to death by mobs—particularly in the South but in other regions of the country as well—lynchings were no longer unusual or shocking events that deviated from the norm. Approximately 4,742 individuals were lynched between 1882 and 1968; of the victims, 3,445 or 73 percent were Black. During the heyday of lynching, between 1889 and 1918, 3,224 individuals were lynched, of whom 2,522 or 78 percent were Black. Typically, the victims were hung or burned to death by mobs of White vigilantes, frequently in front of thousands of spectators, many of whom would take pieces of the dead person's body as souvenirs to help remember the spectacular event...Far from suppressing news about

> lynchings, newspapers embraced them, providing abundant, even graphic, coverage of vigilante violence [44].

As late as 1967, activist, Fannie Lou Hamer on commencing a voter registration drive among African Americans in Sunflower County, Mississippi was quoted, as saying:

> Peoples (sic) need a victory so bad. We've been working here since '62 and we haven't got nothing, except a helluva lot of heartaches [42].

The scars of sin run deep, extending even to the present day. With family structure deliberately destroyed by the system of slavery, men can often be seen as expendable [96]. With opportunities for generations denied [97] (and the Welfare System, itself, imperfect), the work ethic has been impaired. With patience long since eroded (and books actually missing from many inner city classrooms) [98], education is not seen as of value in the inner city. With the goal the same material success the media daily portray as possible for others, the dreams of the young center on easy riches.[19]

Martin Luther King, Jr., too, spoke of having a dream. How long will it take for us finally to make that dream a reality?

As Christians, we are bound to treat others as we ourselves would be treated.

> "'*...you shall love the Lord your God with all your heart, with all your soul, with all your mind, and with all your strength.' This is the first commandment. And the second, like it, is this: 'You shall love your neighbor as yourself.'*" (Mark 12: 29–31).

Why then are there still Ku Klux Klan members? Why are there websites bemoaning the fact that this President is not doing enough for his Conservative supporters, when our brothers and sisters are in such grave need? Why are we not out on the protest lines together?

Racism is not, of course, limited to white/black relations—nor to whites, alone. Pick virtually any color, ethnicity, or race, and it has been hated and/or subject to social injustice in this beloved country of ours—a country which can point with pride to outstanding individuals of every color, ethnicity, and race. Why we fail to recognize that—first and foremost—we are human escapes me. That we fail to see the rich array of these colors, ethnicities, and races as America's greatest strength, remains America's greatest loss.

GANGS: CAN'T WE ALL GET ALONG?

The first street gangs began in the 1600s, when homeless orphans banded together for basic survival needs, and as a substitute for family [141A].

The Irish were the first ethnic group to encounter the hardships of an urban setting [141B]. They clustered in the "Five Points" area of New York City, which became notorious for gang activity [141C]. By the 1840s, this included hand to hand combat, i.e. the beginnings of gang warfare [141D]. Jewish, Italian, and German gangs were to be found on the lower Eastside of New York City [141E]. By 1850, there were 30,000 gang members out of a population of 500,000 [141F]. Guns became more readily available after the Civil War, escalating the level of violence [141G].

During the late 1920s, Mexicans arrived legally in large numbers, the majority becoming laborers and domestic workers. Though born here (and classified as "white" for census purposes), the sons and daughters of these immigrants experienced racism and cultural repression, developing a distinctive look (the "zoot suit") as a response [141H]. In the summer of 1943, Los Angeles erupted in riots between off-duty servicemen and zoot suiters [141I]. These were fueled by press portrayals of the zoot suiters as hoodlums [141J].

Following WWII, Puerto Ricans flooded New York City, with overcrowding contributing to gang formation [141K]. Since jobs for adults were plentiful, the gangs now formed were adolescent-driven [141L]. Military tactics, e.g. intelligence gathering, were admired and adopted [141M], as was a gang lingo. "To bop" meant to fight [1451N].

In 1955 the New York City Youth Board began a Youth Club Project. At its peak, the Youth Club Project had over 200 former gang members as street workers and mentors to some 300 young gang members [141O]. Unfortunately, some active gang members viewed participation in the Youth Club Project as proof that they were sufficiently formidable to warrant intervention [141S].

By the 1950s, the number of girl gangs had, also, risen dramatically [141P]. Female gang members often had to undergo a rite of initiation (sometimes involving sexual intercourse with all the male gang members) [141Q]. Female gang members were typically involved in intelligence gathering and gun smuggling [141R].

The 1960s saw race riots in New York City, Los Angeles, and Newark [141T]. In Chicago, the "Vice Lords" grew to 8000, but in 1967—with Bobby Gore at the helm—they joined the mainstream to undertake constructive community programs [141U]. Becoming the first gang to incorporate (as the "Conservative Vice Lords, Inc."), allowed the Vice Lords access to grant monies which helped fund local businesses, a management training program, and an after-school location catering to young people [141V]. Chicago Mayor Richard Dailey remained unconvinced of the gang's good intentions though the neighborhood blossomed for over two years, under their charge [141W]. Jealousy by rival gangs and Gore's conviction for murder (disputed to this day) ended the idyll [141X].

In Los Angeles, African American gangs in the late 1960s included the Black Panthers from which the CRIPS (Community Revolution in Progress) and Bloods derived [141Y]. These two gangs battled over territory (Compton, Watts, South Central), with their colors blue and red, respectively [141Z]. Leadership was determined by violence which by the late 1980s "crack" cocaine escalated to a new level [141AA]. The battle was not over physical territory now, but market share [141BB]. This led to distrust within the gangs, as well as to many innocent deaths in drive-by shootings [141CC].

Ironically, the high-profile Rodney King beating [142]—of which, outrageously, police were cleared initially (though caught on tape)—led the CRIPS and Bloods to re-examine their situation in Watts [141DD]. The gangs expressed the desire to stop black-on-black violence, and declared a truce as of April 27, 1992 with all boundaries open [141EE]. Although there are 200 affiliate gangs across the country today, deaths have decreased substantially [141FF]. Many former gang members have become involved in positive community activities [141GG].

In San Francisco, Chinese gangs are tied to the adult underworld and used in proxy warfare [141HH]. Descended from centuries old tongs and triads, today's Chinese gangs use materialism to attract new members [141II]. Gang territory is divided by block, but organized along provincial Chinese lines [141JJ].

Neo-Nazi groups ("skinheads") are discussed in Part IV, Chapter 4 In Pursuit of Morality: Whose Darkness? in the context of hate speech.

What can we learn from all this?

- The original reasons for joining a gang remain valid today: security, protection, respect, a sense of family [141KK]. If we can address these, we can reduce the incentive to join a gang. These reasons, as indicated above, have been combined with and undercut by a highly individualist profit motive [141LL]. Every segment of society wants a piece of the American pie. For some, however, the obstacles are too high to make that attainable [141MM]. The promise of ready cash becomes an irresistible lure, no matter how high the price to be paid in innocent blood. Again, if we can make opportunities available to our disadvantaged youth, we will reduce the incentive to seek satisfaction outside the law.
- We can far more easily be divided than united. Yet united we stand; divided we fall (a saying actually attributed to Aesop, a Greek *slave* who lived as long ago as the 6th Century BC [186]). The truth has not changed much in two millenia.
- We find any excuse for division and conflict—color, race, territory, the clothing style of teenage boys. When there is no reason, we will prey on our own. This applies across the spectrum.
- Though there can be legitimate reasons for anger, violence gains nothing. If we want our young people to understand this, we need to make a point of teaching it to them. If we want them to understand that success takes time, but is worth the wait, we have to teach them that, as well.
- It is possible to forge bonds that transcend race, color, and creed. This, however, requires mutual effort and trust. We have role models to follow, if we choose to recall them. Policing will not be

effective, in this context, unless police, too, can be trusted by the community.

Jesus Christ is the King of kings and the Lamb of God, whose shed blood has purchased His people "*out of every tribe, tongue…and nation*" (Revelations 5: 9). He makes no distinctions.

AFRICA TODAY

Our young people need to be sensitized to social injustice because this is the world they will inherit. A world in which slavery still exists; in which 1.3 billion people live on less than a dollar a day, i.e. below the $370 per person per year threshold used by the World Bank to measure poverty in developing nations [94A]; in which AIDS is a death sentence for the poor; in which 15 million children die of hunger annually.

In some parts of Africa—with which we Americans have such close ties of blood, culture, emotion, and (dare I say) ethical responsibility—the per person income is less than $200 per year [94B]. This is abject poverty by any standard.

> Many aspects of [human] trafficking remain poorly understood although it is now a priority issue for many governments. Information available about the magnitude of the problem is limited…The struggle against human trafficking requires a different approach from that of trafficked goods—such as drugs and small arms…Traffickers objectify persons under their control, put them at work without payment, subject them to repeated sale, and may force them to take deadly options to destroy evidence—or murder them (Truong 1998, 2003a). Governments and those civic organizations which seek to free trafficked persons from enslavement or servitude, and to prosecute traffickers, must deal with people who have been placed in such difficult situations that their perception may have been transformed, and their survival mechanisms manipulated in ways that

strengthen rather than weaken dependency. Current efforts to counteract human trafficking fall into three categories: a) prevention and deterrence, b) law enforcement and prosecution of traffickers, c) protection of trafficked persons, "rehabilitation" and assistance in social reintegration. Unfortunately, these official procedures face many problems...such as fragmented evidence...

Coomaraswamy [views]...the lack of rights and the feminization of poverty as causative factors of violence against women (including trafficking)...We locate the main reasons in the economic marginalization of SSA [Sub-Saharan Africa]...The gender-based burdens of women are seen to be increasing in disputes over land-rights...[T]he emergence of autonomous migration over long distances by young people and children (male and female)—to get work, to find care, or to provide care for sick adults—are (sic) clear signals of distress...

[M]onetary measures of income and purchasing power as criteria for drawing what are called "poverty lines"...[fail] to capture the multi-dimensional character of poverty as a lived reality. Chambers (1989, 1995) was among the first to stress this multi-dimensionality and how it can encompass a wide spectrum of deprivation and disadvantage—ranging from the absence of a social base for dignity and self-respect, through isolation, physical weakness and seasonal vulnerability to shock, stress and lack of means to cope with damaging loss...[R]esources [for the poor, overlooked in a monetary assessment of poverty,] may include a variety of support networks—such as clan and kinship...(Elson, 1991; Beneria and Fieldman, 1992). A weakening or disbandment of any of these networks can trigger a downward spiral from relative to chronic poverty...

In the context of HIV/AIDS-related poverty, Ansell and van Blerk pointed out that "coping does not imply that such actions are invariably successful or carry no costs...and strategy does not imply a carefully prepared plan." The manner of coping may be another way of conveying "desperate poverty, social exclusion, and marginalization" (Whiteside, 2002). Where migration is a strategy to diversify household income and enhance personal well-being, it can lead to a downward spiral of destitution, particularly where there is a serious lack of options (De Haan, et al, 2002). Destitution can also be an outcome of risks—taken at the point of decision-making to migrate—which are not assessable...

- Africa's share of world exports decreased from over 3.5% in 1970 to about 1.5% by the end of the 1990s...
- The decline in Africa's exports over the last three decades represents an income loss of US $68 billion annually...
- Flows of Foreign Direct Investment (FDI) are not spread across a broad range of industries but concentrated on high value resource-based industries like oil and diamonds...

Data from Southern Africa—the area worst hit by the HIV-AIDS pandemic—highlights pressure on women on two fronts 1) male sexual demands, and 2) care (for the self and affected relatives)...Studies show that women's health risks stem primarily from the inability to refuse sex or ensure safe sex due to non-negotiable norms about men's entitlements to satisfaction, both in the context of intimacy and commercial sex (Varga, 1997; Weiss, et al, 2002). With the spread of HIV/AIDS the fear of infection has led men to impose sexual demands on young children—believed to be pure (UNICEF, 2003:8)...[This] combined with state failure to respond in a timely manner to the spread of the virus is now known to have allowed the multiple means of transmission further to develop (breast-feeding, blood transfusion, and intra-venal drug use)...Rau points out in his study on child labor and HIV/AIDS in SSA [Sub-Saharan Africa] (2002a: 2) that "girls in particular—whether they are in school, working as domestics, trying to earn cash by hawking, or working in overt prostitution—are subject to sexual coercion, manipulation, and harassment by men." In the three countries involved in his study (Zambia, South Africa, and Tanzania) there is an acknowledgement that poverty is forcing children to leave school and to take up work under conditions which render them more vulnerable to HIV/AIDS. The stigma of the disease is also identified as an important impediment to action [93]...

With this as background:

The President's Advisory Council on HIV/AIDS Endorse[d] the "ABC" HIV/AIDS Prevention Model

..."ABC" represents a three-point message for risk reduction: abstain, be faithful, use condoms...

[Significantly, t]he US Strategy limits condom education and distribution to "high-risk" groups, i.e. "prostitutes" and "sero-discordant couples," couples in which one partner is HIV-positive and the other is HIV-negative. Advocates point out that *in the countries where the US Strategy will provide aid, HIV prevalence rates are so high that every sexually active person can be considered "high risk."* The US Strategy does not support providing information about condoms as part of a broad campaign targeting the general population. "The Bush Administration claims to support the 'ABC' approach when addressing HIV/AIDS in other countries," said Smith [SIECUS, Director of Public Policy] "the *US Strategy, however, redefines 'ABC' by relegating condoms to the very fringes of prevention work."*

Data shows that each piece of the "ABC" model must be promoted in all segments of the population in order for prevention campaigns to be effective. In Uganda, sexuality education occurs in schools, and public radio delivers information on negotiating safer sex and delaying the age at which individuals first have sex. Social marketing of condoms is also a component and has increased condom usage from seven

> percent nationwide to over 50 percent in rural areas and over 85 percent in urban areas.
>
> Sophia Mukasa Monico, a native Ugandan and a senior AIDS officer at the Global Health Council, testified last year to the US Senate Foreign Relations Committee about "ABC" in Uganda. "I am deeply concerned when I hear people taking a single element of our successful national program, like abstinence, out of context and ascribing all of our achievement to that one element. All three elements must be implemented together in order for prevention to work," she said [102]. [Emphasis added.]
>
> —Sexuality Information & Education Council of the United States, 130 West 42nd Street, Suite 350, New York, NY 10036, www.siecus.org. Original Sources including: President's Emergency Plan for AIDS Relief: The US Five-Year Strategy to Fight Global HIV/AIDS, pages 9, 23–24; "Uganda Reverses the Tide of HIV/AIDS," World Health Organization; "Senate Foreign Relations Subcommittee 'Praises' Uganda's 'ABC' HIV/AIDS Prevention Method at Hearing," Kaiser Daily HIV/AIDS Report, May 21, 2003.

By no stretch of the imagination can such an approach be considered anything else, but politically motivated. Presumably, it satisfied the narrow requirements of certain idealogues on the Christian Right—in the process, ignoring biblical principles as to the sanctity of life, with which most of the rest of us are familiar.

Children are a blessing from God. *"...your children like olive plants all around your table. Behold, thus shall the man be blessed who fears the Lord"* (Psalm 128: 3). In the context of our stewardship obligation toward creation, birth control is nowhere expressly forbidden by Scripture. However, God is inextricably involved in the formation of life in the womb (Psalm 139), and any decision to limit or plan childbearing should be in accord with His commands (not merely based on our self-centered desires or convenience). Birth control is not, for instance, permissible to prevent the consequences of sins like adultery (*"You shall not commit adultery"* (Exodus 20: 14)) or fornication, i.e. sex outside marriage.

The moral questions raised here are, as follows:

a) whether, in a culture where migration by men in urgent search of a way to support their families is common, those same men may justify the use of condoms as a means of protecting themselves and their spouses from deadly disease, if and when their intention to remain faithful fails;
b) whether, in situations where women—even young girls—have chosen to enter the sex trade as the only means available to fend off starvation and/or support loved ones (or have been forced into the trade via human trafficking), they are permitted the use of condoms to protect their health and prolong their lives; and
c) whether, in a culture where women are not permitted (or do not recognize themselves as permitted) to decline sex, they are permitted the use of condoms, effectively, as self-defense against HIV/AIDS.

Setting aside any analysis on the basis of situational ethics[20] or moral relativism,[21] these questions can be addressed in reverse order:

Where—as at item c)—there is no choice involved, there is no possibility of sin. The use of condoms here is no mere matter of casual convenience. Self-defense is a God-given right.

Item b) is identical to or comes very close to item c). Here, choice is overcome by coercion—either direct or indirect. Picture kidnappers imposing these same conditions on your wives and daughters. Would that perhaps increase your moral outrage?

Finally, as to item a), I would hope that God in His mercy might forgive any rationalization on the part of these men, far from the comforts of home for months on end. However, the moral choice is that of the actors. For us, the question is simply, do we care enough to save lives?

What a legacy it would be, if Americans—young and old; rich and not-so-rich; Christian and non-Christian; white, black, red, yellow, and brown—reached back across the Atlantic to help restore the future of Africa.

After all, "'God is the color of water [105]...'"

HOMOSEXUALITY AND HOLINESS

"[H]e who is without sin among you, let him throw a stone at her first." (John 8: 7)

I've been thinking about the comments that are always made about the shower rooms and the lack of privacy... How easy it would be just to hang a shower curtain... —Margarethe Cammermeyer, dismissed on having admitted to homosexuality, despite a career in which she earned a Bronze Star for Vietnam War duty, *Time* (July 6, 1992)

When the woman caught in adultery was brought before Jesus, He who was sinless did not condemn her. Rather, He used the moment to convict her accusers of their own sins.

> *Then those who heard it, being convicted by their conscience, went out one by one, beginning with the oldest even to the last. And Jesus was left alone, and the woman standing in the midst. When Jesus had raised Himself up and saw no one but the woman, He said to her, "Woman, where are those accusers of yours? Has no one condemned you?" She said, "No one, Lord." And Jesus said to her, "Neither do I condemn you; go and sin no more"* (John 8: 9–11).

Few of those rabid to condemn homosexuals seem to recall this passage.

Jesus ate with tax collectors. He associated with prostitutes and lepers, the outcasts of society. Jesus' family tree, in fact, included a prostitute (Rahab); an adulteress (Bathsheba); an incest/rape victim (Tamar); and a pagan (Ruth). Jesus forgave a thief, even in His own agony from the cross. *"So speak and so do as those who will be judged by the law of liberty. For judgment is without mercy to the one who has shown no mercy. Mercy triumphs over judgment"* (James 2: 12–13).

GOD'S STANDARD FOR US ALL

The list of sins we *all*—heterosexual and homosexual—are instructed to avoid includes *all* unrighteousness and *all* sexual immorality—heterosexual and homosexual. That list, also, includes hatred and hypocrisy:

> *This people honors Me with their lips,*
> *But their heart is far from Me.*
> *And in vain they worship Me,*
> *Teaching as doctrines the commandments of men* (Mark 7: 7).

The following Scripture passage explains the reason underlying these prohibitions. The full text contains an express prohibition against homosexual activity. However, the passage is clearly not limited to that alone:

> *For the wrath of God is revealed from heaven against all ungodliness and unrighteousness of men, who suppress the truth in unrighteousness, because what may be known of God is manifest in them, for God has shown it to them. For since the creation of the world His invisible attributes are clearly seen, being understood by the things that are made, even His eternal power and Godhead, so that they are without excuse, because, although they knew God, they did not glorify Him as God, nor were thankful, but became futile in their thoughts, and their foolish hearts were darkened... Therefore God also gave them up to uncleanness, in the lusts of their hearts, to dishonor their bodies among themselves, who exchanged the truth of God for the lie and worshiped and served the creature rather than the Creator, who is blessed forever. Amen. For this reason, God gave them up to vile passions...And even as they did not like to retain God in their knowledge, God gave them over to a debased mind, to do*

> *those things which are not fitting; being filled with all unrighteousness, sexual immorality, wickedness, covetousness, maliciousness; full of envy, murder, strife, deceit, evil-mindedness... violent, proud... unloving, unforgiving, unmerciful... (Romans 1: 18–31).*

As Jesus explained, anger without just cause is—from God's perspective—the equivalent of murder; adultery includes not only pre-marital and extra-marital sex, but any sexual thought we voluntarily entertain about anyone other than a spouse (Matthew 5: 21–22, 27–28).

Such is the holiness of God, the extraordinarily high standard to which—heterosexual and homosexual—we are called to aspire. In simple terms, your broad-shouldered, straight as an arrow, football-playing son can no more live with his cutie pie girlfriend, than you can subscribe to *Playboy* and sit contently in church on Sunday while the pastor rants about gays.

Against that high standard, breaking a single Commandment amounts to breaking them all. If we have not had occasion to steal a loaf of bread, but have been angry, we cannot claim to be "better" than the thief. And God, of course, knows whether the thief was desperately attempting to feed his children (having tried every other means but theft, to do so).

By God's standard, which of us can say we are sinless? The central issue is not one of heterosexuality or homosexuality, but of holiness. We cannot deliberately persist in a sinful lifestyle. However—given our flawed nature—all of us fall short on a daily basis (certainly in thought). As such times, we can only throw ourselves on God's mercy, relying on the assurance that our salvation was accomplished through Jesus' sacrifice on the cross.

PERSECUTION AND THE CHURCH'S FAILURE

Homosexuals have been sinned against, and persecuted for centuries. As an example:

> For the late-blossoming Portuguese Inquisition…it was business as usual. This typical *auto de fé* [judicial sentence for heresy, usually death by hanging or burning at the stake] features a bigamist, *two sodomites,* six fornicators, two witches, and 38 alleged Judaizers—22 women and 16 men [82 and 83]. [Emphasis added.]
>
> —Original Sources: *Lista das pessoas, que sahirao, condenaccoes, que tiverao, e sentencas* (Lisbon, 1747). Dorot Jewish Division, The New York Public Library, Astor, Lenox and Tilden Foundations; and "The *'Auto de Fe'* of Madrid in 1680," The New York Public Library, Astor, Lenox and Tilden Foundations.

Homosexuals were among the first Adolph Hitler chose to attack [137A]. The horror of their lives at the Sachsenhausen Concentration Camp is recalled by Dr L.D. Claassen von Neudegg, a gay survivor of the camp:

> After roll call on the evening of June 20, 1942, an order was suddenly given: "All prisoners with the pink triangle will remain standing at attention!" Our detail commander barked: "Three hundred criminal deviants, present as ordered!" We were registered, and then it was revealed to us that in accordance with an order from the Reichsfuehring SS, our category was to be isolated in an intensified-penalty company, and we would be transferred as a unit to the Klinker Brickworks the next morning. The Klinker factory! We shuddered, for the human death mill was more than feared…Forced to drag along twenty corpses, the rest of us encrusted with blood, we entered the Klinker works…We had been here for almost two months, but it seemed like endless years to us. When we were "transferred" here, we had numbered around 300 men. Whips were used more frequently each morning, when we were forced down into the clay pits under the wailing camp sirens. "Only 50 are still alive," whispered the man next to me. "Stay in the middle—then you won't get hit so much [137B]."

It is without question our obligation as Christians to defend homosexuals against hateful behavior and violence. *Under no circumstances should a Christian participate in or condone such activity.*

If anything, we Christians have failed to reach out to these men and women with mercy and compassion, as human beings no more or less deserving of grace than ourselves. We have missed a great opportunity to mirror Christ to them, and have failed to see Christ in their eyes.

Harvest USA [138] is an exception to this. Biblically sound yet welcoming toward gay men and women, it seeks to proclaim Christ to a sexually broken world. Harvest USA distinguishes between sexual orientation and sexual practice. Contact can be made with this ministry at http://www.harvestusa.org.

Angelican Archbishop Benjamin Tutu of South Africa wrote:

> [I]f this sexual orientation were indeed a matter of personal choice, the homosexual persons must be the craziest coots around to choose a way of life that exposes them to so much hostility, discrimination, loss, and suffering [168E].

There are those who—like the Reconciling Ministries Network [171] (which works for full participation of all sexual orientations in the United Methodist Church)—dispute that a homosexual lifestyle is sinful at all [139A and 139B]. A statement entitled, "Here We Stand," by a number of Methodist leaders enunciates this position:

> Especially grievous to us at this time in history is the discrimination created by the statement in the Social Principles that holds that the practice of homosexuality is not condoned and is considered incompatible with Christian teaching. This statement contradicts in the same paragraph the affirmation that *homosexual persons are individuals of sacred worth* and our commitment to be in ministry for and with all persons...So centered in God's unconditional love and justice was Jesus that he offered an inclusive embrace of all people. As he empowered those marginalized and excluded by the dominating social barriers and practices of

> his time, he made visible the Reign of God. Jesus calls us and our church to do the same through personal and social reconciliation and transformation [172]. [Emphasis added.]
>
> —"Here We Stand," a collaborative effort of Methodist Federation for Social Action (MFSA) and Reconciling Ministries Network (RMN).

From a traditional Evangelical perspective, the answer is not for us to redefine God's law (Romans 1: 32). We have no authority to do that [139C].

> It has been suggested...[that what is prohibited] about the activities mentioned in Leviticus 18:22 and 20:13 is not homosexuality *per se*, but rather homosexuality as it is associated with pagan religion. Such associations, and not the homosexual behavior itself, would make those who participated ritually or ceremonially unclean...Consequently, just as the Old Testament sacrificial and dietary laws are no longer binding on believers today...so also these two laws concerning homosexual relations would likewise be defunct. Put another way, it is argued that Leviticus 18:22 and 20:13 are obsolete for two reasons. First, they refer to prostitution or practices associated with pagan worship rather than to the loving and committed same-sex relationships celebrated today. Second, like so much of the Old Testament, these laws are superseded by the New Covenant established by Jesus Christ...[However]it would be patently mistaken to attempt to divorce biblical ethics from their religious context. The threat of spiritual compromise accompanied by sexual immorality is a ubiquitous concern throughout the Bible. Every conceivable aspect of life, not only in the Old Testament but also in the New, has significance for our relationship with our Creator...An attempt to distinguish narrowly ceremonial sexual ethics in the Old Testament is an artificial distinction, foreign to a biblical world view, arising out of a secular mind set that seeks to order life without ref-

> erence to God "*from whom and through whom and to whom are all things*"...
>
> The *Scriptures do not single out homosexual behavior as some peculiarly sinful aberration unlike any other sin. Rather*, homosexual sin...is discussed in the same stern terms as are other sins—sins to which we are all sadly susceptible, and of which we are all, either in principle or practice, guilty. *The sentence of death applied to homosexual sin in Leviticus is in the New Testament applied to us all...*
>
> The interpretation of the Bible requires us to be honest with ourselves and our Maker. Will we yield to the loving lordship of the author of Scripture, whatever he requires of us?...Are we really interested in knowing God's will or are we just looking for affirmation of our beliefs and practices? *Are we willing to be honest about our own failings and forgive the failings of others?* These are the really hard questions that arise out of our study of God's word [140]. [Emphasis added.]

Simon LeVay—a neuroscientist previously with the Salk Institute and proponent of the genetic tie-in—is an evangelist who left scientific research to work primarily as an activist. LeVay views the biological case as *essential* to overcoming claims that homosexual behavior is sinful. According to LeVay, "A genetic component in sexual orientation says, 'This is not a fault, and this is not your fault' [166C]."

Speaking for the Human Rights Campaign, a homosexual-rights political organization, David M. Smith on the other hand told the *Washington Post*, "In the final analysis it should not matter whether there is a biological basis or there is not [166F]."

Whatever premise you start from, seek God out. He has been faithful and forgiving, and He is waiting with open arms.

THE "GAY GENE" THEORY

Indeed, what shapes our sexuality is not yet clear. As with many aspects of human behavior, both nature and nurture seem to play a part. Some homosexuals were molested. Others were not. Some had domineering mothers; absent fathers. Others did not. Some were brought up in strict, legalistic homes. Others had no religious training whatsoever. Some felt "different" from an early age. Others spent years confused over or struggling with their sexuality. No single pattern emerges, except that many homosexuals and lesbians believe it a matter of integrity to come "out of the closet."

The evidence as to existence of a "gay gene" predetermining sexual orientation has been hotly contested [167].

Researchers first began to suspect a genetic basis for homosexuality in the 1950s and 1960s when experiments by Franz J. Kalman and WW Schlegel showed that identical twins had 100% concordance, i.e. similarity to a specified degree, for homosexual orientation [168A]. The case for a biological cause gained credibility in 1991 through research by Michael Bailey, a Northwestern University scientist, and Richard Pillard who studied similar patterns of male homosexuality among identical twins, fraternal twins, and non-genetically related adopted brothers [166A]. Bailey and Pillard found 52% of identical twins gay (48% not) [168B].

The genetic case received international media attention in 1993 when Dean Hamer of the National Cancer Institute and colleagues claimed to have identified a specific genetic link to male homosexuality, and to have isolated the link to the X chromosome [166B]. Hamer drew DNA from the blood samples of a group of forty gay brothers. Among thirty-three of the forty, he found concordance, for five markers on a section of the X chromosome, inherited through the mother. The probability of this happening by chance was less than 1 in 100,000. On repeating the study, he obtained the same results.

Hamer did not isolate a gay gene, but the region in which a gay gene was likely to exist [168C]. Hamer did not, however, complete the control experiment of checking this on the X chromosome of the heterosexual brothers of these gay men [168D]. Additionally, the frequency of homosexuality among fraternal twins (22%) and non-twin brothers (9%) participating in the study should have been the same, since the two groups shared the same percentage of genetic material.

It was not. This was not explained, but suggests that factors apart from genetics can and do influence sexual orientation [169]

Fewer studies have investigated homosexuality in women. A 1990 study at McMaster University in Canada on left-handedness, suggested lesbian women have a different brain organization than heterosexual women (with language centered in the right rather than left hemisphere in gay women, as in women in the population who are left-handed) [168D]. In 1992, Bailey and Pillard followed up their study on homosexual brothers with a similar study on lesbian sisters. They found 48% of identical twins both lesbian (52% not). Based on earlier studies, the researchers hypothesized that higher than normal levels of masculinizing hormones such as testosterone during pregnancy (rather than a gene mandating sexual orientation) might have affected the lesbians' early fetal development [168F].

Clinical neurologists George Rice and George Ebers of Canada's University of Western Ontario failed to find the link between male homosexuality and chromosomal region Xq28 which Hamer had claimed. The Canadian study results (published in *Science* and supported by work at the University of Chicago), according to *Science*, did "not provide strong support for a linkage." Rice stated that the cumulative evidence, "would suggest that if there is a [genetic] linkage it's so weak that it's not important [166D]."

Hamer defended his original research, but conceded the Rice/Ebers study did confirm that some cases of homosexuality were not linked to the X chromosome. In 1997 Hamer stressed, "The trick will be to make sure that sexual orientation is included on a list of 'normal' traits rather that on a list of diseases and disorders." Hamer acknowledged that deciding which list sexual orientation belongs to is a "social judgment, not a scientific one [166E]."

The European Union Directives on Race, Employment and Equal Treatment established a common European framework to prohibit discrimination on the grounds of race, gender, disability, sexual orientation, religion or belief and age [170A]. In reply, the Catholic Bishops' Conference of England and Wales in February 2005 issued a Policy Statement and Guidelines dealing with diversity and equality [170B].

While defending the right of Catholic organizations to "cultivate and preserve" their "vision, mission, and values," the Guidelines contain the following statements:

> 28. The *Catholic community includes people of heterosexual, homosexual and bi-sexual orientation. Every human being, whatever his or her sexual orientation, has the right to live a life free from discrimination and harassment, and we welcome new legislation which protects this right.* Moreover, people of all sexual orientations have a right to take a full and active part in the life of the Catholic community.
>
> 29. Catholic teaching, of course, makes a distinction between sexual orientation and sexual activity, and it holds that all men and women are called to a life of chastity, and to fidelity if they choose to marry [170C]. [Emphasis added.]
>
> —Diversity and Equality Guidelines, prepared by Department for Christian Responsibility and Citizenship, approved for publication by Catholic Bishops' Conference of England & Wales © 2005 CBCEW.

THE SINGLE LIFE

In this sexually saturated culture of ours, we often fail to recognize that we are more than our sexuality. We long for meaning, for purpose, as God intended. We long for union with Him, but strive to fill that void by sexual means. As with Hagar (Part III, Chapter 3), He *sees* us. We are His children; He numbers the hairs on our head (Matthew 10: 30). We are not merely categorized by God as Jane Doe, lesbian; or John Smith, heterosexual male.

We all to varying degrees long for intimacy, for loving support and comfort. We all—heterosexual and homosexual; married or single—struggle with loneliness. This brings up another area in which the organized church has, by and large, failed. That adult singles—heterosexual and homosexual; widowed, divorced, or never married—serve a different, but equally important role to that of married couples is rarely, if ever, acknowledged.

We hear that Christian teens are to keep themselves sexually pure for marriage—to hold their breath till the "right person" comes along (presumably on schedule, between the ages of eighteen and twenty-one or so).[22] Many of us actually live past that age without encountering Mr. or Ms. Right. What long-term strategy are we expected to take? What if he or she never appears?

Some of us have deep desires that God chooses not to fulfill. Solomon, not David, was the one permitted to build the temple. There are men and women—heterosexual and homosexual—who would very much like to marry (or who pray not to lose a partner to illness). Men and women—heterosexual and homosexual—who would give anything for children of their own.

That a heart's desire goes unfulfilled is not a sign that we are worthless in God's eyes—though a desire denied can be experienced that way (even by believers).

We are at first stunned by the denial, then wrenched by pain and anger. Where is our good God? Surely, this marks us out as failures, as second-class. After a long while, we go on with our lives. The wound heals over, but we carry a huge emptiness inside. At unexpected moments, the scab is torn away and we bleed afresh.

These thoughts come to mind:

- We follow in the footsteps of our Lord, Jesus. We bleed as He bled.
- We know He is a good God. We have His Word on that—a Word made flesh.
- We grow in faith through grace, by trial.
- We are called to obedience.
- We are being shaped by our loss for the very purpose God intends.

Our cultural ideal is to give in to passion, to be swept away. Anything less is unsatisfactory. The Bible, however, teaches that sexual behavior—heterosexual and homosexual—is always subject to the will. At first this seems unrealistic, counter-intuitive. We are, after all, sexual human beings (Christians no less so). We buy cars based on sex appeal. We react to moonlit nights and Georgia O'Keefe.

Passion can be held in check by principle, but the goal is not to convert us into repressed neurotics. It is to deepen our love for God to such an extent that we are willing to make the necessary sacrifices out of that profound love (Philippians 1: 9–10). For "...*those who are Christ's have crucified the flesh with its passions and desires*" (Galatians 5: 24).

Jesus went willingly to the cross, out of love for us, and obedience to the Father. We, in turn, are asked to live sacrificial lives (Romans 12: 1). Sacrifices are bound to be difficult and painful. Only overwhelmed by the enormity of Christ's love can we attempt to comply.

God hears our prayers, spoken and unspoken. He knows our longings, even those unfulfilled. "*I said in my hast, 'I am cut off from before Your eyes;' nevertheless, You heard the voice of my supplications when I cried out to You*" (Psalm 31: 22).

Singles—male or female; heterosexual or homosexual—are in the position to offer a unique level of service to those in need, and the community as a whole. We have much more freedom at our disposal than do our married friends. Though single, we are never alone with God by our side, and—whether we realize it or not—never without purpose.

> *Then one of the Pharisees asked [Jesus] to eat with him. And He went to the Pharisee's house, and sat down to eat. And behold, a woman in the city who was a sinner, when she knew that Jesus sat at the table...brought an alabaster flask of fragrant oil, and stood at His feet behind Him weeping; and she began to wash His feet with her tears, and wiped them with the hair of her head; and she kissed His feet and anointed them with the fragrant oil. Now when the Pharisee who had invited Him saw this, he spoke to himself, saying "This Man, if He were a prophet, would know who and what manner of woman this is who is touching Him, for she is a sinner."*
>
> *And Jesus answered and said to him, "Simon, I have something to say to you."*
>
> *So he said, "Teacher, say it."*
>
> *"There was a certain creditor who had two debtors. One owed five hundred denarii, and the other fifty. And when they had*

nothing with which to repay, he freely forgave them both. Tell Me, therefore, which of them will love him more?"

Simon answered and said, "I suppose the one whom he forgave more."

And He said to him, "You have rightly judged." Then He turned to the woman and said to Simon, "Do you see this woman?... You did not anoint My head with oil, but this woman has anointed My feet with fragrant oil. Therefore I say to you, her sins, which are many, are forgiven, for she loved much. But to whom little is forgiven, the same loves little."... Then He said to the woman, "Your faith has saved you. Go in peace" (Luke 7: 36–44, 46–47, 50).

STEM CELL RESEARCH AND THE DISABLED

But as for me, I trust in You, O Lord; I say, "You are my God." My times are in Your hand... (Psalm 31: 14–15)

Congress acknowledged that society's accumulated myths and fears about disability and disease are as handicapping as are the physical limitations that flow from actual impairment. —William J. Brennan, Associate Justice, US Supreme Court

Some of you may know this poem, said to be by a Civil War veteran, badly injured as a young soldier. Having long waited for God to show His purpose, the crippled soldier wrote toward the end of his struggles:

I asked for strength that I might achieve;
I was made weak that I might obey.
I asked for health that I might do greater things;
I was given infirmity that I might do better things.
I asked for riches that I might be happy;
I was given poverty that I might be wise.
I asked for power that I might have the praise of men;
I was given weakness that I might feel the need of God.
I asked for all things that I might enjoy life;
I was given life that I might enjoy all things.
I have received nothing I asked for, all that I hoped for.
My prayer is answered.

As theologian, Martin Luther put it, "We pray for silver, but God often gives us gold instead."

With loving care, God guides our footsteps, even in desert places. When we can no longer go forward on our own, He carries us.

Classical composer, Ludwig van Beethovan; President Franklin Delano Roosevelt; Irish novelist and poet, Christy Brown; Ray Charles, the musician perhaps most responsible for developing soul music; actress, Marlee Matlin; and Nicole Johnson, Miss America 1998, could all be termed disabled ("physically challenged") in one way or another [157]. That is hardly the first thing that would come to mind about any of them.

What each did was pursue a life—develop talents, follow dreams, overcome obstacles. It was just that those obstacles included deafness, polio, blindness, cerebral palsy, and diabetes—oh, and poverty, in some cases.

We focus on the talent, but it is the heroism which is astounding. And it is the heroism required for daily living by ordinary people that should be the real focus when we discuss disabilities. That term—"heroism"—is embarrassing. Those of us with disabilities do not want accolades, we want the chance to work; we want to be treated as normal by the world. But our daily struggles do not go unnoticed by God, and they may have greater significance than we recognize.

This does *not* require that we forego the hope science may offer. Laudable ends cannot, however, justify immoral means. That principle applies to the abortion debate, as well.

Hear me out. Christopher Reeve was a remarkable man. An advocate for the disabled and an outspoken proponent of stem cell research, Reeve, nonetheless, continued his work in film and television following the accident which left him paralyzed. No one would have wished that trauma on Reeve or his family. Anyone of us would have spared him that grief, if we could. However, Reeve's impact for good was exponentially increased by it. The world will be forever grateful.

There are World Paralympics. There is a World Blind Sailing Championship, and are disabled sailing organizations throughout the globe [154]. These are not for sissies. On the other hand, struggling with such basic human functions as eating, dressing one's self, and bowel and bladder control, can have devastating effects on self-esteem [158].

Joni Eareckson Tada is a woman who was left paraplegic at age 17, following a diving accident. Initially, stunned and bitter, Joni has since come to terms with her condition. She now runs "Wheels for the World," an organization which collects and refurbishes wheelchairs for distribution in third-world countries. Also, a writer and the host of a radio program titled, "Joni and Friends," Eareckson Tada has addressed extensively the question of why God allows suffering:

> God will fulfill His purpose for you. He'll do it *for* you because He keeps His promise. He'll fulfill His plan *in* you by creating in you the image of His Son. Also, God will fulfill His plan *through* you as you touch others with His love and faithfulness. Nothing ever thwarts the purpose of God. Nothing can ruin His plan...A woman I had been counseling shook her head and said to me, "I could never live in a wheelchair totally paralyzed." "Relax," I replied with a smile, "because you'll probably never have to." "How can you be so sure?" she said suspiciously. I had her flip open her Bible and read Jeremiah 29: 11. *["For I know the thoughts that I think toward you, says the Lord, thoughts of peace and not of evil, to give you a future and a hope."]* "But what about you? Look at your wheelchair. You don't think God's plan harmed you?" I sighed and smiled at the woman, realizing there was no way I could humanly convince her...Because God is love, His plans can only be loving. Because God is good, His plans for you are of the highest good. Because He is the Lord of Hope, His purpose is to always give you hope...God will only permit in your life those trials that, with His grace, you can handle. That includes everything from emotional pain to physical paralysis. And this is why you have the assurance that His plans only mean spiritual prosperity and a hopeful future [159].
>
> —Taken from *Diamonds in the Dust*, by Joni Eareckson Tada. Copyright © 1993 by Joni Eareckson Tada. Used by Permission of Zondervan.

We need not be classical composers or public figures to count in God's eyes. We are not assessed by what we can "do," but by who we are. After all, Jesus restored sight to the blind, cured epileptics of seizures, and gave paralytics the power to walk. More even than that, He died to give us life everlasting. Had there been only one of us in need of salvation, He would have died for that one alone.

When we cry out in pain, we know He understands. When we complain about the unfairness of our situation, we recall that a good and holy God gave His only begotten Son as atonement on our behalf, with no requirement that He do so.

Archbishop Fulton J. Sheen expressed these thoughts in poetic form in *Cross-Ways* [160]:

> When we suffer, we do not want one
> Who stands over us like a physician,
> Who touches us as tongs touch hot coals,
> Who washes in antiseptic after contact,
> And who parrots, "Keep your chin up."
> We want One Who left footprints
> In the dark forest—so we can follow.
> A Surgeon Who, before He cuts,
> Says: "I had the same—see My Scars!"
> Someone Who stumbled to a Throne
> And walked not unfallen to the Hill.
> We want One Who, as we question:
> "Does God know what it is to suffer?"
> Can point to riven Side and open Heart,
> Saying: "Wouldst thou not be nobler than I
> If thou couldst suffer for Love,
> And I could not?"...

—"When We Suffer." From *Cross-Ways* by Fulton J. Sheen (originally published in 1967 under the title *Lenten and Easter Inspirations*). Reprinted by permission of the Society for the Propagation of the Faith on behalf of the Estate of Fulton J. Sheen.

> ...did not Christ on the Cross complain:

"My God! Why hast Thou abandoned Me?"
If the Son asked the Father...
Why should not you?
But let your wails be to God
And not to man,
Asking not: "Why does God do this to me?"
But, "Why, O God, dost Thou treat me so?"...
And at the end of your sweet complaining prayer...
You will not so much ask to be taken down
As the thief on the left,
But to be taken up as the thief
Who heard: "This Day, Paradise"...

—"Complain." From *Cross-Ways* by Fulton J. Sheen (originally published in 1967 under the title *Lenten and Easter Inspirations*). Reprinted by permission of the Society for the Propagation of the Faith on behalf of the Estate of Fulton J. Sheen.

Please, do not think I lack comprehension—or compassion—for suffering on this scale. Or, for that matter, that I jumped to some stock conclusion about the morality or immorality of stem cell research. I recommend that to no one. This is a critical and complex issue requiring careful consideration.

As for myself, I had spinal surgery at the cervical level, and have for years endured back pain. I have something known as chronic urticaria (CU). This is an autoimmune condition in which the body makes anti-bodies against itself—producing severe hives. The hives can progress to shock, if not controlled. Along with the medications I take daily for the CU, I travel with an epinephrine injector for emergencies. I suffer from severe migraines, and have lain on the floor in anguish, unable to reach the phone to call for help. I have experienced enough side-effects from medication over the years to fill an encyclopedia; and have made more emergency room visits than I can count.

I lost a friend to melanoma; saw another friend through breast cancer; and have one now wrestling with colon cancer.

I do not compare any of this on my part to paralysis or blindness. I do though feel I have some standing to speak.

STEM CELLS DEFINED

Stem cells are the precursors of all specialized cells in the body [174A]. Blood stem cells are found in the bone marrow and continuously produce blood and immune system cells. Mesenchymal stem cells are the source of new bone and cartilage. Neuronal stem cells are the source of nerve tissue, both during the embryonic stage and later in life [174B].

These more specialized stem cells are, themselves, preceded in the inner cell mass of the pre-implantation embryo and certain areas of the early fetus by more general stem cells (sometimes called "pluripotential stem cells" or PSCs) [174C]. In 1998, two independent research groups—headed by Dr. James Thomson of the University of Wisconsin and John Gearhart of Johns Hopkins University, respectively—isolated these early stem cells and succeeded in culturing them [174D].

Stem cell research has enormous potential (in human, medical, and commercial terms) [174E].

STEM CELL SOURCES

There are three sources of stem cells:

1. adult stem cells, present from infancy and onward [174L], as well as in umbilical cord blood;
2. embryonic germ cells, derived from aborted fetuses or discarded human embryos available at fertility clinics [174M]; and
3. embryonic stem (ES) cells, from the inner cell mass of blastocyst stage embryos (formed four or five days after the egg is fertilized) [174F and 178A].

The first of these is multipotent, i.e. capable of producing a range of cells (as, for instance, blood stem cells can). The second and third are pluripotent, i.e. capable of producing any type of cell [174G].

For cell replacement therapies to live up to their potential, cell lines must be produced which will not be rejected by the recipient's immune system. To accomplish this would require either:

a) That the immune system factors within the donor stem cell be manipulated to suit; or
b) that on each intervention, tissues be prepared compatible with the patient [174H].

Somatic Cell Nuclear Transfer Technology is a method allowing for the latter [174I]. This method uses the cloning developed by Ian Wilmut and his colleagues at the Roslin Institute [174J]. The nucleus is removed from a donor egg and replaced with the nucleus from one of the recipient's somatic cells, e.g. from the skin. This egg is then stimulated to divide. The result is a blastocyst stage embryo which is then dismantled ("disaggregated") to produce an ES cell line made to order for the patient [174K].

ETHICAL AND MORAL ISSUES

- "Like several other recent studies, the new work with hearts suggests that stem cells retrieved from adults have unexpected and perhaps equal flexibility of their own, perhaps precluding the need for the more ethically contentious [embryonic] cells [183]."

  —Original Source: Rick Weiss, "Studies Raise Hopes of Cardiac Rejuvenation," *Washington Post,* March 31, 2001.

- On June 15, 2001, the *Globe and Mail* (Canada) reported a story that could provide great hope to those with spinal cord injuries. Israeli doctors injected paraplegic Melissa Holley, age 18, with her own white blood cells. Disabled when her spinal cord was severed in an auto accident, Holley regained the ability to move her toes and control her bladder. Note that this was the result of *adult* stem cell research, and barely reported, if at all, in the US [182A].
- On July 19, 2001, the *Harvard University Gazette* reported that mice with Type 1 diabetes (an autoimmune disorder) were *completely cured* of their disease using adult stem cells. This was accomplished by destroying the cells responsible for the disease, after which the animals' own adult stem cells replaced the missing

cells with healthy ones. Dr. Denise Faustman commented that, if the therapy worked in humans, "[W]e should be able to replace damaged organs and tissues by using adult stem cells, thus eliminating, at least temporarily, the need to harvest and transplant stem cells from embryos and fetuses." No general media reported the story [182B].

- In December 2001, *Tissue Engineering*, a peer–reviewed journal, reported that researchers believed they would be able to use adult stem cells found in the fat to rebuild bone. The researchers were about to conduct animal studies. If these studies were successful, osteoporosis and other degenerative bone conditions could benefit greatly. This development was essentially ignored by the mainstream press [182C].

The *New Scientist* in 2002 reported successful work by Catherine Verfaillie of Minnesota University in locating adult stems cells, dubbed MAPCs ("multipotent adult progenitor cells"), in bone marrow [176]. The ethical question was raised even then as to why most researchers insisted *embryonic* stem cell research should continue. However, as of January 2001, at least 123 patient, research, and academic institutions were committed to advancing ES cells (in the belief it was still too early to know whether adult stems cells would have the same potential as embryonic) [177].

> Most research proponents feel that the rights of a blastocyst are far outweighed by the need for new treatments and potential cures. And they do not consider blastocysts to be human beings *per se*. "I believe that the human embryo has some moral status, but it is quite different from the status of a living, breathing human who is desperately ill," explains Hank Greely, JD, a law professor with the Stanford Center for Biomedical Ethics. "I think human life is too sacred to let it be lost for lack of pursuing promising research avenues [178B]."

Dr. Irving Weissman, Director of Stanford University's Stem Cell Institute sought a workable middle ground [178D]. Opposed to reproductive cloning, he argued that it should be banned, as is in a small number of states, but that Somatic Cell Nuclear Transfer Technology to create new stem cell lines for research and therapy a/k/a "therapeutic cloning" should remain legal [178E].

Without that technology, researchers would be left with excess embryos from fertility clinics as their only source of embryonic stem cells. These embryos are a poor source for medical research, since most carry just the genes of healthy white couples. Somatic Cell Nuclear Transfer Technology allows researchers to use nuclei from non-white patients, and patients with genetic diseases, to develop pluripotent stem cell lines, and better represent the diversity of the population [178F].

Carole Hogan, spokeswoman of the California Catholic Conference takes this position:

> There's no way to get [ES] cells out without killing embryos...An embryo is the earliest form of human life—it's not just a fertilized egg. People who are in support...[of ES cell research] minimize the embryo and make it sound like a building block or product [178C].

Scientists do not currently believe that embryos are capable of experiencing pain until further along in their development [175A]. For that reason, some who consider themselves religiously and morally sensitive, nonetheless, can characterize embryos as merely a "form" of human life [175B], and assess the moral worth of embryos as residing exclusively in their future potential [175C].

These individuals argue that so-called symbolic issues and concern for the sanctity of human life should not outweigh the possible benefits of ES cell research [175D]. Having convinced themselves that morality derives principally from the balance of competing interests—and seeing embryos as possessing no such interests, at least in the present moment—they recommend a morality which is said to evolve "on the ground" [175E].

However sincere it may be, this morality changes with the times. God's does not.

We may not wish to acknowledge the real nature of our choices.

We may not want to accept them, but the bottom line is simple. Some of us are here, and can speak for ourselves. Others cannot. They would live only if given time to develop fully (or would not have come into being at all, if we did not wish to make use of their cells—cells which under different circumstances would become their body parts).

We may be more sympathetic to those whose voices we can hear, whose faces we can see, for that reason arguing that their interests far outweigh those in the group unable to speak. If so, let us at least be honest with ourselves.

The misleading argument is sometimes put forward that stem cell research on aborted fetuses and the discarded embryos from fertility clinics would give meaning to lives already lost. Any woman who has miscarried knows the reality of a life in the womb, and the mourning associated with loss. The possibility of giving meaning to such loss, understandably, holds great appeal. A majority in our society have conceded that the lives of aborted fetuses and discarded embryos are forfeit. Moreover, because of the nature of *in vitro* fertilization, we have become inured as a society to the concept of frozen embryos.

Of course, in God's eyes, these lives had meaning before even they came into being.

What if our new technologies do not succeed? How many lives will have been allowed to expire in a Petri dish or have been dropped into a lethal solution, in the interim?

And if our technologies do succeed, do we create a class of beings that never reach maturity, solely for the purpose of servicing our needs? Would the perverse human experiments performed in Nazi concentration camps have been morally justified, if they had produced scientifically useful results?

From a human perspective, the comparison may sound melodramatic, excessive. Not so from God's perspective:

> *My frame was not hidden from You,*
> *When I was made in secret,*
> *And skillfully wrought in the lowest parts of the earth.*
> *Your eyes saw my substance, being yet unformed.*
> *And in Your book they all were written,*
> *The days fashioned for me,*

When as yet there were none of them (Psalm 139: 15–16).

Dan Perry, President of the Coalition for the Advancement of Medical Research, a stem cell research advocacy group, takes this view:

> With therapeutic cloning, no egg and sperm ever meet, there is no implantation of a cloned structure into the uterus and there is no fetus, no pregnancy, no birth...Yet for ideological reasons some blur the line between reproductive cloning and therapeutic cloning [178G].

Now, this is a cleverly circular argument!

No sperm is required because the entire nucleus of the donor egg (containing one-half the normal set of chromosomes from the female parent, in expectation of being paired with one-half the normal set of chromosomes from the male parent) is replaced by a full set of chromosomes from a somatic cell. It is then stimulated to begin blastocyst formation.

That disaggregation is required for the production of cell lines is, itself, proof that the immensely intricate and beautiful process of cell organization—which ultimately results in the formation and birth of a child, if an infant is conceived in the womb—has begun. There is no fetus, no pregnancy, and no birth because these are terminated by the researchers?! For Perry to make this argument is for a patricide to request mercy from the court, on the basis of his orphan status.

And if by ideology Perry means that "inconvenient" or outdated beliefs are being applied, we use those same inconvenient beliefs to regulate experimentation on adults. We saw the abhorrent results, when Adolf Hitler chose to ignore those outdated beliefs.

Calling the procedure "therapeutic" is icing on the cake! It is certainly not therapeutic for the embryo.

Resort to the utilitarian argument ("the greater good"), as a fallback, is extremely dangerous—particularly from the perspective of the disabled. Who makes the decision as to which of us "matter" to society? Are we dispensable, if we are disabled? What if we are fully capable, but there were too many engineers trained in a given year for the jobs available? What if we are over 60? Over 40? What if we do not have the requisite blue eyes and blond hair?

And since certain of our characteristics can now be determined from our genes, will there come a time that it is more cost effective simply to abort those children who do not fit the requisite mold?

We are already told that boys are favored in China. The state imposed "one child policy" there (enforced since the 1980s) has had parents favoring boys and aborting female infants or disposing of them shortly after birth [266]. According to International Planned Parenthood, there were 750,000 abortions in China in 1999 alone, over 70% of these female infants. How precisely can this be said to have advanced women's rights, reproductive or otherwise?

Remarks in June 2005 by Princeton University's Robert P. George, a member of the Administration's Council on Bioethics, are particularly significant, in this connection:

> ...[T]he question of *whether a human embryo is* or is not a *whole living member of the species Homo sapiens* is not one to be resolved in the mind of any conscientious citizen or morally serious policymaker by examining public-opinion polling data...There is no mystery about when the life of a new human individual begins. It is *not a matter of* subjective opinion or *private religious belief.* One finds the *answer not* by consulting one's viscera or *searching through the Bible or the Koran*; one finds it, rather, in the basic texts of the relevant scientific disciplines. Those texts are clear. Although none of us was ever a sperm cell or an ovum, *each of us was, at an earlier stage of development, an embryo,* just as each of us was an adolescent, a child, an infant, and a fetus...One's *identity as a human being does not vary with or depend upon one's location, environment, age, size, stage of development, or condition of dependency.* Of course, science cannot by itself settle questions of value, or dignity, or morality. And there are, to be sure, *people such as* my colleague *Peter Singer* who understand the science, but who *deny the ethical proposition that human beings have inherent dignity and equal rights.* They are *willing to license the killing of* certain innocent human beings (the

very young, the severely retarded, the gravely debilitated), distinguishing those whom they regard as "persons" from those whom they believe are not, or are not yet, or are no longer "persons." Hence, Singer's notorious advocacy not only of abortion but of infanticide and euthanasia as well...Surely [we] would wish to uphold against the Singers of the world Jefferson's "self-evident" proposition that all human beings are created equal...The *truth is that we do not know when, or even whether, embryonic stem cells will prove to be useful in treating any disease.* Leading authorities on Alzheimer's disease, including many scientists in the field who personally favor embryonic-stem-cell research and its public funding, say that Alzheimer's will almost certainly *never* be treated (much less cured) by embryonic-stem-cell therapies...We cannot say with certainty that embryonic cells will never prove therapeutically useful in treating other diseases, but as a matter of sheer fact *not a single embryonic-stem-cell therapy is even in clinical trials. No one knows how to prevent tumor formation and other problems arising from* the use of *embryonic stem cells.* No one knows whether these problems will be solved or solved before other research strategies render embryonic research obsolete...*Oocyte assisted reprogramming (OAR)* is *among* the most exciting *proposals for obtaining pluripotent stem cells without killing or harming human embryos.* OAR is a *variation of* a broader concept known as "*altered nuclear transfer.*" It combines basic cloning technology with epigenetic reprogramming...In OAR...the somatic-cell nucleus or the egg cytoplasm or both would first be altered before the nucleus is transferred. The modifications would change the expression of certain "master genes"—transcription factors that control expression of many other genes by switching them on or off. These genetic alterations *would permit the egg to reprogram the somatic-cell nucleus directly to a pluripotent, but not a totipotent (i.e., embryonic) state.* The altered expression of the powerful control gene would ensure that the characteristics of the newly produced cell are immediately different from, and incompatible with, those

> of an embryo...[W]e would reasonably expect to obtain precisely the type of stem cells desired by advocates of embryonic stem-cell research, without ever creating or killing embryos...William Hurlbut of Stanford University and the President's Council on Bioethics has been the leading voice urging scientists and policy makers to explore altered nuclear transfer [181]...[Emphasis added.]
>
>

Thereafter, scientists at the Whitehead Institute for Biomedical Research in October 2005 demonstrated that altered nuclear transfer (ANT)—proposed by Hurlbut and discussed by George (above)—was possible in mice [185A]. The Whitehead Institute is a nonprofit research and educational facility, with a teaching affiliation to MIT [185D]. In an attempt to avoid the ethical controversy surrounding embryonic stem cell research, Rudolf Jaenisch and Alexander Meissner, a graduate student in his laboratory, created a blastocyst unable to implant in a uterus, by disabling Cdx2, the gene which allows an embryo to grow a placenta [185B]. They achieved this using a technique known as RNA interference, publishing their findings in the online edition of the journal, *Nature* [185C].

With all this still in dispute, the *Journal of Stem Cells and Development* subsequently reported that the University of Minnesota Medical School (which conducts adult stem cell research) had discovered a new group of cells in human umbilical cord blood with the properties of primitive stem cells and the potential to produce a large variety of cell types [179A]. Umbilical cord blood is known to contain stem cells that can produce the cells found in blood. It has been so highly successful in curing and treating disease and illness [179B] that umbilical cord blood banking was already becoming common in 1998 [180A]. The New England Journal of Medicine the same year reported that recipients from unrelated donors accounted for almost all transplants using adult stem cell lines from umbilical cord blood [180B].

A *New York Times* article as recently as February 21, 2006, reported on the outcome of cancer research by Dr. Michael Clarke at Stanford University in 2003; Dr. Peter Dirks of the University of Toronto in 2004; and Dr. Peter Gibbs at the University of Florida. All three found stem cells or stem-like cells (in human breast tumors, brain tumors, and bone cancer, respectively) [267A].

This suggests that aberrant adult stem cells may be the cause for some cancers. Biologists theorize either:

a) That the adult stem cells allowing for routine cell regeneration are, themselves, somehow damaged by mutation, or
b) that their immediate progeny (known as progenitor cells) are damaged, regaining the ability to self-renew, i.e. divide unevenly (in the process losing the ability to control population size) [267B].

There is a great deal yet to learn before any chance for a cure, but the theory (if proven correct) would explain why cancers after being almost destroyed by radiation and/or chemotherapy can sometimes return [267C].

It appears that we may have found a viable alternative to embryonic stem cell research.

Still, a line comes to mind which the prophet Jeremiah is believed to have authored after the fall of Jerusalem. *"The hands of the compassionate women have cooked their own children; they became food for them in the destruction of the daughter of my people"* (Lamentations 4: 10).

Is this our story, as well? In the face of suffering here on earth, are we pursuing the unthinkable, when God has promised us an eternity free from sorrow and pain?

ARTIFICIAL LIFE SUPPORT AND ASSISTED SUICIDE

Therefore you now have sorrow; but I will see you again and your heart will rejoice… (John 16: 22)

Any man's death diminishes me, because I am involved in Mankind; And therefore never send to know for whom the bell tolls; it tolls for thee. —John Donne

There is an old (by current standards, ancient) Neil Diamond song entitled "Done Too Soon" which remains a favorite of mine.

The body of the song consists of a lively and diverse recitation of names. The list includes everyone from Mozart, Humphrey Bogart, Genghis Khan, and HG Wells; to Ho Chi Minh, Karl and Chico Marx, Rousseau, Buster Keaton, and "Alexanders (King and Graham Bell)," as Diamond puts it.

By contrast, the refrain to the song is slow and haunting. It goes:

> And each one there
> Has one thing shared:
> They have sweated beneath the same sun,
> Looked up in wonder at the same moon,
> And wept when it was all done
> For bein' done too soon [264]…

The song ends abruptly, in mid-sentence.

God numbers our days. Our lives are His, from beginning to end. We live, however, in a culture that does not understand suffering can have purpose.

In pain, grief, or despair we may feel as Shakespeare's anti-hero did:

> Out, out, brief candle!
> Life's but a walking shadow, a poor player
> That struts and frets his hour upon the stage
> And then is heard no more.
> It is a tale
> Told by an idiot, full of sound and fury,
> Signifying nothing [265].
>
> —"Macbeth," Act V, Scene 5.

Archbishop Fulton J. Sheen wrote in *Cross-Ways* [161]:

> You can save a sinner in India, give courage to a leper in Africa, console the bereaved in [war torn countries] by offering your cross. You can be like the clouds that gather up moisture from one body of water and then transport it over mountain heights, letting it fall as gentle dew on distant parched lands...The tragedy of any life is not what happens, it is rather how we react to what happens. Those who do not profit from the things that happen to them generally carry around with them through life open infectious wounds. But those who know that God is working out a Plan in them that one day will be revealed learn from the incidents of life...
>
> —"Transmute Your Pain." From *Cross-Ways* by Fulton J. Sheen (originally published in 1967 under the title *Lenten and Easter Inspirations*). Reprinted by permission of the Society for the Propagation of the Faith on behalf of the Estate of Fulton J. Sheen.

Or as the Apostle Paul said:

> …[*W*]*e also glorify in tribulations, knowing that tribulation produces perseverance; and perseverance, character; and character, hope. Now hope does not disappoint, because the love of God has been poured out in our hearts by the Holy Spirit who was given to us* (Romans 5: 3–5).

This does not justify the extrajudicial interference (or blatant self-promotion) seen in the Terri Schiavo case. Nor are we required to use extraordinary means to extend life.

Contrary to what the culture tells us, however, our bodies are not our own. They belong to God. This deprives us of the right to dispose of them as and when we may wish.

Sometimes the point of suffering takes generations to become clear:

- The Israelites during their years of bondage in Egypt were a great light to the Egyptians who, sadly, continued in darkness with the worship of many false gods. Whatever else, the 400 years of bondage in Egypt reflect God's mercy toward the unbelieving.
- *"Also you shall not oppress a stranger, for you know the heart of a stranger, because you were strangers in the land of Egypt"* (Exodus 23: 9). This lesson resonated as far as the 20th Century Civil Rights Movement.
- Consider Joan of Arc. Her impact as a martyr has been far greater than any military victory could have been.
- The horror of the Holocaust led to the re-establishment of the state of Israel after an interval of 2000 years.

Other times when we presume to "judge" God, we fail to take into account His numberless hidden offsets to what we see as unjust suffering. How many people could have died in the World Trade Center on 9/11, but did not? What prompted those who so selflessly ran toward the flames, or spent months amid the debris? The darkness that seemed to reign for a moment could not overshadow the thousands of acts of courage and compassion.

We will each of us experience evil in some form during our lives. Grief and loss need not be inflicted by terrorists to tear at our confidence, undermine our faith. Yet it is in the furnace of just such trials that faith is forged. The circumstances may not be of our making. The choice of how to respond is ours.

How presumptuous of us to think our sense of justice greater than God's! Job learned this. God specifically spoke to Job of creating the living world which fact (like Genesis, itself) points to a time before time.

> *Where were you when I laid the foundations of the earth... Who determined its measurements? Surely you know!... Can you bind the cluster of the Pleiades, or loose the belt of Orion?... Does the hawk fly by your wisdom...* (Job 38: 4–5, 31; 39:26).

Why then would God be hampered in the administration of justice by time? Certainly, His covenant extends from generation to generation.

If we assume our lives merely end in the grave, then what are we to make of the repeated references in Scriptures to everlasting life?

> *The Lord...brings down to the grave and brings up* (1 Samuel 2: 6).
>
> *He [the king] asked life from You, and You gave it to him—length of days forever and ever* (Psalm 21:4).
>
> *The Lord shall preserve your going out and your coming in from this time forth, and even forevermore* (Psalm 121: 8).
>
> *It is like the dew of Hermon, descending upon the mountains of Zion; for there the Lord commanded the blessing—life forevermore* (Psalm 133: 3).
>
> *He will swallow up death forever,*
> *And the Lord God will wipe away tears from all faces;*
> *The rebuke of His people*
> *He will take away from all the earth;*
> *For the Lord has spoken* (Isaiah 25: 8).
>
> *Then He said to me, "Son of man, these bones are the whole house of Israel. They indeed say, 'Our bones are dry, our hope is lost, and we ourselves are cut off!' Therefore prophesy and say to them, 'Thus says the Lord God: "Behold, O My people, I will*

> *open your graves and cause you to come up from your graves, and bring you into the land of Israel"'* (Ezekiel 37: 11).
>
> *And many of those who sleep in the dust of the earth shall awake,*
> *Some to everlasting life,*
> *Some to shame and everlasting contempt* (Daniel 12: 2).
> *I will ransom them from the power of the grave;*
> *I will redeem them from death.*
> *O Death, I will be your plagues!*
> *O Grave, I will be your destruction!* (Hosea 13:14).
> *So when this corruptible has put on incorruption, and this mortal has put on immortality, then shall be brought to pass the saying that is written "Death is swallowed up in victory. O Death, where is your sting?"* (1 Corinthians 15: 54–55).

Against the backdrop of eternity, surely God can appropriately render justice to the innocent and guilty alike. Or is this all wishful thinking?

> The moral law is not only disquieting…it can be downright frightening. Once its demands assert themselves no one can help but recall he has used them to judge other people. And the behavior he has condemned in others he himself has done. "By the measure you measure, it shall be measured back to you," said Jesus. We stand condemned not by some arbitrary, external law, but by a law we have in our own hearts and use daily.
>
> The dismissal of believers in the after-life as comfort seekers can easily be turned around. I myself have thought how comforting it would be to simply fall into a perfect, dreamless sleep. Shakespeare's Hamlet would have wanted nothing more than to put an end to the "sea of troubles… the heartache and the thousand natural shocks that flesh is heir to." But he was stopped by a further reflection: "To die, to sleep. To sleep, perchance to dream. Ay, there is the rub." At the conclusion of the "To be or not to be" soliloquy, Shakespeare movingly describes the power of conscience. Wouldn't living (or even ending) this life be so simple if

> we did not have within us nagging compunction about the moral law? If we did not feel its present demands and fear possible future consequences of breaking it?...Do you feel within you the claims of the moral law? Do they make you tremble, even slightly when you consider your own life? And is there someone who can lift those burdens? Someone who can give you true comfort, the forgiveness of sins? If so, come to Him [132B].

So is God only to be considered a good God, if no child ever again dies, and the righteous are assured long and pleasant lives? These days we overlook the full extent of sin in replying to this. We deny the existence of an Eden, but hold God accountable for the fact we were expelled. We proudly proclaim our free will, but disclaim such consequences of that free will as, for instance, war.

Whether you picture it as first having occurred in a garden or not, sin when it came into the world impacted the whole of creation, which to this day groans under the weight and longs for renewal. Thus, we have tsunamis and cancer. Thus, we have death.

The original sin was prompted by a lack of trust in God. Daily, we are offered the priceless chance to trust Him again—in spite of doubt, in spite of pain, in spite of fear. We have the example of countless nameless saints who preceded us (Hebrews 12:1).

PART IV:

A HOUSE DIVIDED

FEAR AS A POLITICAL TACTIC

The Lord is my light, and my salvation; whom shall I fear? (Psalm 27: 1)

You gain strength, courage, and confidence by every experience in which you really stop to look fear in the face. You are able to say to yourself, "I have lived through this horror. I can take the next thing that comes along"... You must do the thing you think you cannot do. —Eleanor Roosevelt

The Bible, Old and New Testaments, is replete with admonitions not to fear. These are but a handful:

> *Be strong and of good courage, do not fear nor be afraid...for the Lord your God, He is the One who goes with you. He will not leave you nor forsake you* (Deuteronomy 31: 6).
> *I will not leave you nor forsake you* (Joshua 1: 5).
> *Fear not, for I am with you...* (Isaiah 41: 10).
> *For He Himself has said, "I will never leave you nor forsake you." So we may boldly say: "The Lord is my helper: I will not fear. What can man do to me?"* (Hebrews 13: 5–6).

How ironic then that the Christian Right would choose to be associated with an Administration that deliberately utilizes fear as a political tactic.

> Upon this a question arises: whether it be better to be

> loved than feared or feared than loved? It may be answered that one should wish to be both, but, because it is difficult to unite them in one person, is much safer to be feared than loved, when, of the two, either must be dispensed with. Because this is to be asserted in general of men, that they are ungrateful, fickle, false, cowardly, covetous, and as long as you succeed they are yours entirely; they will offer you their blood, property, life and children, as is said above, when the need is far distant; but when it approaches they turn against you. And that prince who, relying entirely on their promises, has neglected other precautions, is ruined; because friendships that are obtained by payments, and not by greatness or nobility of mind, may indeed be earned, but they are not secured, and in time of need cannot be relied upon; and men have less scruple in offending one who is beloved than one who is feared, for love is preserved by the link of obligation which, owing to the baseness of men, is broken at every opportunity for their advantage; but fear preserves you by a dread of punishment which never fails [249].
>
> —Niccolo Machiavelli, *The Prince,* Chapter XVII "Concerning Cruelty And Clemency, And Whether It Is Better To Be Loved Than Feared."

If President George W. Bush has not studied Machiavelli, those around him certainly have. It has been chilling to hear Vice President Richard "Dick" Cheney threaten the political careers of any who might oppose Bush's policies.

Moreover:

> The siege mentality average Americans are suffering as they smother behind yards of plastic sheeting and duct tape will increase by orders of magnitude as our aggressions bring forth new terrorist attacks against the homeland. These attacks will require the implementation of the newly drafted Patriot Act II, an augmentation of the previous Act that has profoundly sharper teeth. The sun will set

> on the Constitution and Bill of Rights…Germany, France and the other nations resisting this Iraq war…are not acting out of cowardice or because they love Saddam Hussein, but because they mean to resist this rising American empire, lest they face economic and military serfdom at the hands of George W. Bush [220A]…
>
> —William Rivers Pitt, *The Project for the New American Century,* February 25, 2003.

Have we ever before allowed fear to dominate our actions to this extent? What has become of our country? When did we agree to submit to this? Can no one else see the dangers of this course of action? The beautiful turn of phrase President George W. Bush, himself, used in 1999 could not be in sharper contrast:

> America has never been an empire. We may be the only great power in history that had the chance, and refused—preferring greatness to power and justice to glory.

If that has not been wholly true, let us strive to make it so. We can take our direction from Civil Rights activist, Rosa Parks who said: "I have learned over the years that when one's mind is made up, this diminishes fear; knowing what must be done does away with fear."

PARTISAN POLITICS

...if your brother sins against you, go and tell him his fault between you and him alone. If he hears you, you have gained your brother. But if he will not hear, take with you one or two more, that "by the mouth of two or three witnesses every word may be established." (Mathew 18: 15–16)

To announce that there must be no criticism of the president... is morally treasonable to the American public. —Theodore Roosevelt, Republican President

Since Republicans characterize Democrats as demonic and Democrats characterize Republicans as moronic, it may be worthwhile actually to compare the two parties.

This lengthy excerpt on the history of the Republican Party is taken from *Wikipedia Encyclopedia*:

> The Republican Party...was established in 1854 by Northerners who opposed the expansion of slavery...The party founders adopted the name "Republican" to indicate it was the carrier of...beliefs about civic virtue, and opposition to aristocracy and corruption...Besides opposition to slavery, the new party put forward a vision of modernization—emphasizing higher education, banking, railroads, industry and cities, while promising free homesteads to farmers... Republicans still often refer to their party as the "party of Lincoln" in honor of the first Republican president...
>
> In Reconstruction how to deal with the ex-Confederates and the freed slaves or Freedmen were the major issues. By 1864 Radical Republicans controlled Congress and demanded...more vengeance toward the Confederates.

Lincoln held them off just barely. Republicans at first welcomed President Andrew Johnson; the Radicals thought he was one of them and would take a hard line in punishing the South. Johnson however broke with them...[When] in the Congressional elections of 1866...Radicals won a sweeping victory and took full control of Reconstruction...Johnson was impeached by the House, but acquitted by the Senate. With the election of Ulysses S. Grant in 1868 the radicals had control of Congress, the party and the Army, and attempted to build a solid Republican base in the South... Grant supported...the 14th Amendment, equal civil and voting rights for the Freedmen; most of all he was the hero of the war veterans...

As the Northern post-bellum economy boomed with heavy and light industry, railroads, mines, and fast-growing cities, as well as prosperous agriculture, the Republicans took credit and promoted policies to keep the fast growth going. They supported big business generally...By 1890, however, the Republicans had agreed to the Sherman Anti-Trust Act and the Interstate Commerce Commission in response to complaints from owners of small businesses and farmers...

The election of William McKinley in 1896 is widely seen as a resurgence of Republican dominance and is sometimes cited as a realigning election. He relied heavily on industry and the middle classes for his support and cemented the Republicans as the party of business...This emphasis on business was in part mitigated by Theodore Roosevelt, McKinley's successor after assassination, who engaged in trust-busting. McKinley was the first president to promote pluralism, arguing that prosperity would be shared by all ethnic and religious groups, but they must not attack each other...

The term "Rockefeller Republican" was used 1960–80 to designate a faction of the party holding "moderate" views similar to those of the late Nelson Rockefeller...After Rockefeller left the national stage in 1976, this faction of the party was more often called "moderate Republicans," in

> contrast to the conservatives who rallied to Ronald Reagan. Historically Rockefeller Republicans were moderate or liberal on domestic and social policies. They favored New Deal programs, including regulation and welfare. They were very strong supporters of civil rights. They were strongly supported by big business on Wall Street (New York City). In fiscal policy they favored balanced budgets and relatively high tax levels to keep the budget balanced. They sought long-term economic growth through entrepreneurships, not tax cuts. In state politics, they were strong supporters of state colleges and universities, low tuition, and large research budgets. They favored infrastructure improvements, such as highway projects. In foreign policy they were internationalists, and anti-Communists. They felt the best way to counter Communism was sponsoring economic growth (through foreign aid), maintatining a strong military, and keeping close ties to NATO...
>
> The Reagan Democrats were Democrats before the Reagan years, and afterwards, but who voted for Ronald Reagan in 1980 and 1984 (and for George W. Bush in 1988), producing their landslide victories. They were mostly white ethnics in the Northeast who were attracted to Reagan's social conservatism on issues such as abortion, and to his hawkish foreign policy. They did not continue to vote Republican in 1992 or 1996, so the term fell into disuse...
>
> Stanley Greenberg, a Democratic pollster, analyzed white ethnic voters, largely unionized auto workers, in suburban Macomb County, Michigan, just north of Detroit. The county voted 63 percent for Kennedy in 1960 and 66 percent for Reagan in 1984. He concluded that Reagan Democrats no longer saw Democrats as champions of their middle class aspirations, but instead saw [the Democratic Party] as being a party working primarily for the benefit of others, especially African Americans and the very poor [251].

This history of the Democratic Party is taken from the same source:

The Democratic Party...traces its beginnings to Thomas Jefferson in the early 1790s, and is one of the two longest-standing political parties in the world...[S]ome scholars date the party's beginnings to 1828 when...supporters of Andrew Jackson...formed the Democratic Party along with former members of the Federalist Party...The old party and the new...shared the same anti-elite rhetoric of opposition to "aristocracy" and faith in "the people"...The Democratic Party of the 1830s was a complex coalition...[comprised of] farmers in all parts of the country, together with working-men's groups in the cities...

In the 1850s...the Democratic Party became increasingly divided, with its Southern wing staunchly advocating the expansion of slavery into new territories...At the 1860 nominating convention the Party split and a rival convention was held. The Northern Democrats nominated Stephen A. Douglas and the Southern Democrats nominated John Breckenridge...As a result, Republican Abraham Lincoln won, and seven southern states seceded from the Union, leading to the Civil War. During the war, Northern Democrats divided into two [further] factions, War Democrats, who supported the military policies of President Lincoln, and Copperheads, who strongly opposed them...

The Democrats were shattered by the war but nevertheless benefited from white Southerners' resentment of Reconstruction and consequent hostility to the Republican Party. Once Reconstruction was ended by the Compromise of 1877, and the disenfranchisement of blacks took place in the 1890s, the region was known as the "Solid South" for nearly a century because it reliably voted Democratic...

In the presidential election of 1896, widely regarded as a political realignment, Democrats...lost to Republican William McKinley in an election which was to prove decisive: the Republicans controlled the presidency for 28 of the following 36 years...

Democrats...elected the intellectual reformer Woodrow Wilson in 1912 and 1916. Wilson successfully led Congress to [adopt]...stronger antitrust laws, the Federal Reserve System, pay benefits for railroad workers, and [the] outlawing of child labor...[C]onstitutional amendments for prohibition and woman's suffrage were passed in [Wilson's] second term...Wilson led the US to victory in the First World War, and helped write the Versailles Treaty, which included the League of Nations...

The Great Depression set the stage for a more liberal government and Franklin D. Roosevelt won a landslide victory in the election of 1932...Roosevelt came forth with a massive array of programs, soon known as the New Deal. These focused on...relief of unemployment and rural distress, recovery of the economy back to normal, and long-term structural reforms to prevent any repetition...Roosevelt sought to move the party away from laissez-faire capitalism, and towards an ideology of economic regulation and insurance against hardship...by building up labor unions, nationalizing welfare by the WPA, setting up Social Security, imposing more regulations on business (especially transportation and communications), and raising taxes on business profits...[This was followed, under Harry Truman by] the Truman Doctrine, Marshall Plan, and NATO...

In 1960 Senator John F. Kennedy won the presidential election defeating then Vice-President Richard Nixon. Even though Kennedy's term in office only lasted 34 months he guided America through the Bay of Pigs Invasion, the construction of the Berlin Wall, the Cuban Missile Crisis, racial integration, and America's space race against the Soviet Union...Democratic President Lyndon B. Johnson [subsequently] signed into law the Civil Rights Act of 1964...

The degree to which white and black southerners had reversed their historic parties became evident in the 1968 presidential election...President Nixon, facing impeachment in the Watergate scandal, resigned...Prior to that... Nixon appointed Gerald Ford as Vice President. Ford soon pardoned Nixon, giving the Democrats a "corruption" issue...[This together with] a combination of economic

> recession and inflation…led to Ford's defeat in 1976. The winner was a little-known outsider who promised honesty in Washington, Jimmy Carter…Carter…[created] two new cabinet departments, the…Department of Energy and the…Department of Education. Carter also successfully deregulated the trucking, airline, rail, finance, communications, and oil industries, bolstered the social security system, and appointed record numbers of women and minorities to significant government and judicial posts…In foreign affairs…[Carter was responsible for] the Camp David Accords…and the negotiation of the SALT II Treaty. In addition, he championed human rights throughout the world and used human rights as the center of his administration's foreign policy…[However] Iranians held 52 Americans hostage for 444 days, and Carter's diplomatic and military rescue attempts failed…
>
> In 1992, for the first time in 12 years, the United States elected a Democrat to the White House. President Bill Clinton created a balanced federal budget and welfare reform…enacted the NAFTA free trade agreement with Canada and Mexico over the strong objection of…labor unions [250]…

Both parties claim to represent the people. Both have significant achievements to their credit. Both had mistakes, failures, and scandals in their past. Why would this surprise any of us? They are made up and led by human beings, all of whom—like the rest of us—are flawed.

As Will Rogers put it, humorously, in *Illiterate Digest*:

> The more you read and observe about this Politics thing, you got to admit that each party is worse than the other. The one that's out always looks the best [87].

Nonetheless—Republicans with Lincoln, opposition to slavery, and Teddy Roosevelt; Democrats with Jefferson, FDR, social security, and integration—the parties have given the American people a rich political heritage. There is no reason those same parties should not be able to work together to find common ground. There must be a few sane men and women on both sides, willing to put their country first and set petty squabbles aside.

Sadly, our President has not made this a priority. Far from it, in fact.

> *From Don Friedman:*
>
> Why do you allow senior members of your administration to accuse the Democratic Party of being "soft" on terrorism [Mr. President]? Why have you not spoken out publicly to criticize statements like this? Isn't your administration, in effect, politicizing the war on terror and seeking to use it for political gain? Shouldn't the president have the responsibility to foster an atmosphere of bipartisanship when it comes to national security issues [111O]?

Samuel Johnson might have responded, "Patriotism is the last refuge of the scoundrel." We can only assume there is some advantage to the Executive Branch from disarray in the Legislative Branch. This reflects the ongoing struggle for power among the three branches of our government—the very reason the Founding Fathers created a "checks and balance" system.

Non-Christians may be surprised and Christians should be reminded that the Bible actually speaks to this:

> *Now I urge you, brethren, note those who cause divisions and offenses, contrary to the doctrine which you learned, and avoid them. For those who are such do not serve our Lord Jesus Christ, but their own belly, and by smooth words and flattering speech deceive the hearts of the simple* (Romans 16: 17–18).

It is not an individual's honeyed words that matter, but his actions. I am not certain whether politicians can grasp this concept, but I will make the attempt.

- We elected you as our representatives. Our taxes pay your salaries. That means—like postal employees—you work for *us*. Every last one of you: president on down.
- You wanted these positions, thankless though they may be. You actually ran for them. Don't complain if it is troublesome to do them right. Try working in a coal mine sometime, or standing in an unemployment line.
- Somewhere along the way, you decided we could be lied to at will. Henry Fountain Ashurst said that "voters never grow weary of illusory promises." Don't imagine we're not aware of your contempt. It's just that we've had so few choices among you. Hope is engineered into our genes. Elections are far enough apart that a glimmer of it resurfaces and, a few of us at least, head to the polls again.
- Try and imagine your jobs actually matter. In point of fact, they do. We don't need your "spin doctors" to tell us what to think. Just do your jobs, and we can manage all on our own to figure out if you've done them right.

What is called for at this critical juncture is the rare quality of statesmanship. That may require sacrificing local interests, in favor of national. Though hard to believe, such a sacrifice might actually involve foregoing "pork."

Statesmanship would require placing long-term goals before short-term, and the country's interests before the party's. If this is not something our representatives can stomach, one day soon, we may wake up to find all we have left are their honeyed words.

The parties will not and need not agree on all things. Two of Christ's original twelve Apostles were, themselves, at opposite ends of the political spectrum [187A]. Simon the Zealot was a member of a fanatically patriotic party, with the goal of complete freedom for the kingdom of Israel.

> Any opposition to the nation's sovereignty was seen as an act of war, and any Jewish sympathy for their Roman oppressors was seen as an act of treason...Some of the more

> extreme members of the Zealots even executed fellow Jews whom they suspected of Roman sympathies. In short, these were extremely motivated, intense, and often dangerous men [187B].

Matthew, on the other hand, was a publican or tax collector on behalf of Rome.

> As such, he worked for the political oppressors, taking tax money from the Jews and delivering it to the authorities... Thievery was common, as publicans often exacted exorbitant unauthorized fees...[More than this] in the opinion of his fellow Jews...Matthew, the publican, was a traitor [187C].

How did these two men coexist? "Such a relationship demonstrates that no relationship exists that cannot be reconciled in and by the power of the love of Christ [187D]." Every senator, every House member who claims to be Christian has an obligation to step forward and seek reconciliation. Nor can denominational differences be any excuse, for the Bible, itself, forbids sectarianism (1 Corinthians 1: 10–17).

This would not, of course, bar any one else from taking part in the process. It was Abraham Lincoln who said, "As a peacemaker the lawyer has superior opportunity of being a good man [188]." All we lawyers—in government and outside it—might do well to take note.

IN PURSUIT OF SECURITY: AT WHAT COST?

And do not seek what you should eat or what you should drink, nor have an anxious mind. For all these things the nations of the world seek after, and Your Father knows that you need these things. But seek the kingdom of God, and all these things shall be added to you. (Luke 12: 29–31)

The true danger is when liberty is nibbled away, for expedience, and by parts. —Edmund Burke

On November 25, 2002 the legislation creating the Homeland Security Department was signed into law. Called for in the aftermath of the terrorist attacks of September 11, 2001, the new department merged 22 different government agencies and over 170,000 employees into a single unit, with the goal of streamlining communications, and better defending America against future terrorist attacks [189A].

President George W. Bush's proposed $2.57 trillion Budget for 2006 substantially increased the amount of money spent on surveillance equipment and manpower [196]. Homeland Security was to receive $41.1 billion (an increase of almost 7% over 2005).

PRIVACY

Initially, the Total Information Awareness (TIA) database was made an integral part of Homeland Security [189B]. This database was intended to gather vast amounts of highly personal information including academic grades, medical procedures, financial records, property and credit card purchases, magazine subscriptions, phone calls, websites visited, surveys taken, sweepstakes entered, and more from lawful American citizens and foreign visitors [189C]. The data was intended to reveal "not only shopping habits but an overall picture of personal lifestyle, including everything from pets owned to religious preferences [189D]." All in the name of national security.

The TIA database was to be run by—of all people—Admiral John Poindexter, criminally convicted in 1990 of lying to Congress, destroying official documents, and obstruction of justice in the Iran/Contra scandal [189E]. Thankfully, in September 2003 Congress eliminated funding for the controversial project, and closed the Information Awareness Office [189F]. Some of the TIA's high tech tools were shifted to agencies involved in foreign intelligence gathering (the CIA, State Department, and Defense Department). Which items remains classified.

This did not, however, end government "data mining" activities as regards American citizens.

A report by the General Accounting Office dated May 4, 2004 [194A and 195A] revealed almost 200 federal "data mining" projects either under way or planned (many using personally identifiable information). Sen. Daniel Akaka, who had requested the study, said, "The federal government collects and uses Americans' personal information and shares it with other agencies to an astonishing degree, raising serious privacy concerns [195B]." The Technology and Privacy Advisory Committee recommended that federal agencies obtain special authorization before using personally identifiable information to engage in data mining on American citizens [194B].

The *New York Times* in December 2005 brought to light the fact that President George W. Bush had authorized the National Security Agency (NSA) to obtain information from American citizens without first obtaining a warrant or court order, as specified by statute [197A]. The full extent of this surveillance is not yet known. The President's authority to supersede the requirement of court approval is under serious question.

According to Attorney General, Alberto Gonzales, President Bush in 2002 issued a secret order allowing the interception of communications with a party outside the US if the government had a reasonable basis to conclude that one of the parties to the communications was "a member of al Queda, affiliated with al Queda…a member of an organization affiliated with al Queda, or working in support of al Queda" [197B]. Per the Attorney General, the President based his actions on the inherent powers of his office, and the joint resolution authorizing the use of "all necessary and appropriate force" to engage militarily those responsible for 9/11 [197C].[23]

The case of *Youngstown Sheet and Tube Co. v. Sawyer*[24] laid out (in dissent) what is now considered the leading opinion on separation of presidential and congressional powers:

1. When the President acts pursuant to an express or implied authorization of Congress, his authority is at its maximum, for it includes all that he possesses in his own right plus all that Congress can delegate…
2. When the President acts in absence of either a congressional grant or denial of authority, he can only rely upon his own independent powers, but there is a zone of twilight in which he and Congress may have concurrent authority, or in which its distribution is uncertain. Therefore, congressional inertia, indifference or quiescence may sometimes, at least as a practical matter, enable, if not invite, measures on independent presidential responsibility. In this area, any actual test of power is likely to depend on the imperatives of events and contemporary imponderables rather than on abstract theories of law.
3. When the President takes measures incompatible with the expressed or implied will of Congress, his power is at its lowest ebb, for then he can rely only upon his own constitutional powers minus any constitutional powers of Congress over the matter. Courts can sustain exclusive presidential control in such a case only by disabling the Congress from acting upon the subject. Presidential claim to a power at once so conclusive and preclusive must be scrutinized with caution, for what is at stake is the equilibrium established by our constitutional system.

Under this view, if the Constitution forbids the conduct, then the court must find it invalid, even if the President and Congress have acted in concert. The President may sometimes have the effective power to take unilateral action in the absence of any action on the part of Congress to indicate its will, but this should not be understood to mean that the President has the inherent authority to exercise full authority in a particular field, without Congress' ability to encroach [197D].

Presidents have, historically, contended that the ability to conduct surveillance for intelligence purposes is purely an executive function, and have tended to make broad assertions of authority while resisting efforts on the part of Congress or the courts to impose restrictions. Congress has asserted, itself, with respect to domestic surveillance, but has largely left matters involving overseas surveillance to executive self-regulation (subject to congressional oversight and willingness to provide funds) [197E].

Acknowledging that electronic surveillance had enabled intelligence agencies to obtain valuable information, the Senate Judiciary Committee, nonetheless, commented on the "chilling effect" of warrantless electronic surveillance. The Senate Judiciary Committee pointed out that "[t]he exercise of political freedom depends in large measure on citizens' understanding that they will be able to be publicly active and dissent from official policy, within lawful limits, without having to sacrifice the expectation of privacy that they rightfully hold [197F]."

The interception of wire, oral, or electronic communications is regulated by Title III of the Omnibus Crime Control and Safe Streets Act of 1968 ("Title III"). Government surveillance for the gathering of foreign intelligence information is covered by The Foreign Intelligence Surveillance Act of 1978 (FISA) [197G].

If FISA leaves room for NSA surveillance outside its confines, then the power the President claims can fall into the first or second categories, as either condoned by Congress (expressly or impliedly) or left untouched. If FISA (and Title III) are found to occupy the entire field, then for a court to sustain the President's authorization of electronic surveillance to obtain foreign intelligence outside the FISA framework, FISA will have to be ruled an unconstitutional encroachment by Congress on the President's inherent power—that is, assuming a political compromise is not reached first [197H].

TRANSPARENCY

The Freedom of Information Act (FOIA) was passed in 1966 to allow the public access to records and documents created and maintained by federal agencies [189G]. Since its passage, all fifty states have passed their own versions [189H]. The US Supreme Court addressed the importance of the FOIA over a quarter century ago in a case entitled *NLRB v. Robbins Tire Co.*: "The basic purpose of FOIA is to ensure an informed citizenry, vital to the functioning of a democratic society, needed to check against corruption and to hold the governors accountable to the governed [189I]."

Since then, the FOIA has been severely hampered by Homeland Security legislation. Public data on the actions of federal agencies is now considered a potential security risk [189J].

We know today that a full year before the al Qaeda attacks on 9/11, an Army military intelligence unit known as "Able Danger" under the command of Special Operations identified a terrorist cell in Brooklyn, New York, and recommended to superiors that the FBI be called in to "take the cell out [227A and 228A]." Among the cell's members were Mohamed Atta, ringleader of the September 11 attacks [227B], and three other al Qaeda members [228B]. Department of Defense attorneys working for Special Operations recommended that the FBI not be informed because Atta at the time had a valid "green card [227C]."

Republican Pete Hoekstra, Chairman of the House Permanent Select Committee on Intelligence, himself, had difficulty obtaining this information. The Pentagon initially declined to acknowledge that the Able Danger Unit had ever existed [227D]. The Bush Administration appeared uninterested in exposing this enormous oversight [227E]. Peter Zelikow (former Executive Director of the 9/11 Commission; now counselor to Secretary of State, Condoleeza Rice) is believed to have been personally informed of the matter by the intelligence officer involved in transmitting the relevant documents up the chain of command [227H]. For unknown reasons, however, Zelikow failed to pass the information on to other 9/11 Commission members [227F].

A small local paper—the *Times Herald* of Norristown, Pennsylvania—broke the story in June 2005 [227G]. Unaccountably, a Defense Department investigation concluded that Able Danger did not identify either Atta or any hijackers before 9/11.

HABEAS CORPUS

> Nasser Ahmed spends over three years in prison as a national security threat. "Secret evidence" in a "secret" government proceeding marks him a bona fide threat to the nation's security. An Egyptian father of four US citizen children, Ahmed is never charged with a crime. Even so, the Immigration and Naturalization Service imprisons and then seeks to deport him based on evidence hidden from Ahmed and his attorney. For an entire year, the government refuses to even furnish Ahmed's lawyer with a summary of the evidence. Finally, the government provides a one-line summary, asserting only that it has evidence "concerning respondent's association with a known terrorist organization." The government refuses to identify the organization. Unable to defend himself against nonexistent charges on the basis of undisclosed evidence in a secret proceeding, Ahmed languishes in solitary confinement. After years of incarceration the actual "secret" evidence is revealed, and it shows that Ahmed has not engaged in any kind of terrorist activity. Nor has he supported any terrorist organizations. The government imprisoned and sought to deport Ahmed on national security grounds because of his "associations." And what were the government's allegations of those associations? Ahmed once was appointed by a US court to serve as a paralegal and translator for the defense team of Sheik Abdel Rahman, who was being tried in a US court for seditious conspiracy. Three years of secret incarceration for doing what the court asked and indeed authorized him to do.
>
> Ahmed's civil liberties nightmare sounds like tortured Kafkaesque imaginings. It is, however, reality. United States reality...

Today, in response to the horrific killing of thousands of Americans and people from countries around the world, the President, Congress and federal agencies, like the Immigration and Naturalization Service, are creating a new regime of national security measures. Some of these measures are needed and only reasonably burdensome—like added checks at airports and increased security at nuclear power plants and government buildings. But others, like secret detentions, are immensely troubling. When the government abuses its national security powers, particularly by targeting members of vulnerable groups, and is challenged, how are the US courts likely to rule?...

Recall the potentially prescient dissent of Supreme Court Justice Jackson in the 1944 *Korematsu* case, which upheld the legality of the [Japanese] internment: "The Court has for all time validated the principle of racial discrimination in criminal procedure and of transplanting citizens. The principle stands as a loaded weapon ready for the hand of any authority that can bring forward a plausible claim of urgent need [193]."

—Original Source: Eric K. Yamamoto and Susan Kiyomi Serrano, "*The Loaded Weapon,*" *Amerasia Journal,* 27:3 (2001)/28:1 (2002): 51–62, 51–53.

IN PURSUIT OF MORALITY: WHOSE DARKNESS?

"But woe to you Pharisees! For you tithe mint and rue and all manner of herbs, and pass by justice and the love of God." (Luke 11: 42)

America will never be destroyed from the outside. If we falter and lose our freedoms, it will be because we destroyed ourselves.
—Abraham Lincoln

Every generation must face its own darkness. What we choose to condemn may not be the enemy at all. "[The] ideals and convictions that have become [our] basic democratic principles…must be understood and [re-]affirmed by every generation, if the American experiment in liberty is to endure [206B]."

WITCHCRAFT

Between June and September 1692, nineteen men and women—all convicted of witchcraft—were taken to Gallows Hill near Salem Village and hanged. An 80 year old man was pressed to death beneath heavy stones for refusing to submit to trial. Five others, including an infant, died in prison [199]. Hundreds faced accusations. Dozens were jailed for months while the hysteria held sway [198A].[25]

There have been a number of theories put forth for this period of madness.

Disease and natural disasters were directly attributed to Satan. As the frequency of these ills (in the form of small pox, congregational strife, and frontier wars with the Native Americans) mounted, the community became desperate to identify and eliminate their cause [198B]. Given the limited knowledge of medicine and science, it seemed logical that one or more individuals in the community might be conspiring with the forces of evil. Superstitious practices (as on the part of slave, Tituba) and a misguided text by preacher, Cotton Mather (entitled "Memorable Providences") [198C] contributed to this belief.

Teenagers may have been bored by the restrictive religious regimen [198D] and girls—the least influential members of society, apart from slaves—particularly pleased (if unconsciously) at the attention their symptoms produced and the power derived from them.

An underlying property dispute may have fueled the trials [198E]. Alternatively, some have suggested that the entire series of events was the result of mass (psychogenic) hysteria [200] or that the symptoms the girls exhibited were real, but the result of ergotism infection [201].

Like witchcraft in the 17th Century, some allegations today are so heinous that they tarnish the reputation beyond recovery, whether proven or not. Child molestation is one; sedition, another. More than that, the murders in Salem were committed under color of law by people who considered themselves outstanding Christians.

That fact by itself should serve as a penultimate cautionary tale.

MCCARTHYISM

US Senator Joseph McCarthy managed to ruin the lives of the people on his list just by claiming they were or had once been Communists. McCarthy's reign was finally brought to an end when he accused the US Military of harboring Communists, and the Military were able to prove his allegations false [202A].

This country had good reason to fear the Communists in the 1940s and 1950s. Communism was growing in Eastern Europe and China, as my own family—which fled to the West in the immediate aftermath of WWII—can attest. We would still, when I was a very young girl, send packages of food and clothing to relatives behind the Iron Curtain.

McCarthy saw in this human tragedy the opportunity to carve out a reputation for himself [202B]. Though he was eventually censured by the Senate [202C], McCarthy's paranoid hunt for Communist infiltrators and the climate of fear it created, permanently destroyed the careers of some of America's most famous writers and entertainers.

Among those accused of Communist sympathies and/or called before the House Un-American Activities Committee were: Lillian Hellman (author of "The Little Foxes"), the incomparable Lena Horne, Paul Robeson (African American athlete/actor/singer/scholar/political activist), Arthur Miller (author of "Death of a Salesman"), Aaron Copeland (one of the 20th Century's most respected classical composers), and renowned symphony conductor, Leonard Bernstein [202D].

There are lessons of McCarthyism that should not be forgotten [203]:

1. That McCarthy caused irreparable harm without credible evidence. This was not justified, even in a time of crisis.
2. That McCarthy used accusations of Communist sympathies against anyone who disagreed with his methods. This was merely a bullying tactic, but we see it resurfacing today with references to al Qaeda, rather than the Communist Party.
3. That McCarthy viewed freedom of speech, itself, as a danger (believing that even the ideas of Communism should not be discussed). Regrettably, this seems to be the view of some individuals on the extreme Right.
4. That McCarthy was defeated by the courage of those who spoke up against him, regardless of the consequences. Among these was Edward R. Murrow whose reputation for integrity we hold up as a model, even today.

HATE SPEECH

No body of law has yet developed by the US Supreme Court on the issue of "hate speech" specifically on the Internet. The high court's rulings as to other means of expression are, however, binding [190A].

Many would argue that racial and ethnic slurs are types of speech that (like "fighting words," defined in 1942, in *Chaplinsky v. New Hampshire*[26]), have "no redeeming value." We know that such slurs can incite violence. The Supreme Court, however, has been highly protective of the right to free speech—so much so, that the Court has been reluctant to regulate hate speech. The Court has said that any such regulation must be "strictly scrutinized" to ensure that it does not, also, forbid protected speech [190B].

As a consequence, the *Chaplinsky* "fighting words" doctrine as applied to hate speech has evolved into a "speech" vs. "action" dichotomy [190C], discussed in the following five cases.

Two-Pronged *Brandenburg* Test:
1) Directed and
2) Likely to Incite Imminent Lawless Action

In the 1969 case of *Brandenburg v. Ohio,* the court explained its modern incitement test [190D]. Speech does not create the classic "clear and present danger" to citizens unless it is "directed to inciting or producing imminent lawless action and is likely to incite or produce such action." The case centered around a videotaped and broadcast news piece on an Ohio Ku Klux Klan rally. The viewer could hear racial and anti-Semitic remarks (such as "Freedom for the whites" and "Send the Jews back to Israel") in the background. Though offensive, this was not considered likely to produce imminent lawless action by the public [190E].

Nazi Party v. Skokie: Hostile Audience Insufficient for Prior Restraint

The famous 1977 case of *National Socialist Party v. Skokie* centered on the efforts of residents of a predominantly Jewish town to prevent the Nazi Party from holding a demonstration there. The Supreme Court denied the residents' attempts to block the march, because to do so, it said, would suppress the Nazis' First Amendment rights [190F]. According to the court: "[A]nticipation of a hostile audience [cannot] justify the prior restraint…[I]t is [the] burden of [Skokie residents] to avoid the [offensive march] if they can do so without unreasonable inconvenience."

Symbolism as Speech

In 1992, the city of St. Paul banned the placing on public or private property of any "symbol, object, appellation, characterization or graffiti, including, but not limited to, a burning cross or Nazi swastika, which one knows or has reasonable grounds to know arouses anger, alarm, or resentment in others on the basis of race, color, creed, religion, or gender." This gave rise to the case of *RAV v. City of St. Paul.* The plaintiff in that case was arrested for placing a burning cross on the front lawn of an African American family's house. The court held St. Paul's ban invalid both because it was overbroad and because it was underinclusive. The Court considered the ban overbroad since the speech used by "proponents of all views" whatever its context would be prohibited [190G]. The ban was underinclusive since it did not prohibit all fighting words, for example, homophobic slurs or "aspersions about one's mother [190H]."

Though one might disagree with the outcome of this case as applicable to the particular set of facts, it is clear that the court was not attempting deliberately to undermine legislative authority or the "will of the people." If anything, it was attempting to protect the voice of the people, even the voice of ugly sentiments.

Speech v. Acts Distinction Reaffirmed

In 1993 the Supreme Court in *Wisconsin v. Mitchell* reinforced the speech/action distinction [190I]. The case concerned young African American men convicted under a hate-crime statute for severely beating a white person after becoming outraged by racist depictions in the movie "Mississippi Burning." The Wisconsin Supreme Court overturned these convictions on the basis of *RAV* because the actions constituted "offensive [yet protected] thought." The Supreme Court reversed the state decision, saying that there was a difference between speech and conduct [190J].

Indefinite Future Illegal Acts Constitutionally Protected

Parenthood of the Columbia/Willamette, Inc. v. American Coalition of Life Activists is the leading case on the speech/action distinction as applied to the Internet [190K]. This case involved the "Nuremberg Files" website by the American Coalition of Life Activists. The names and home addresses of abortion doctors were posted on the site, then crossed out (or turned gray) if the doctors were killed or wounded by anti-abortion zealots [190L].

The "Nuremberg Files" site did not explicitly threaten the doctors, but the ACLA applauded and possibly encouraged the killings [190M].

Some of the doctors whose names appeared on the website sued the ACLA on the grounds that this speech robbed them of their anonymity and "gave violent anti-abortion activists the information to find them." The doctors argued this was a true threat.

The US Court of Appeals for the 9th Circuit held that the ACLA's speech on the website was constitutionally protected by the First Amendment [190N]. The Court said that "advocating illegal action at some indefinite future time is protected [by the First Amendment]. If the First Amendment protects speech advocating violence, then it must also protect speech that does not advocate violence but still makes it more likely [190O]."

With 9/11 and the recent violence against our Judiciary, the FBI has increased its monitoring of hate group websites. "Federal officials won't tolerate anyone crossing the line from protected free speech to advocating violence in the wake of Matthew Hale's conviction," said Richard K. Ruminski, the FBI's Assistant Special Agent in Charge of Counter-Terrorism Investigations in Chicago [190P].

Neo-Nazism

Historically, fascist leaders at times used terrorist tactics with the goal of provoking demands for a stronger state. By contrast, a new form of terrorism identifies the state, itself, as the enemy [191C]. This concept gained popularity with Neo-Nazis in the late 1980s and 1990s [191D].

American racists gradually transformed old anti-Semitic ideas into a terrorist doctrine about "racial war" against the "Zionist Occupation Government" (ZOG) and so called "racial traitors" ("ZOG agents"), such as the Liberal press [191A]. Targets under this perverse ideology include newspapers and journalists, along with judges, jurors, prosecutors, witnesses and police [191I]. Immigration is perceived as a "strategic weapon" of the Jews, in their alleged war with the "Aryan race [191J]." This is actually very telling, since it suggests that fear underlies the hatred expressed.

The Turner Diaries, a violent 1980 novel by US racist leader, William Pierce (pseudonym, Andrew Macdonald) and *Hunter*, a novel nine years later by Pierce, were extremely influential, in this regard [191E]. *The Turner Diaries* describe revenge by the white "resistance movement" after its seizure of power. *Hunter*, by comparison, focuses on a single individual (or "lone hunter") who wages a one-man war against Jews, the media, politicians, etc. [191F]. These have been virtual handbooks of terrorist tactics for the Neo-Nazi subculture [191O].

The extreme right-wing terrorism fostered by the ZOG ideology made its entrance on the public stage in April 1995 with the deaths of 169 men, women, and children, in a car bombing at the Federal Office Building in Oklahoma. There were more than 400 others wounded, as well [191B]. *The Turner Diaries* described the Oklahoma City bombing in detail, before the event [191G]. However, the idea of a large organization was replaced by that of "leaderless resistance" which authorities were less likely to uncover, as in *Hunter* [191H].

Among Neo-Nazi gangs, there are two common variants: those groups with members between the ages of 13 and 18; and those with members between the ages of 17 and 25 [191K]. The concerns of younger Neo-Nazi gang members generally center on belonging and protection (whether from bullies, rival gangs, or perceived enemies) [191L]. This is not far different from the motivation of other gangs (discussed at Part III, Chapter 3B Gangs: Can't We All Get Along?).

Though troubled, gang members in this age range may be from well-off middle class families. This distinguishes them from the members of older Neo-Nazi gangs, who are usually marginalized individuals with working-class backgrounds, low educational levels, and lengthy criminal records [191M]. Both groups view immigrants as threatening—younger gang members seeing them as a physical threat; older gang members seeing immigrants as an economic threat [191N].

How do we respond to such terrorism, whether by Neo-Nazis or radical Islamic fundamentalists [192]? Law Professor, Bill Quigley of Loyola University in New Orleans made the following points in an article written following September 11, 2001:

- *Courage is critical.* There is a concerted effort to try to intimidate and silence people interested in justice and peace. Conservatives challenge the patriotism of all who dare to examine and question the root causes of why all that America does is not universally admired. Conservatives are setting up cardboard liberals who excuse the terrorists, hate America, do not support democracy, and are just as intolerant as Jerry Falwell...If working for peace and justice does not meet some conservative's narrow definition of patriotism, then they have created too weak a form of patriotism. By that definition, Sojourner Truth was not a patriot, Abraham Lincoln was not a patriot...Martin Luther King was not a patriot. I want to be what they are...*True patriotism should allow an appreciation for both what is great about our country and what we need to work to improve* [209A]...
- Prior to September 11...[t]he people organizing around welfare reform worked apart from those organizing against the death penalty. People working on living wages were isolated from those working on voting rights and redistricting. When times get tough, they are tougher when you are alone...*As members of a community we are much stronger and wiser than when we are alone* [209B]...
- There has been an upsurge in people seeking consolation and leadership and direction from their churches. *The religious community has a big opportunity as people search for new meaning: linkages between faith and justice and peace.* Some churches have spoken eloquently about peace and justice issues...In my experience, all faiths place justice and peace and sacrifice and respect and the common good at the very center of their beliefs. The problem is that many churches preach and practice

a very weak form of their faith...*Work for social justice is replaced by church tithing. Working for peace is replaced by supporting the church school or church suppers. The faith which is meant to afflict the comfortable and comfort the afflicted, weakly ends up comforting the comfortable.* We need to work with people whose interests in justice and peace are faith-based. We also need to challenge our church leaders, who tend to mute the justice issues in order to accommodate their congregations [209C]...

- [We]...should respond to questions [on the basis of] values central to both the peace and social justice movement and the majority of the general public: Thus, "How can we hunt down the terrorists" can be recast as "How can we be safe?" "How do we protect America" can be "How can we be strong?" Instead of "How can we wipe these fanatics out?" we can discuss "How can we arrive at justice?"...*Martin Luther King spoke about the three evils of racism, militarism, and materialism, for a reason.* Attempts to blame these tragedies on Islam, Muslims, Arabs, Jews, liberals, and gays and lesbians show us the *need to stand up for the civil and human rights of all people* [209D]...[Emphasis added.]

—From an article entitled, "Ten Ideas for Social Justice Organizing in a Time of Crisis."

PART V:

IDOLATRY

EXECUTIVE ETHICS ABANDONED: THE SO-CALLED LIBERAL CONSPIRACY

I am the Lord your God…You shall have no other gods before Me… (Exodus 20: 2–3)

I am not bound to win, but I am bound to be true. I am not bound to succeed, but I am bound to live by the light that I have. I must stand with anybody that stands right, and stand with him while he is right, and part with him when he goes wrong. —Abraham Lincoln

There is a long history of vigorous political debate in this country—with mudslinging having involved even Thomas Jefferson.

What is more disturbing is that apparent ethical violations by members of the Bush Administration have been ignored—even defended—by the Christian Right without further examination. Again and again on Christian radio and television, reference has been made to the political Left as the source of (supposedly) unfounded allegations, and to a so-called "liberal conspiracy" by the media.

The New Hampshire Gazette—founded in 1756, before the nation, itself—described the purpose of the press this way:

> Back in the 1790s, when our form of government was being hammered out, a prevailing theory held that newspapers could, should, and would tell the public what was going on. That way, if the nation's leaders were driving it towards a precipice, the public might be able to replace them before the whole shebang went over the edge [217A].

In explaining the approach he, personally, takes toward fact-finding, reporter, Lou Dobbs of CNN spoke in terms Christians should understand better than most:

> There's no question that there is a bias in the media, one that sometimes is perceived as liberal. But...[a]n even worse bias has grown up—"he says, she says"—journalism. Reporters are...not...doing...rigorous newsgathering...I always tell my people that we're interested in the one side of the story that counts, and that is the truth...The fact is, the truth usually is not fair or balanced. Truth stands by itself. The idea that fair and balanced is a substitute for truth and fact is mindless nonsense that has captured much of the national media. There are two political sides to every story. Does that mean if we had three major political parties there would be three sides to the truth?...It's utter nonsense...[I]n every story...it is our obligation to report...the non-partisan reality that exists for 98 percent of the population of this country—a country that is first American, and only secondarily—and ancillarily—Republican or Democrat [213].

A conspiracy is defined as an agreement between two or more persons to perform a wrongful or subversive act; commit a crime; or accomplish a legal purpose through illegal means. The political Left (always a civil rights proponent) seems to have lost favor defending the rights of certain groups of which the Conservative Right does not approve. Among these are gays. Granted certain members of the media may have their biases—Right and Left.

The prerequisite of an agreement is not, however, met. Nor is the definitional requirement met of intention to perform a wrongful or subversive act; commit a crime or a legal act by illegal means. Instead, a series of major events involving elected officials have taken place in which the public has had a legitimate interest.

Forgive me, if I utilize news reporting to reiterate a few of these events and the questionable ethical responses to them. From all indications, these events were truthfully reported (if not always truthfully or fully described by the Administration). For those who—like the

President—may not recall, the First Amendment protects freedom of the press.

WMD

"Official intelligence on Iraqi weapons programs was flawed, but even with its flaws, it was not what led to the war," Pillar wr[ites] in the upcoming issue of the *Journal on Foreign Affairs*. Instead, he assert[s], the Administration "went to war without requesting—and evidently without being influenced by—any strategic-level intelligence assessments on any aspect of Iraq [111A]."

Walter Pincus writes in *The Washington Post*: "The former CIA official who coordinated US intelligence on the Middle East until last year has accused the Bush administration of 'cherry-picking' intelligence on Iraq to justify a decision it had already reached to go to war, and of ignoring warnings that the country could easily fall into violence and chaos after an invasion to overthrow Saddam Hussein [111B]."

VALERIE PLAME DISCLOSURE

Investigative reporter Murray Waas, now a staff writer for the *National Journal*, spots two lines no one else noticed in a document that was made public 11 days ago…The two lines are from a Jan[uary] 23 letter from Special Prosecutor, Patrick J. Fitzgerald to the lawyers for former White House Aide, I. Lewis "Scooter" Libby…Fitzgerald wrote: "Mr. Libby testified in the grand jury that he had contact with reporters in which he disclosed the content of the National Intelligence Estimate…in the course of his interaction with reporters in June and July 2003…We also note that it is our understanding that Mr. Libby testified that he was authorized to disclose information about the NIE to the press by his superiors…The public correspondence does not mention the identities of the 'superiors' who authorized the leak-

> ing of the classified information, but people with firsthand knowledge of the matter identified one of them as Cheney. Libby also testified that he worked closely with then-Deputy National Security Adviser, Stephen Hadley and White House Deputy Chief of Staff, Karl Rove in deciding what information to leak to the press to build public support for the war, and later, postwar, to defend the administration's use of prewar intelligence [111C]...."

Note that President George W. Bush had initially promised to fire anyone involved in leaking CIA Agent, Valerie Plame's name. We were apparently expected to forget this. His standard at the time was not the commission of a crime and guilt beyond a reasonable doubt, but any involvement with the leak. Nonetheless, the President praised Libby following his indictment. Though the defense may argue that the information was disclosed for national security reasons, it appears obvious this was political payback aimed at Joe Wilson.

HURRICANE KATRINA

The Associated Press on March 1, 2006 made public secret government videotape of the final briefing August 28, 2005, the day before Hurricane Katrina struck the Gulf Coast. Both President George W. Bush and Homeland Security Director, Michael Chertoff are shown participating (the President from his vacation ranch home in Texas). Warnings of the pending disaster—including specific mention of breached or overrun levees, deaths at the Superdome, and the dire need for post-storm rescue—were conveyed in urgent terms. Former FEMA Director, Michael Brown during this meeting expressed his concern that there were not enough teams to assist evacuees at the Superdome. An additional seven days of briefing transcripts clearly show that federal officials anticipated the tragedy [246].

> Eric Lipton writes in the *New York Times*: "In the aftermath of Hurricane Katrina, Bush administration officials said they had been caught by surprise when they were

> told on Tuesday, Aug. 30, that a levee had broken, allowing floodwaters to engulf New Orleans. But Congressional investigators have now learned that an eyewitness account of the flooding from a federal emergency official reached the Homeland Security Department's headquarters starting at 9:27 p.m. the day before, and the White House itself at midnight [111D]."

President George W. Bush on September 1, 2005 blandly said on the ABC program, *Good Morning America*, "I don't think anyone anticipated the breach of the levees." [224A]. In stark contrast, the *Chicago Tribune* reported, "Despite continuous warnings that a catastrophic hurricane could hit New Orleans, the Bush administration and Congress in recent years have repeatedly denied full funding for hurricane preparation and flood control. That has delayed construction of levees around the city [224B]..."

FEMA Director, Michael Brown's assertion that FEMA was unaware as late as September 1, 2005 that thousands of refugees were trapped in the New Orleans Convention Center without food or water was nothing less than astounding [224C]. Evidently, no one in the entire agency owned—or was acquainted with anyone who owned or had access to—a television, radio, or computer with Internet capability.

> ...[W]hile government emergency planners scrambled to get relief to stricken communities, the USS Bataan—a 844-foot ship with 1,200 sailors, helicopters, doctors, hospital beds for 600 patients, six operating rooms, food and water—was cruising in the Gulf of Mexico, awaiting relief orders [224G].

Was the slow response to Hurricane Katrina merely the result of incompetence; a reflection of misplaced priorities (insofar as an overcommitment of resources to terrorism-prevention, at the expense of natural disaster relief); casual, albeit callous, disregard by this Administration for the lives of the poor, i.e. those most likely to be impacted by a catastrophe—and most at risk from cronyism—or something even colder? In that distinction lies the difference between gross negligence and outright criminality, stemming from party politics.

The prodigous population shift which followed on Hurricanes Katrina and Rita is virtually certain to result in a permanent reduction in the concentration of Black voters in Louisiana and a negative impact on the Democratic Party [214A]. Over one million residents fled their homes, and are scattered throughout the country. Many will never return [214B]. The issue is not only whether this could have been foreseen, but whether it was the intended goal, all along. That—in my view at least—would be a "conspiracy" worth investigating.

NSA

From Bradford H. Gray:

Mr. Bush: In your speech on the Patriot Act in Buffalo on April 20, 2004, you said the following:
"Now, by the way, any time you hear the United States government talking about wiretap, it requires—a wiretap requires a court order. Nothing has changed, by the way. When we're talking about chasing down terrorists, we're talking about getting a court order before we do so. It's important for our fellow citizens to understand, when you think Patriot Act, constitutional guarantees are in place when it comes to doing what is necessary to protect our homeland, because we value the Constitution."
Is that the same Constitution that you now say authorizes wiretaps without a court order [111H]?

From Geoff Tyrrell:

Have you ever used NSA derived information for political purposes [111I]?

From W. S. Dixon:

Mr. Bush, if only known al Qaeda members or suspected al Qaeda members are having their telephone, e-mail or other communications intercepted, why is it necessary to do it

> without the FISA court approval? The NSA must have their names to allow such surveillance now and the court can give approval to intercept all messages going to them so there would be no urgency in obtaining warrants and there could be no constitutional question raised [111J].
>
> *From Kevin Hoover:*
>
> Did you actually read the August 6, 2001 PDB, "Bin Laden determined to strike in the United States?"
> If so, why did you not act on it?
> If not, why is it necessary to spy on Americans when you don't even use the information you already have [111K]?
>
> *From Kurt W. Kolasinski:*
>
> Why is the FISA law from 1978 old and outdated but you insist that the Constitution written in 1787 can only be interpreted by strict constructionalists [111L]?
>
> *From J. Smith:*
>
> Mr. President, when it comes to interpreting the Constitution you claim to be a strict constructionist, insisting that JUDGES not read things into the Constitution that aren't there. Yet when it comes to interpreting your powers under Article II, you want to interpret the phrase "Commander-in-Chief of the armed forces" so broadly that that phrase becomes virtually a blank check to do anything you want—such as tap phones without warrants or imprison people forever without trials. Mr. President, how can you seriously claim that YOU PERSONALLY aren't also guilty of reading things into the Constitution that clearly aren't there [111M]?

Since these questions were all posed by ordinary citizens, I am curious where we are all supposed to have met, for the purpose of conspiring? My social life would be far more active, were I acquainted with all these people.

PORT SECURITY

On February 21, 2006 the President promised to veto any legislation—even by Republicans—to block the takeover by Dubai Ports World (a government-owned company controlled by United Arab Emirates, a dictatorship) of P&O (the privately-owned British company which currently runs commercial operations at several of the nation's busiest ports) [210A]. The ports in question were: New York/ New Jersey; Philadelphia; Baltimore; Miami; and New Orleans [210B]. It is fair to say that the public was at a loss to understand why American ports (already a security risk) were in foreign hands at all. Then came the other shoe:

> No one in this administration has talked about the fact that Dubai Ports World could be partially responsible for the shipment of military equipment through the Texas ports of Beaumont and Corpus Christi. There are also charges tonight that the Bush administration violated US law by rushing this port sale through the Committee on Foreign Investments without a properly and legally-mandated review.
>
> At the same time, the White House, from the President on down, seems to be in complete denial about the risk to our national security from the sale of US port operations to a country with ties to the 9/11 hijackers and nuclear proliferation [211A].
>
> —Reporter, Lou Dobbs on *Lou Dobbs Tonight*, aired February 23, 2006. Courtesy of CNN.

Democratic Senator Carl Levin complained that the Armed Services Committee had not been notified of the change, learning of it only from the media [211B]. The September 11 Commission Report had cited United Arab Emirates as both a valued counterterrorism ally and an ongoing concern [211C]. Astonishingly, White House Homeland Security Adviser, Frances Townsend saw no problem with the takeover and no need for an investigation of the security aspects of the deal [211D]—this though only 5% of cargo containers are ever x-rayed to confirm that their contents are as listed [211E].

Biblical heroes, such as Moses and David, had feet of clay to remind us that only God is perfect. We are not to make idols of mortal men. Edmund Burke reminded us, in simpler terms, that "[o]ne that confounds good and evil is an enemy to good."

THE CHRISTIAN WITNESS TAINTED

Now I saw heaven opened, and behold, a white horse. And He who sat on him was called Faithful and True, and in righteousness He judges and makes war. (Revelation 19: 11)

Great is the guilt of an unnecessary war. —John Adams

The history of mankind is the history of warfare. At the outset there were no rules. The winner took all: the loser's life and the spoils of war [236]. This continued even into biblical times. *See*, for example, the war on Midian at Numbers 31: 7–10.

Gradually, unwritten rules became accepted practice. These distinguished among the types of enemies; determined the situations warranting war; provided the authority for starting and ending wars; placed limitations on the time, place, and nature of combat; and even outlawed war altogether. We know this because surviving hunter-gatherers still utilize unwritten rules on these subjects today [235A].

As civilization developed, texts began to appear with rules urging respect for the enemy. These included the Bible, the Mahabharata, and the Koran [235B].

From ancient days onward, we have over 500 covenants, codes of conduct, and other texts governing combat and/or the treatment of prisoners and non-combatants [235C]. These include the 13th Century Viqayet (written while the Arabs ruled Spain) and the Lieber Code (adopted for use by Union troops during the Civil War) [235D].

Since September 11, 2001 the concept of the "just war" has received new attention [232E].

THE JUST WAR

From earliest times, the Western tradition attempted to put war in a legal context by formulating a doctrine of the "just war." The goal was to reconcile might and right [237I], i.e. to justify ethically how and why wars are fought [232A].

With time, the principles of the "just war" evolved into the following: just cause, declared by a proper authority; right intention; a reasonable chance of success; and an end proportional to the means used [232E].

JUS AD BELLUM

The terms now used in relation to war—*jus ad bellum* and *jus in bello*—did not exist in the Middle Ages, and were unknown to canon and civil lawyers of that time [237A]. War was simply seen as a just response to unprovoked aggression and, more broadly, as the method for restoring a legitimate right which had been violated [237B]. There were originally four causes for which a "just war" could be waged: defense, recovery of property, recovery of debts, and punishment [237C].

In the doctrine of *bellum justum,* legal analysis focused entirely on the act of going to war and, more especially, on the causes for war, from the subjective perspective of the belligerent [237F]. In other words, did this particular belligerent (from his perspective) have the right to resort to force [237D]? A belligerent without just cause had no rights; he was merely a criminal, and could be executed as such, if caught [237E].

Unless a nation is, itself, attacked (or intervenes to assist another in resisting internal or external oppression [232K]), a "just war" can only be pursued as a last resort [233A]. All non-violent options must be exhausted first [233B].

Self-defense in response to aggression qualifies as *just cause.* The question arises whether aggression requires the physical injury of a nation's citizens (or whether the invasion of a nation's territory is sufficient). These two grounds are the most well recognized [232G]. However, the definition of "aggression" has, at times, been extended by rationalization [232F].

What if there are legal issues surrounding title to the disputed territory? Does an insult to national honor constitute sufficient aggression, so that a military response would be seen as self defense [232H]? Does a trade embargo qualify as aggression, perhaps against a nation's economic interests [232I]? Would an oil embargo suffice? Can a nation's prosperity alone qualify as aggression against a neighbor, perhaps by way of social injustice [232J]?

This last would seem the rationale employed by al-Qaeda for its violence against the US.

If a government is just, i.e. is accountable to the governed and does not rule arbitrarily, then giving the officers of the state the right to declare war is reasonable. However, the farther from a proper and just government the ruling authority is, the more its sovereignty disintegrates. A historical example would be the Vichy puppet regime established in France by the Nazis [232L].

Military action taken by a group (such as al-Qaeda) which does not constitute a *legitimate authority*, i.e. one sanctioned by society and outsiders as appropriate, cannot be in furtherance of a "just war," no matter how "just" that group may believe its cause [233C].

A "just" war cannot be pursued for reasons of self-interest or self-aggrandizement [232M], but only to redress a wrong [233D]. That alone is considered *right intention.*

The next principle is that of *reasonable probability of success.* This is a necessary condition for waging a "just war," but is not sufficient by itself. It, also, raises moral issues. How is success to be defined? Do we never assist in a hopeless cause? Is it not sometimes morally necessary to stand up to a bully [232N]?

Finally, the desired *end* should be *proportional to* the *means* used [232O]. This principle (which overlaps *jus in bello*) generally involves minimizing war's destructive impact [232P]. The ultimate goal of a just war is to re-establish a peace preferable to that peace which would have prevailed if the war had not been fought [233E]. Whether this goal has been (or can be) achieved in Iraq—indeed, whether it was even considered—is for each American to decide.

JUS IN BELLO

*Jus in bello (*the twin doctrine *to jus ad bellum)* was initially a body of law applied objectively to all belligerents [237G].

As the rules of war developed, some consideration was given to women, children, and prisoners of war [232B]. Soldiers, also, invoked the concept of "honor." Some acts were in every war deemed dishonorable [232C]. The specifics changed from century to century, and place to place. However, the fact that even one virtue was sought after, early on infused warfare with moral concerns [232D].

Throughout the 17th and 18th Centuries the doctrine of the "just war" lost ground to the idea that nation states had the discretionary power to wage war as a means of pursuing national policy [237J]. Subsequently the philosopher, Immanuel Kant, made a distinction between the right to wage war and the use of just methods during war (what we understand as *jus in bello* today) [237H].

The Law of War incorporates the concept of the "just war" and is applicable to all cases of declared war; to armed conflicts between the US and other nations (even if the state of war is not recognized by one of them); and to partial or total occupation [238A]. It includes all international law binding on the US, e.g. treaties, Hague Regulations, and Geneva Conventions [238B].

For training purposes, these extensive materials are "boiled down" to 10 rules that 18-year old soldiers can easily comprehend and recall [238E]. A copy of these "Soldier's Rules" is *attached* at **Appendix** VII.

The difficulty lies not in the comprehension of these rules, but their application under war time conditions. To say that emotions during wartime can run high—certainly under fire and immediately after—is a vast understatement. Situations are often ambiguous and can change from moment to moment. Soldiers realize that they are staking their lives and the lives of their comrades on the outcome of decisions taken.

In modern terms, the principles of the Law of War a/k/a Humanitarian Law [235F] can be enunciated, as follows [238C]:

1. Requirement of Military Necessity. A civilian bridge over which munitions must travel can become a legitimate military objective.
2. Prohibition Against Unnecessary Suffering. Even in a good cause, the right to injure the enemy is not unlimited.
3. Requirement of Proportionality. As applied here, this would mandate that a battle end before it becomes a massacre. For instance, at Omdurman in the Sudan, six machine gunners killed thousands of primitively-armed dervishes [232Q]. The Requirement of Proportionality would prohibit such an outcome.
4. Distinction Between Combatants and Non-Combatants. When soldiers turn their weapons against non-combatants, they are no longer committing legitimate acts of war, but rather acts of murder.

It is Department of Defense policy to apply the Law of War principles to any conflict, regardless of how it is characterized (declared war, international "peacekeeping" mission, internal armed conflict, or other military operation) [238D].[27]

Among other things, this prevents the deterioration of order within our military units; maintains the humanity of our own soldiers;[28] and maintains public support for the efforts of our soldiers and marines [238F]. It is intended—though not guaranteed—to reduce retaliation against our troops, and allow for the earlier restoration of peace [238G].

I have not attempted to set out every philosophic view of war here, only to provide an understanding of the basics, so that we Americans will not be as easily misled by lofty sounding rhetoric or false accusations in future.

IRAQ: HOW MANY LEGS DOES A DOG HAVE?

In September 2001 Bishop Joseph Fiorenza, President of the US

Conference of Catholic Bishops, Office of Social Development & World Peace, wrote President George W. Bush to confirm that the use of force against Afghanistan would be justified, if carried out in accord with "just war" norms, and as one element of a broader—primarily non-military—effort to address terrorism [231A].

In September of the following year, Bishop Fiorenza's successor, Bishop Wilton D. Gregory, wrote the President again on behalf of the US Conference of Catholic Bishops. This time the 60 member Administrative Committee of the Bishops Conference had met to consider the morality of our unilateral, preemptive use of military force to overthrow the government of Iraq.

Despite the September 11 attacks a year earlier, the Bishops Conference was unable to find moral grounds to support such action on our part, in the absence of "clear and adequate evidence of Iraqi involvement in the attacks of September 11th or of a [further] imminent attack of a grave nature [231B]."[29] Bishop Gregory then applied the "just war" criteria of just cause, right authority, probability of success, proportionality and noncombatant immunity to the situation.

- *Just Cause (casus belli)*—Damage by the aggressor must be lasting, grave, and certain. The Bishops Conference asked whether there was evidence of a direct connection between Iraq and the September 11 attacks (expressing reservations at the concept of a preemptive strike, even should such evidence exist) [231C].
- *Legitimate Authority*—For legitimacy, the Bishops Conference felt there should be constitutional compliance, a broad national consensus, and international approval (particularly in light of the preemptive nature of the action contemplated) [231D].
- *Probability of Success and Proportionality*—For moral justification, the use of force must not produce evil greater than that to be eliminated, and must have realistic prospects for success [231E]. The Bishops Conference—presumably not international affairs experts—nonetheless, thought to inquire:

> Would...preemptive force succeed in thwarting serious threats or, instead, provoke the very kind of attacks that it is intended to prevent [231F]?

> Would the United States…commit to the arduous, long-term task of ensuring a just peace or would a post-Saddam Iraq continue to be plagued by civil conflict [231G]…?
>
> Would the use of military force lead to wider conflict and instability [231H]?
>
> Would war against Iraq…undermine the broader coalition against terrorism [231I]?

- *Norms Governing the Conduct of War*—The Bishops Conference expressed concern for the welfare of civilians [231J].

It is deplorable that the President and his advisors did not have as much insight.

A few questions from the American people:

From Steve Walach:

> Referring to intelligence that claimed Iraq had an extensive program to construct and use weapons of mass destruction, you, Mr. President, now sheepishly admit that those assertions were plain wrong. However, by way of disclaimer, Mr. President, you attach this bizarre epilogue: "Knowing what I know today, I'd make the decision again." Taken to its logical conclusion, Mr. President, your statement means that the casus belli—the WMDs—mattered not a lick in your decision to invade. Doesn't your statement mean that you would have invaded Iraq regardless what the CIA and all the other spy agencies said about WMDs, making the war in Iraq your decision entirely and a decision based only on your desire to attack Iraq and eliminate Saddam [230A]?

From Steve Shepherd:

> You repeatedly said you had not made any decision to invade Iraq in the run-up to the actual invasion. Yet numerous sources, including administration insiders such as Richard Clarke and Paul O'Neil, say otherwise. And for more than 10 years, invading Iraq had been a publicly stated goal

> of the so-called "neoconservatives," including Paul Wolfowitz and Donald Rumsfeld, within your administration. Wasn't it always your intention to invade Iraq [230B]...
>
> *From Phillip Daniel:*
>
> President Bush, many times you and your administration ha[ve] claimed that a significant fraction of the Al-Qaeda leadership has been captured or killed. But when you consider that none of those persons were captured or killed in Iraq, were from Iraq, or, to the best of our knowledge, have ever been to Iraq, how can Iraq be "the central front in the War on Terror [230C]?"

A war against terrorism? A just war? How many legs does a dog have? Lincoln knew the answer.

> How many legs does a dog have, if you call the tail a leg? Four. Calling a tail a leg doesn't make it a leg.
>
> —Abraham Lincoln

THE VETERANS' REWARD

> Many of our troops are listening tonight. And I want you and your families to know, my administration, and this Congress, will give you the resources you need to fight and win the war on terror [218B].
>
> —Source: President George W. Bush, State of the Union Speech, 2004

Let us examine what this has actually meant, in practical terms.

Back-End Draft

Nearly 40% of those now deployed in Iraq and Afghanistan are National Guard or Reserve troops [218A]. Tours of duty were unilaterally extended—inflicting unexpected hardships on military families, and making Guard Members and Reservists unavailable for disaster relief when Hurricanes Katrina and Rita hit.

> Starr: *Fifty-eight-year-old* Ray Johnson *flew Huey helicopters 37 years ago in Vietnam*. Now, he is *headed back into combat*, this time in northern Iraq.
>
> R. Johnson: Since I'm a Black Hawk instructor and everything, you know, I've trained a lot of helicopter pilots in my years in the service, and now my number's come up, so, you know, I feel that I must serve.
>
> Starr: We met him last year, flying for the Maryland State Police, but always a member of the Army National Guard.
>
> R. Johnson: As long as I signed up, and, you know, received the benefits, I felt that whenever they need me, where they need me, I had to pay back [211F]. [Emphasis added.]
>
> —Interview with Army National Guard Member, returning to Active Duty, *Lou Dobbs Tonight,* February 24, 2006. Courtesy of CNN.

Inadequate and Shoddy Gear

The Pentagon has failed to provide critical equipment needed by our troops in Iraq and Afghanistan—from life-saving body armor to warm gloves and cushioned socks, from cargo belts to padded rucksack straps, from flashlights to hydration systems, satellite position-finders, and rifles that function?!

Families have received desperate phone calls, letters, and emails from their loved ones at the front lines. Far beyond knitting socks, family members have literally had to go to their local stores, purchase the necessary equipment out of their own pockets, and ship it overseas [218C].

Can a more damning statement be made?

Yes, the same Pentagon that sops up $400 billion of our tax dollars every year (plus the $87 billion add-on it was given last year to pay for Bush's Iraqi occupation) is shamelessly short-changing the grunts who are putting their lives on the line every day.

...One important innovation for ground troops is a simple, relatively lightweight [*Kevlar*] vest that contains ceramic plates of boron carbide capable of stopping powerful AK-47 bullets and flying shrapnel. Simply put, these *vests are lifesavers in a firefight or a bomb blast*—and they were readily available to the Pentagon from US manufacturers...*Instead, the troops had been issued Vietnam- era flak jackets* that, as one soldier put it, "couldn't stop a rock."..Enraged military families later learned that even the small contingent of troops that Mongolia sent to Iraq came with the lifesaving vests. Hauled *before a House committee, General John Abizaid, the head of US forces in Iraq, said he couldn't "answer for the record why we started this war with protective vests that were in short supply."* Thanks to the howl and heat from the grass-roots, Congress added money to the Pentagon's already bloated budget last fall, requiring body armor for all soldiers in Iraq. Finally, nearly a year after Bush started his war—and after an untold number of unnecessary deaths—our troops are receiving the vests...

Families of these GIs were forced to buy...basics to send to the troops—things the Pentagon chose not to provide, even *though it spent some $690 million* that *same year just on the cost-overrun charged by Lockheed-Martin for the unnecessary F-22 jet fighter it is developing...*

[O]ur troops have also *found* that *many of their weapons don't work...*The *M-16 rifle that "jammed up" on [Jessica] Lynch was infamous for having the exact same problem in the Vietnam War, 35 years before. Back then*, the complaints from the field were so many and so angry that *Congress held hearings, concluding* that the gun had "serious and excessive malfunctions" and that the Army's behavior in sending soldiers

into combat with a weapon that had such *known defects "bordered on criminal negligence."* Isn't the same true now?

...Last November 2, 16 American soldiers were killed and 20 wounded when a missile hit their Chinook helicopter. *Missing from* that *Chinook, and many* other *helicopters* under fire in this war, was an *"aircraft survivability" package* that includes an infrared jammer and flare dispenser to decoy heat-seeking missiles. Sen. Dick Durbin (D-Illinois) learned that copter crews had been beseeching higher-ups for months to get these packages, to no avail. In an email to Durbin, one of the copter pilots said: "So we were essentially flying around for *five months with no anti-missile equipment.* For the life of me, I cannot understand what goes through the head of commanders that would load 30 soldiers into an aircraft with no protection against a credible threat [218D]." [Emphasis added.]

—Source: Jim Hightower, *The Lowdown,* February 2004.

...The Army has been slow to acknowledge the vulnerability of its thin-skinned Humvees, say critics in Congress and elsewhere. Now, Army officials acknowledge the problem will not be fixed for another three months. Meanwhile, soldiers in Iraq are hanging flak vests and even plywood on their Humvees in desperate attempts at protection, Army officials say. And the casualties mount week by week [218H]...

—David Wood, *Newhouse News Service,* February 18, 2004.

"We weren't as effective as we could be," the Army's logistics chief, Lt. Gen. Claude V. Christianson, acknowledged in an interview. In a devastating self-critique, Christianson and his staff have produced an analysis that concludes...that the *Army's logisticians can't see what is needed on the battlefield, can't respond rapidly when they do find out what's needed, and can't distribute what they have when it's needed...*But the *supply problems* were *exacerbated*, officers said, *by* the *decision*

> *of Defense Secretary Donald Rumsfeld to deploy mostly combat units in the weeks before the invasion, and to hold back Army and Marine Corps logistics and support units until weeks or months later*—gambling that the war would be over quickly enough that sustained resupply wouldn't be needed [229B]. [Emphasis added.]
>
> —David Wood, *Newhouse News Service*, January 22, 2004.

Rumsfeld's involvement may explain why General Abizaid was unable to answer "on the record" why such necessary items as Kevlar vests were unavailable.

Early Greek and Roman soldiers had to provide their own equipment. It seems we are returning to that barbaric approach. Evidently, the Bush Administration sees it as a way of "starving the beast" of large government, while simultaneously establishing Pax Americana and allowing corporations and the very wealthy to root at the trough. This is the Administration with which the Christian Right has chosen to ally, itself.

Inadequate Medical Equipment

The insurgency appears not to have been notified that combat has officially ended in Iraq. In fact, as of this writing, Iraq is on the verge—if not in the early stages—of civil war. Apart from those killed outright, there have been well over 3000 of our soldiers wounded by gunfire, mortar rounds, car bombs, and other incidents [218G].

> The doctors and nurses [at the 28th Combat Support Hospital in Baghdad, to which the wounded are first taken] are excellent—but, again, they are shorthanded and often short on supplies. CSH Commander Beverly Pritchett says, "It's very frustrating when a physician or surgeon comes to me and says, 'I need this,' and eight weeks later I still can't give him that. I know *if I got on the phone and used my own credit card, I could get it here.*"
>
> In the best can-do spirit of the US military, the CSH staff is creative. For example, after soldiers go through sur-

> gery, their bodies can become dangerously cold, sometimes resulting in death. Having been issued no equipment to deal with this, a *nurse set up* a *cardboard box big enough to hold a person* (*like the homeless use on the streets*), went out and bought a hair dryer, and rigged it to blow warm air on the patient. Dubbed the "Chief Cuddler," it has saved more than 50 lives. While proud of such innovations, Commander Pritchett is angry that her staff has to resort to them [218I]. [Emphasis added.]

In a day and age when we can communicate in real time with climbers on Mount Everest, when we have the technology to photograph galaxies 60 million light years away, must our soldiers settle for medical care that harks back to the Crimean War?

Follow-Up Care: Delayed/Reduced/Denied

Combat in Iraq and Afghanistan is producing about three soldiers, marines, and others a week who have suffered traumatic or surgical amputation of at least one limb [229A].

The Bush Administration's 2006 Budget proposed major reductions in Veterans' benefits, insofar as the elimination of funding for state programs providing long-term care (this resulting, among other things, in increased prescription drug co-payments for some veterans, and an annual enrollment fee of $250). The Administration, also, proposed trimming nursing home care for veterans by $351 million in 2006, thereby eliminating approximately 5,000 beds run by the Veterans Administration [75].

Veterans' programs under the Bush Administration's proposed 2007 Budget would be cut a total of $10.3 billion over the next five years (these cuts reaching 13% in 2011). Again, the programs in question primarily supply health care to veterans [241M].

> ...Last fall, Bill Moyers' *Now* program reported on the case of Billy Bisel.
>
> Under mortar fire in Afghanistan, Billy dove for cover and broke his neck. He required two surgeries to install

> a metal plate, and was left so debilitated that he couldn't return to his carpentry and welding work. Seeking rehab and the disability benefits he was due, Billy started calling up the VA's bureaucracy. He says they told him to "shut up." Here's an excerpt from his *Now* interview:
> Now: They didn't say, "Shut up."
> Bisel: Yes, they did.
> Now: They said, "Shut up"?
> Bisel: Literally, yes. I needed to quit bitchin'; I needed to quit complainin'; I needed to just go home and wait until the paperwork comes in.
>
> *Now* went on to report: "Nineteen months after he got back from Afghanistan, Billy Bisel was still waiting [218E]."

In fact, as of February 2004 the average wait by a veteran for a medical appointment at a VA hospital was *seven months* [218F]. VA systems have always been overburdened, but by late 2003, about 300,000 veterans were waiting simply to get enrolled. With an election on the horizon, the Bush Administration announced it would eliminate those enrollment lists and did. A campaign promise kept, just in time for the President to take credit for it before the election.

Unfortunately, waiting lists for primary care first appointments grew longer. As of 2006 these now take *up to 18 months* (more than twice the time they did before). And the *wait for "medically necessary surgery"* is currently *between 18 and 24 months* at many VA facilities [217C].

Now, it appears the Bush Administration is attempting to shorten the lists of those finally receiving care.

> Last fall it was reported in the press—as opposed to announced by the government—that the Veterans Administration would be reviewing [i.e. reviewing with an eye toward dismissing] the cases of 72,000 veterans who were rated disabled for Post-Traumatic Stress Disorder. It was also reported that a new rule change would require an additional level of review before future ratings would be granted. Some old-school Congress members concerned about their

> constituents looked into the changes and found that *problems perceived by VA bureaucrats were actually the result of VA screw-ups, not greedy veterans*. The proposed changes were rescinded, but late in the year the issue arose again. The *Washington Post* reported December 27 that the *VA* was "*in negotiations with* the *Institute of Medicine over* a review of the 'utility and objectiveness' of *PTSD diagnostic criteria* and the validity of screening techniques, a process that *could have profound implications for returning soldiers.*" The *Post* quoted Jeff Schrade, a "communications director for the Senate Veterans Affairs Committee," saying that "[o]n the one hand," a recent 150 percent jump in PTSD claims was "good" because it meant "people are reaching out for help." "At the same time," Schrade told the *Post*, "as more people reach out for help, it squeezes the budget further." "*Among the issues* being discussed," the *Post's* Shankar Vedantam wrote "was *whether veterans who show signs of recovery should continue to receive disability compensation*: 'Whether anyone has the political courage to cut them off—I don't know that Congress has that will, but we'll see.' The *Post* quoted an anonymous *VA official* as saying '*If we show that PTSD is prevalent and severe, that becomes one more little reason we should stop waging war. If, on the other hand, PTSD rates are low...that is convenient for the Bush administration...*' .According to Terence M. Keane, whom the *Post* calls 'one of the nation's best-known PTSD researchers,' a 1988 study determined that '[1]ess than one fourth of people with combat-related PTSD have used VA-related services'...[apparently, among other reasons, because of the long wait] [217D]." [Emphasis added.]

I am grateful for (and humbled by) our veterans' sacrifice. How many others may share this unnamed veteran's sentiments, I do not know.

> Speaking as an amputee, we...[ha]ve suffered enough and continue to be exploited by the right and by the left!

> From the beginning of this war campaign, I've said that there isn't enough media coverage of the carnage and I do feel if our country is going to continue this occupation, we should at least see the horrors that are being produced by it. It seems to me that the Bush administration has done a good job of playing down this aspect...I am a veteran, an amputee, and I feel for all those who have lost sons and daughters, husbands and wives, and significant others in this senseless war.
>
> I try to afford those who have given their lives, the dignity and honor that they deserve, but at the same time I think we should hold the person or persons responsible for this accountable and that would be our president, his administration and congress for acquiescing their responsibility and not maintaining the oversight and asking the difficult questions all along that could have prevented this tragedy from occurring in the first place...
>
> [I]f we don't expect from our leaders the very best that they can give us—well, then we deserve to be deceived and lied to...
>
> I love my country [the USA], but I certainly do not agree with all of our policies and this one was truly a disaster, even if things turn out for the better in Iraq and they achieve some form of democracy: [26,000 to 30,000 civilians killed and thousands of our own soldiers killed and/or maimed for life] to topple a dictator that WE are at least partially responsible for creating...[is a high price to pay] [155].

In memory of those no longer here to speak, I offer 24 familiar notes:[30]

> Day is done, gone the sun,
> From the hills, from the lake,
> From the sky.
> All is well, safely rest,
> God is nigh.

PART VI:

THE CROSSROADS OF HISTORY

THE ROMAN EMPIRE AS PRECEDENT: MIGHT STILL DOES NOT MAKE RIGHT

Woe to you who plunder, though you have not been plundered; and you who deal treacherously, though they have not dealt treacherously with you! (Isaiah 33: 1)

Let us have faith that right makes might; and in that faith let us, to the end, dare to do our duty as we understand it. —Abraham Lincoln

Few these days have read Thomas Paine's 1776 pamphlet, "The Crisis." The pamphlet was written during one of our country's darkest hours, with enlistments in the Continental Army about to run out. Paine struggled over the wording—wondering what he could say to keep the troops from disbanding, and what right he had to ask such a high degree of devotion from them.

Recall that he had no assurance the American cause would triumph, when he penned this stirring passage:

> These are the times that try men's souls. The summer soldier and the sunshine patriot will in this crisis shrink from the service of their country. But he that stands it now deserves the love of men and women. Tyranny like hell is not easily conquered...Though the flame of liberty may sometimes cease to shine, the embers will never be extinguished [262].

These are the times that try men's souls. The flame of liberty is flickering. It is not our troops who are losing heart. Gallant men and women, they will fight and die wherever we send them. Rather, it is our leaders who are abandoning the ideals on which this country was founded.

A recent blog inquiry read:

> *From Phillip Daniel:*
>
> President Bush, you are currently exhorting the Shiite majority (about 60 percent of Iraqis) to include the Sunni minority (about 20 percent) in the new government's structure and policies. Yet in the United States, where your best showing in an election was a minimal majority of 51 percent, you and your party have ignored and excluded Democrats whose percentage of the voting population is twice that of Iraq's Sunnis. Aren't you and the rest of the Republican leadership setting a bad example for inclusive democracy? Can you fault the Iraqis for considering you a "do as I say, not as I do" hypocrite [111P]?"

The Bush Administration seems to be under the impression that democracy can be exported as if it were a commodity—assuming the spread of democracy is its intention at all.

> ...*Dick Cheney's* masterwork...has taken several forms over the last decade...The Plan was published in unclassified form most recently under the title of *Defense Strategy for the 1990s*...as Cheney ended his term as secretary of defense under the elder George Bush in early 1993...It was the controversial Defense Planning Guidance draft of 1992—from which Cheney, unconvincingly, tried to distance himself... [I]t was leaked to the press as yet another Defense Planning Guidance (this time under the pen name of Defense Secretary Donald Rumsfeld). It will take its ultimate form, though, as America's new national security strategy...*The Plan is for the United States to rule the world.* The overt theme

> is unilateralism, but it is ultimately a story of domination. It calls for the United States to maintain its overwhelming military superiority and prevent new rivals from rising up to challenge it on the world stage. It calls for *dominion over friends and enemies alike.* It says not that the United States must be more powerful, or most powerful, but that it must be absolutely powerful...[The Plan] is being sold now as an answer to the "new realities" of the post-September 11 world, even as it was sold previously as the answer to the new realities of the post-Cold War world...This country once rejected "unwarned" attacks such as Pearl Harbor as barbarous and unworthy of a civilized nation. Today many cheer the prospect of conducting sneak attacks—potentially with nuclear weapons—on piddling powers run by tin-pot despots. We also once denounced those who tried to rule the world. Our primary objection (at least officially) to the Soviet Union was its quest for global domination. *Through* the successful employment of the tools of *containment, deterrence, collective security*, and *diplomacy*—the very *methods we now reject—we rid ourselves and the world of the Evil Empire.* Having done so, *we now pursue the very thing for which we opposed it.* And now that the Soviet Union is gone, there appears to be no one left to stop us...The *Bush Administration and its loyal opposition seem not to grasp that the quests for dominance generate backlash. Those threatened with preemption may themselves launch preemptory strikes.* And even those who are successfully "preempted" or dominated may object and find means to strike back. Pursuing such strategies may, paradoxically, result in greater factionalism and rivalry, precisely the things we seek to end [219]...[Emphasis added.]
>
> —David Armstrong, excerpted from "Dick Cheney's Song of America," *Harper's Magazine*, Vol. 305, Issue 1829, October 2002

Lest the above be viewed as an exaggeration of some sort:

The Project for the New American Century, or PNAC, is a Washington-based think tank created in 1997. Above all else, PNAC desires and demands one thing: The establishment of a global American empire to bend the will of all nations. They chafe at the idea that the United States, the last remaining superpower, does not do more by way of economic and military force to bring the rest of the world under the umbrella of a new socio-economic Pax Americana.

The fundamental essence of PNAC's ideology can be found in a White Paper produced in September of 2000 entitled "Rebuilding America's Defenses: Strategy, Forces and Resources for a New Century." In it, PNAC outlines what is required of America to create the global empire they envision.

According to PNAC, America must:

- Reposition permanently based forces to Southern Europe, Southeast Asia and the Middle East;
- Modernize US forces, including enhancing our fighter aircraft, submarine and surface fleet capabilities;
- Develop and deploy a global missile defense system, and develop a strategic dominance of space;
- Control the "International Commons" of cyberspace;
- Increase defense spending to a minimum of 3.8 percent of gross domestic product, up from the 3 percent currently spent.

Most ominously...[t]he two central requirements are for American forces to "fight and decisively win *multiple, simultaneous major theater wars*," and to "perform the '*constabulary' duties* associated with shaping the security environment in critical regions." Note well that PNAC does not want America to be prepared to fight simultaneous major wars. That is old school. In order to bring this plan to fruition, the military must fight these wars one way or the other *to establish American dominance...*

Vice President Dick Cheney is a founding member of PNAC,

> *along with Defense Secretary Donald Rumsfeld* and Defense Policy Board chairman Richard Perle. *Deputy Defense Secretary Paul Wolfowitz is the ideological father of the group.* Bruce Jackson, a PNAC director, served as a Pentagon official for Ronald Reagan before leaving government service to take a leading position with the weapons manufacturer Lockheed-Martin...
>
> PNAC has recently given birth to a new group, The Committee for the Liberation of Iraq, which met with National Security Advisor Condoleezza Rice in order to formulate a plan to "educate" the American populace about the need for war in Iraq. CLI has funneled millions of taxpayer dollars to support the Iraqi National Congress and the Iraqi heir presumptive, Ahmed Chalabi. Chalabi was sentenced in absentia by a Jordanian court in 1992 to 22 years in prison for bank fraud after the collapse of Petra Bank, which he founded in 1977. Chalabi has not set foot in Iraq since 1956, but his Enron-like business credentials apparently make him a good match for the Bush Administration's plans [220B]...[31] [32] [Emphasis added.]
>
> —William Rivers Pitt, *The Project for the New American Century,* February 25, 2003.

A bully is a small mean man, no matter his size. The bully's friend is no one to be trusted, and himself grows more fearful every day. All Vice President Dick Cheney can propose for this great nation is the role of a bully. What a limited imagination! What a failure of vision.

Abraham Lincoln, I believe, would respond, as he once did: "As I would not be a slave, so I would not be a master. This expresses my idea of democracy."

President George W. Bush appears to have confused capitalism (as enforced by American military dominance) for democracy. These are not one and the same.

Indeed, this type of confusion is something one would expect from a foreign society, unfamiliar with democracy. As an illustration, it is clearly the longing for America's material well-being which has spurred China's recent economic experiment with capitalism—not any concern for individual rights.

Or is Tiannamen Square already so dim a memory that we in the West are at risk of believing the revisionist history now being propounded, as to China's never having been an aggressor nation?

I ask this for the following reasons:

- First, because the Bush Administration is relying on the American public's notoriously short memory and notorious disinterest in history in general (and foreign affairs in particular), to turn truth into fiction before our eyes.
- Second, because the Bush Administration and Conservatives to which it is allied see nothing bizarre in the concept of forcing democracy on a people who give every indication they have no interest in or understanding of it, when democracy cannot be forced at all.
- Third, because the Bush Administration and the large corporate interests to which it is allied evidently lose no sleep at investing in a nation which still utilizes slavery as a political weapon.
- Fourth, because the Bush Administration and Christian Right to which it is allied see no irony in investing in a nation which continues active religious persecution.
- Fifth, because the Bush Administration seems, itself, to have forgotten that China (which has always taken a long-range view) has plans of its own.

Add to these concerns, the following:

> **Peter Leitner, Center For Advanced Defense Studies:** China has been and still is the greatest proliferator on the planet. We're buying their pocket combs and their little tape decks, and they're using that same money to steal our F-16 engines and satellite technology and night vision equipment and everything else that isn't nailed down.
>
> **Romans:** Through arms brokers, students, and scientists, and a vast network of spies, approximately 4,000 front

> companies and legitimate joint ventures, funneling nuclear and missile technology to Iran, North Korea and countless other countries and groups. ICE [Immigration & Customs Enforcement] says China is getting even more aggressive in its attempts to steal or smuggle U.S. military gear [212].
>
> —Videotaped Interview by Reporter, Christine Romans on *Lou Dobbs Tonight*, aired February 13, 2006. Courtesy of CNN.

As aspirations for global military and economic conquest will have dreadful long-term consequences abroad, so will a return to laissez-faire capitalism and casual abuse of the national economy have dreadful long-term consequences at home.

> *Bush Economy: Temporary Growth, Lasting Damage*
>
> The *Globe* describes the economic policies of the Bush administration as a "crude and destructive cocktail of stimulants." Even if the recent positive economic signals temporarily take hold, "the administration's policies will weaken the economy over time, fall particularly harshly on its working middle- and low-income citizens, and fail to prepare the nation for a century of far more intense global competition [92]."
>
> —Source: *Boston Globe*, "Boom and Bust," November 9, 2003.

We would do well to remember that the Roman Empire—originally a republic—had become a dictatorship by the time it fell.

THE MIDDLE CLASS: THE GREAT DIVIDE

Remember, O Lord, what has come upon us; look, and behold our reproach!... We labor and have no rest. (Lamentations 5: 1, 5)

Government is not reason, it is not eloquence, it is force; like fire, a troublesome servant and a fearful master. Never for a moment should it be left to irresponsible action. —George Washington

There is a plaintive line from the Simon and Garfunkel song, "*El Condor Pasa*" that runs: "I'd rather be a hammer than a nail. Yes, I would, if I could, I surely would [263]." Sometimes we feel that way, Christians and non-Christians alike. So beleaguered that any road seems a better one. If only we could leave our burdens behind.

It is worth remembering that nails hold things together. Tables, chairs. Even skyscrapers. Maybe you are the "nail" holding a family or an organization together. Maybe you are the one "nail" on whom someone's life hangs.

A certain Carpenter we all know used nails. In fact, He continues to use them. He was hung on a cross by—and for—them.

TAXATION WITHOUT REPRESENTATION

> *...if there should come into your assembly a man with gold rings, in fine apparel, and there should also come in a poor man in filthy clothes, and you pay attention to the one wearing the fine clothes and say to him, "You sit here in a good place," and say to the poor man, "You stand there," or, "Sit here at my footstool,"*

have you not shown partiality among yourselves, and become judges with evil thoughts? Listen, my beloved brethren: Has God not chosen the poor of this world to be rich in faith and heirs of the kingdom which He promised to those who love Him? (James 2: 2–5).

Bush Attempts to Give Tax Breaks Worth Hundreds of Millions to Corporations. Bush tried to repeal the corporate Alternative Minimum Tax (AMT). Had he been successful in repealing the AMT, corporations would have received the following retroactive tax breaks:

$1.4 billion to IBM
$371 million to United Airlines
$1 billion to Ford
$254 million to Enron
$833 million to General Motors
$241 million to Phillips Petroleum
$671 million to General Electric
$184 million to American Airlines
$608 million to Texas Utilities
$155 million to IMC Global
$600 million to Daimler Chrysler
$144 million to Comdisco
$572 million to Chevron Texaco
$136 million to CMS Energy
$102 million to Kmart [85]

—Original Source: Citizens For Tax Justice, Corporate Annual Reports.

Propertied men though our Founding Fathers were, they could never have envisioned the overwhelming power that monied special interests would attain over the electoral process.

We always prefer to give the money directly to the guy, or the woman, that you're going to support. You like to walk in,

> to give them the check, you like to look in their eye and say "I'm here to help you." You always do [106].
>
> —Rodney Smith, PAC Director, SBC Communications.

Information as to campaign contributions by Political Action Committees (PACs) and donations to PACs is readily available by industry and sector, e.g. defense, as well as by individual PAC [107A]. Top organizational contributors include:

- Unions and union associations, e.g. American Federation of State, County & Municipal Employees; International Brotherhood of Electrical Workers; Teamsters Union; National Education Association.
- Trade organizations, e.g. National Association of Realtors.
- Professional organizations, e.g. Association of Trial Lawyers of America; American Medical Association.
- Banks and securities firms, e.g. Goldman Sachs; Citigroup Inc., Merrill Lynch.
- Financial services and/or tax consulting, e.g. General Electric; Deloitte Touche.
- Air delivery and freight services, e.g. FedEx Corp.; United Parcel Service.
- Communications companies, e.g. AT&T; Time Warner.
- Tobacco interests, e.g. RJR Nabisco/RJ Reynolds Tobacco.
- Auto manufacturers, e.g. General Motors.
- Health insurance carriers, e.g. Blue Cross/Blue Shield.
- Drug manufacturers, e.g. Pfizer Inc.; Eli Lilly and Co.
- Oil, gas, and energy corporations, e.g. Exxon Mobil; Enron.
- Declared interest, e.g. National Rifle Association [107B].

How many of us take the time to track this information is questionable. Who benefits most from which PAC contributions might be in the forefront of our consciousness were the principal results perhaps regularly posted like box scores, on the sports pages. Or the League of Women Voters might circulate the information, prior to election, as it has done with other basic data on the candidates.

This is not information we can afford to overlook. While we may not be in a position to counter the influence to which a particular politician is subject, we should at least be able to identify that influence, so as to cast an informed vote.

At times, PAC contributions may actually benefit us. Frequently, however, they dilute our votes—in effect, taxation without representation, repeated. In calling for campaign finance reform, the *New Hampshire Gazette* blasted Congress, characterizing the situation as a "Darwinian free-for-all in which money takes the place of beneficial mutations, and widows and orphans who fail to hire their own lobbyists [are viewed by their elected representatives as] deserv[ing] whatever they get [217B]."

Democrat or Republican, Liberal or Conservative, Christian or non-Christian, are we satisfied with this?

If not, we have the following options:

- We can work for real election reform.
- We can support candidates with more integrity.
- We can run for office ourselves.
- We can strive to replace one or both the major parties with a better one.

The PACs are sufficiently motivated. The question is, are we?

One final thought, in this connection:

> *From Charles Posner:*
>
> The turmoil of the Iraq war, since 2003, has contributed significantly to the tightening of the world oil market and a steep run-up in the price of oil. During this war, major US oil companies have reaped record profits and US consumers have paid inflated fuel prices because of this. Please explain why a portion of the oil profits should not be recouped by the US government (e.g. windfall tax) to help pay for the $2 trillion war debt [111N]?

It's an idea.

GLOBALIZATION: JOB SECURITY NOW DISPOSABLE

As of May 2005, there had been 893,000 jobs created over the first 52 months of the Bush presidency, the 917,000 jobs created in the government sector offsetting the 24,000 jobs lost in the private sector. Since the Great Depression, no other president who served at least 52 months has overseen a net loss in private sector jobs through this point. In addition to lack of job growth, real weekly and hourly wages have declined since the start of the recession. At a time when middle-class Americans are experiencing stagnant wages and vanishing benefits, CEO pay continues to rise [91].

—Source: Center for American Progress, Economic Policy Weekly, Jenna Churchman, June 6, 2005.

The Administration Refuses to Support Unemployed Workers and Their Families. The administration indicated that, despite the weakening job market, it refuses to support legislation to extend unemployment benefits to the estimated 1.5 million workers who will have exhausted their benefits by the end of September. An additional 700,000 workers are expected to exhaust their unemployment benefits by the end of the year [86].

—Source: Gannett News Service, "Senate Panel Considers Renewal of Extended Jobless Benefits," Brian Tumulty, September 12, 2002.

...Key business issues—including corporate competitiveness, flexibility and productivity—as well as macro-issues—global job growth and economic development—are all tied to the outsourcing discussion. It is clear that the business case for outsourcing has been proven, through many examples. Cost savings for companies often can be in upwards of 50 or 60 percent [46]...

There is no question that we are in the midst of a Second Industrial Revolution with globalization its engine. Represented to us as an inevitable economic process—as irresistible as gravity, as beneficial as rain—globalization is merely a means by which corporations can decrease costs while increasing customer base. It is neither inevitable, nor beyond our control.

As an illustration, having eliminated numerous permanent positions, legal contract work has reduced costs, thereby becoming a permanent feature on the landscape. Allowing large law firms the flexibility to size up or down on short notice, it affords attorneys temporary, if precarious, employment.

Frequently, however, contract work is tedious and underpaid; without benefits; and performed under physical conditions which paralegals and legal secretaries would not—and rightfully should not—tolerate. Attorneys fresh out of school find this particularly discouraging, since they have hundreds of thousands of dollars in school loans to repay. There is every possibility portions of the work will shortly be sent overseas, eliminating still further jobs.

Many non-attorneys will shrug at this (even cheer!). And, as a group, we attorneys have earned that disapprobation. Law schools urge students toward Wall Street, not legal aid. Countless lawyer jokes exist because, at their core, they contain a grain of truth about the callousness and avarice of the profession.

Nonetheless, if this is occurring in a profession which as a whole never before experienced significant financial concerns, what of other areas of employment? Re-training has been urged upon us. However, no politician of either party has—as far as I am aware—addressed what precisely all of us should be re-training for and how we, individually or as a country, can survive the globalization process.

This is not vision; it is short-sightedness. It is the triumph of greed over the common good in what appears the 21st Century version of 19th Century Social Darwinism, a crackpot theory even when it was first hatched. Professor S. Shermis of Purdue University summarized the origins of Social Darwinism, as follows:

> Social Darwinism is a quasi-philosophical, quasi-religious, quasi-sociological view that came from the mind

of Herbert Spencer, an English philosopher in the 19th century...[I]t is the use...some people made of biological evolution which concerns us. Some simplified the idea to "survival of the fittest." Others believed that an identical process took place among human beings...[T]he followers of Herbert Spencer, took it one step further. Human society is always in a kind of evolutionary process in which *the fittest*—which happened to be those who can *make lots of money*—were chosen to dominate. There were armies of unfit, the *poor*, who *simply could not compete*. And just as nature weeds out the unfit, an enlightened society ought to weed out its unfit and permit them to die off so as not to weaken the racial stock.

This idea eventually led to...Nordic Racism, used by German anthropologists and later Nazi theoreticians. It also led to eugenics...A breeding program for human beings would see to it that the unfit did not transmit their undesirable characteristics.

Another [mis]application of a biological concept to human behavior was the notion that any attempt to provide welfare for the poor was a tragically misguided mistake. Feeding or housing the poor simply permitted them to survive and to transmit their unfitness to their children, who in turn would pass it on to their children. A spurious piece of sociology about two families known as the Jukes and the Kallikaks purported to trace a race of criminals and prostitutes to two persons in the Revolutionary War. This study was used for many years to demonstrate that "inferiority" was inherited...

The point is that a piece of ideology got into American life and assumed considerable importance. What is also significant is that some, e.g. wealthy industrialists, believed that what they were doing was supported by science. Yes, they said, the Caucasian, European-derived male industrialist was at the apex of evolution. And yes, they said, it is *undesirable to provide, as public policy, governmental sup-*

> *port* for any plan that would perpetuate racial weakness [216]. [Emphasis added.]
>
> —"Social Darwinism" from *Introduction to Social Justice.*

Whatever name we give it (and whether racially motivated or merely materialistic), this approach is clearly reflected in the Bush Administration's shameful social policies.

We cannot stick our heads in the sand and pretend this is not happening. We cannot simply leave this to our children and their children to sort out.

Nor am I urging isolationism. There is no safety associated with that either.

If we cannot turn back the clock, what we can do is use this as an opportunity. We Americans are an ingenious, determined, and courageous people; blessed with enormous natural resources. We have known hardship before. This is nothing new. We crossed oceans and prairies—often with little more than the shirts on our backs. We endured centuries of slavery; the Trail of Tears; Elmira [56] and Andersonville [55]; forced feeding for the sake of the vote; and internment at Tule, for the shape of our eyes [57]. We fought drought, hailstorms, polio [58], and segregation. We invented the phone [49], the skyscraper [53 and 54], the blood bank [52], the artificial heart [51], and the computer [50]—not to mention jazz [59 and 60], hip hop [61], Broadway [47], and the lights on it [48]. We flew at Kitty Hawk and walked on the moon. We have simply forgotten that.

First and foremost, we must prevent further drain.

To do that, we must band together and recognize our strength. North, south, east, and west. Cities, suburbs, and small towns. Cowboys and insurance salesmen, truckers, traders, and the waitresses who proudly serve them both, plumbers and professors, football players and armchair quarterbacks, sailors and scientists, doctors, nurses, and patients alike. This is our country. We have to take it back.

Not the violent or divisive way Neo-Nazis think to do that, but in the best possible American tradition.

That cannot be as difficult for us as it was for those who carved a nation out of wilderness; who fought a great empire to a standstill on the basis of a belief that human beings can actually govern themselves. A shimmering ribbon of internet highway has already been laid down for us. All we have to do is put our self-interests aside, and reach out to one another.

We must decide under what circumstances we will allow jobs to be sent overseas, and how best America (and the world) can benefit when that occurs. We must then regulate the process, rather than submitting like victims to it. Corporations are fictional entities. They exist only on paper, while impacting the lives of millions. Since corporations have argued that this is now a global economy, they must shoulder their share of global responsibility.

The corporate decision to send jobs overseas should trigger:

- The filing equivalent to an Environmental Impact Statement. Call it a Labor Impact Statement (LIS). Responsibility for review of the LIS be could placed under jurisdiction of the Federal Reserve, with input from the Senate and House Joint Economic Committee as to policy.
- A hefty tax, dedicated to social services, if the LIS is approved. There is always a cost/benefit analysis when major business decisions are undertaken. This would simply shift that analysis slightly more in America's favor.
- Payment by the corporation (rather than the taxpayer) of all re-education and relocation costs for its employees, at a rate to be determined by the state.
- Payment by the corporation of transition counseling fees for its employees.
- An Unemployment Compensation Extension, until the re-education process is complete (with a cut-off, in the event of demonstrable employee malingering).
- A prohibition against corporate bankruptcy, at least until out-sourced workers have been provided the above benefits (or a secured right to recover these benefits, exempt from bankruptcy protection).

The corporate decision to send jobs overseas should, also, be accompanied by the enforceable requirement to ensure product safety, along with a safe working environment, equivalent to that in the US. Responsible corporations would not sell sub-par products abroad, simply because overseas markets are unregulated. They should not tolerate child labor or sweat shops abroad. Taking the high road is one of the simplest and most direct ways of conveying US values to those unfamiliar with them.

Indeed, there is an enormous and obvious need for unions overseas. Under totalitarian regimes, of course, it may not be possible for unions to exist. That fact alone makes one wonder why we would choose to invest there.

As for the re-education question, what has been overlooked is job satisfaction. Should the engineer or manufacturing supervisor be asked to work behind a fast food counter? Are we all now to rush to the malls for jobs selling cologne or lingerie?

Adaptability and inclination aside, there is a deep-seated anger at being asked to make this transition—along with fear that the change may not be possible. Age can play a role. We have responsibilities: a mortgage, children in need of braces. We have worked for decades towards something. Now that goal is undermined or gone, leaving behind an enormous sense of loss.

In many parts of the world life is so hard that job satisfaction is an unknown luxury. In India, for example, children sell sexual favors to commuters at train stations, to avoid starvation. Globalization is perhaps America's reminder of that terrible fact.

God made each of us for a special purpose. We ache to use the talents we were given. So, too, do those children in India. What does their future hold?

Perhaps God's purpose for America is not what we thought. Perhaps the challenge is far greater.

The mantle of leadership demands far more of America than mere military might. Any bully can land a punch on a weaker or unwary foe. That has never been what we Americans have seen as greatness. Someone should explain that to Vice President Dick Cheney.

If we are to lead the world into the next century and beyond, we cannot afford—generation after generation—to leave a significant portion of our own population behind, as if that portion were expendable.

We need to think in a radically different manner than we have to this point. Ralph Waldo Emerson put it this way: "Do not go where the path may lead, go instead where there is no path and leave a trail."

- We need to revise the method by which we fund schools, so that children in poorer districts are not denied a quality education. Since all our children are of value, funding should be on a statewide basis, creating a more level playing field.
- We need to invest in our teachers, where necessary raising salaries to reflect the significant and ennobling task with which they have been entrusted. We likewise need to create incentives to draw the best minds into secondary education.
- We need to identify those subjects which will make America more competitive in the global marketplace. These will undoubtedly include science, medicine, and technology. They may well include music, art, literature, poetry, philosophy. There is no reason we cannot create a nation of scholars, if we set that as a goal. This does not rule out the finest business education. However, we need to convey to our sons and daughters that business ethics really do matter; that business success is not just measured in dollars and cents, or by the short-term. Regrettably, our behavior has demonstrated the very opposite of that, thus far.
- We need to extend the school year (certainly for older students) and raise our performance standards far higher than they are now. We need to keep our school buildings open for multiple use purposes beyond the ordinary school day.
- We need to mandate a minimum of one year's public service by our students upon graduation, so that those fortunate enough to have grown up in affluent surroundings can see what life is like for those not so fortunate, and the energies of our young people may be devoted to improving the nation, as a whole. This would be a far better lesson in values than any force-fed ideas.

Note that the word I have used is "need." Whether we have the will to do these things is another matter. There would be trade-offs involved. The pie is only so large. The suggestions here would require hard decisions from those we elect, not mere pandering to special interests. They would certainly require reductions in our military spending.

The American people are fully capable of making the necessary sacrifices. The question is whether our elected officials are up to the task. To stand any hope of success, we cannot vacillate and we cannot delay. We cannot cross the Grand Canyon by building a bridge half-way.

UNIVERSAL HEALTH CARE DENIED

Of the 50 most economically advanced nations around the globe, only the United States and South Africa do not provide universal health insurance [223A]. Estimates place the number of uninsured Americans between 43 and 60 million [223B]. Although the United States leads the world in healthcare spending (approximately 10% of Gross Domestic Product [223C]), large disparities exist based on wealth, race, and state of residence [221A].

The UN's Annual Development Report for 2005 showed the following:

More than one in six adults of working age lack health insurance coverage [221B].

One in three families living below the poverty line in the US is uninsured. More than 40% of the uninsured have no regular place to obtain medical care, frequently deferring or doing without treatment due to lack of funds [221C].

On average, our infant mortality rate is now the same as that of Malaysia, a Third World country. The rate has actually climbed since 2000 [221D].

With African Americans giving birth to roughly twice the number of ELBW infants that Caucasians do, the mortality rate for Black infants in the nation's capital is higher than infant mortality in the Indian state of Kerala. Throughout the US, Black children are twice as likely as whites are to die before reaching their first birthday [221E].

According to a 2003 World Health Organization report, life expectancy in the US was 77.3 years compared with 79.8 years in

Canada [222A]. There are several possible reasons for this. There is less drug use and less violence in Canada [222B]. Canada's health care system is weighted in the direction of primary care physicians [222C] (who may be in a better position than specialists to become familiar with their patients).

More importantly, since it is universally available, the Canadian system narrows the gap between rich and poor, allowing for earlier treatment [222D]. In the US, for instance, there are 9.8 maternal deaths for every 100,000 births. In Canada, by contrast, there are only 3.4 [222E]. Little more than a third of US citizens with severe mental disorders obtain treatment. In Canada, more than half do [222F]. For all this, we spend more than twice per capita what Canadians do ($4887 v. $2163) [222G]. And health care costs keep rising.

We could afford universal health care...if we chose to reduce our military budget. At present, some fifty two cents of every dollar in the Federal Treasury are committed to the Pentagon. Our total military expenditures far exceed those of our nearest competitors.

I am not advocating that the US become vulnerable, militarily. Because of bad choices by our leaders, I frankly think we are much more vulnerable, than we should be—at least to terrorism. (Unlike Vice President Dick Cheney, I have no desire to conquer the world.)

We have invested huge sums in technology—sometimes useless technology, at that. We have invested very little in people—including, by the way, our troops.

Republican President and respected WWII General, Dwight D. Eisenhower, had this to say:

> Every gun that is made, every warship launched, every rocket fired signifies, in the final sense, a theft from those who hunger and are not fed, those who are cold and are not clothed. This world in arms is not spending money alone. It is spending the sweat of its laborers, the genius of its scientists, the hopes of its children [234]...

There may still be time to reorder our priorities.

LABOR PROTECTIONS DISMANTLED

Conservatives speak frequently about their belief that government interferes with the liberty of the individual; over-regulates business to the point of strangulation; and is far less efficient than the private sector. There is no doubt that we have seen government waste; and that government power must, itself, be controlled. Natural disasters, however, demonstrate the need for government—a need encompassing more than military goals.

Occidental College's Urban & Environmental Policy Program Director, Professor Peter Dreier spoke eloquently of this in a recent issue of *Dissent Magazine*:

> [Government] is needed to provide things that individuals and the private sector simply cannot. It is needed to build the public infrastructure necessary for a civilized society, to help deal with risk, to help relieve the immediate suffering, and to help people and communities restore some level of normalcy and decency. This role sometimes means imposing government regulations on people and institutions (such as making buildings earthquake proof, or having basic housing codes, or requiring factories and cars to limit pollution). These regulations add short-term costs, but are necessary to insure public safety and health. Government is also needed to build dams, levees, bridges, roads, and public transit—as well as schools, parks, and playgrounds. These, too, are long-term investments that make society more livable as well as safer.
>
> The Katrina disaster also underscores the need for a strong federal government, the only level of government with the resources to deal with the prevention, rescue, and rebuilding of areas faced with major disasters. Local and state governments lack the resources for this task, although they should be part of the planning and implementation [224D].

What prompted the very writing of our Constitution was the

abject failure of the Articles of Confederation, under which the states had operated beforehand. That failure was due to the absence of a strong central government—another historic reality right-wing Conservatives seem to have overlooked.

Where the central government abrogates its responsibilities, we see the effects immediately. Greed, like power, abhors a vacuum.

This is again well-illustrated in New Orleans. The private sector is poised to make a financial killing, in what the *New York Times* characterized as, "the largest domestic rebuilding effort ever undertaken [224H]." Three large companies—the Shaw Group, Kellogg Brown & Root (a subsidiary of Halliburton, at which Vice President Dick Cheney served as CEO), and Boh Brothers—have already been awarded "no bid" contracts. Halliburton, of course, is under fire for allegedly overcharging in Iraq [224I]. In theory, this was to expedite repair and reconstruction. In reality, politically connected firms (rather than, for instance, locally owned minority businesses) were moved to the head of the list.

Long unhappy with the Davis-Bacon Act mandating that contractors employed on reconstruction pay their employees a fair minimum wage, the Bush Administration sweetened this deal by suspending the Act [224J]. Dating from the Depression Era, the law imposes the going rate in the region. In New Orleans, that rate is only $9/hour for construction work [224K].

According to the National Audit Office, deaths in the construction industry accounted for over 30% of workplace deaths in 2003 [225].

The consequence of the Bush Administration's favoritism may be that laborers risk their very lives for less than minimum wage, while corporate profits rise still higher, and the local economy (which lost some 400,000 jobs to Hurricanes Katrina and Rita) is depressed yet further by these reconstruction efforts [224L].

According to the US Census Bureau, Louisiana (with 19.4% of her population living below the poverty line) was already before Hurricane Katrina one of the two poorest states in the nation [224M]. Party city, New Orleans—the home of Mardi Gras—was already the nation's twelfth poorest city (with 23.2% living below the poverty line) [224N].

Efficiency is not the word that comes to mind. Rape may be closer to the truth.

There is a price to be paid for all this—a price that those who have grown fat, at Halliburton and the like, would do well to recall.

> *"If my land cries out against me, And its furrows weep together; If I have eaten its fruit without money, Or caused its owners to lose their lives; Then let thistles grow instead of wheat, And weeds instead of barley"* (Job 31: 38–40).

OLD AGE SECURITY DAMAGED

That American culture is so youth-oriented has made it particularly easy to pit one generation against another in the debate over Social Security and Medicare Reform.

> Our society must make it right and possible for old people not to fear the young or be deserted by them, for the test of a civilization is the way that it cares for its helpless members.
>
> —Pearl Buck, *My Several Worlds* (1954).

The Concord Coalition, a nonpartisan organization which describes itself as "dedicated to informing the public about the need for generationally responsible fiscal policy"[33] has the following to say about Social Security, Medicare, and the Bush Administration's proposals for same:

- Today, Social Security taxes are running ahead of benefits by about $70 billion. But by 2009, the annual excess will start to fall…
- At first, the gap between promised benefits and dedicated revenues will be relatively small—$9 billion in 2017—but it will grow very quickly as those who were born in the peak of the baby boom begin to retire in large numbers… The Social Security Trustees project that the annual

shortfall will grow to $256 billion by 2030 in inflation adjusted dollars and that the program's cost will grow from roughly 4.3 percent of the nation's gross domestic product (GDP) today to 6.1 percent in 2030…Expressed as a share of workers' pay (taxable payroll), Social Security will grow from about 11 percent today to nearly 17 percent in 2030 [108A]…"

- "There are 37 million people in the population age 65 and older today. By 2025, this number is estimated to rise to 62 million. By 2045, it will rise to nearly 80 million, or more than double the current number. In contrast, by 2025 the number of workers is estimated to rise by only 13 percent, and by 2045, only 20 percent. As a result, the number of workers paying into the Social Security system relative to the number of beneficiaries is estimated to fall from 3.3 today to just 2 by 2040.
- This dynamic has consequences that go beyond Social Security. For Medicare and Medicaid it is even more troublesome…Health care prices continue to outpace economic growth and this phenomenon will simply compound the growing costs attributable to the rising number of beneficiaries. The Congressional Budget Office (CBO) projects that the combined cost of Medicare and Medicaid could increase from 4.2 percent of GDP today to 11.5 percent in 2030 [108B].
- Some commentators have suggested that the financial problems confronting Social Security are overblown because the large balance building up in the Social Security trust funds will carry the program for decades. Projections made by the Social Security trustees show that the balance of the trust funds will grow from $1.7 trillion today to $3.9 trillion in 2022…[However, "t]rust funds have no particular economic significance. They do not hold separate cash balances; instead they function primarily as accounting mechanisms"…The key point is that the same trust fund "assets" are a future liability for the Treasury. So while it may be comforting to think of the trust funds

accumulating trillions in federal government bonds over the next twenty years, in reality that just means the government will owe itself a lot of money [108C]...

- Much of the recent Social Security debate has revolved around the question of how to establish claims on future resources rather than on how to increase saving that will produce those resources...What legal, political, and fiscal incentives best ensure that resources are actually reallocated from the present to the future? Perhaps the most persuasive case for adding personal accounts to the Social Security system is that it would put the funds involved beyond the reach of government to spend on other programs [108D].
- Running budget surpluses and using them to pay down the federal debt, constraining government expenditures that add to consumption, adopting policies that advance productive technology and investment in education, eliminating regulations that inhibit productivity, adopting tax measures that reward personal saving and work, and creating a funded system of personally owned accounts are the types of policies that are likely to have the greatest chance of spurring growth. That said, even if the economy were to grow at greater than expected rates, it is unlikely by itself to solve Social Security's problem since the program's benefits are automatically tied to wage growth, meaning that if the economy grows faster than expected, future benefits will too [108E].
- Governments, businesses and individuals can do two things with their money: they can buy things that are consumed immediately, or they can invest the money to enable them to produce more in the future. Simply put, there is no free lunch in achieving national saving...[P]eople can spend their money or save it. The same is true when making government policy [108F]."
- "...Very few economists believe that you can generate new wealth simply by shuffling assets from one financial instrument to another...If this kind of large scale finan-

> cial arbitrage could work, why should government stop at putting a thousand borrowed dollars per year into each worker's personal account? Why not, in the first year, put a million borrowed dollars into each account?...In fairness, the administration does not itself claim it will be able to cash in on the spread between stocks and bonds. The administration, however, wants it both ways. To the public, it implies that the personal accounts will more than make up for the reduction in traditional benefits—which is another way of saying that stocks will outperform bonds. To the experts, it denies that its plan is dependent on the spread. But if the administration thinks that workers will lose as much in traditional benefits as they gain in their personal accounts, what's the point [108G]?"

I have quoted the Concord Coalition's analysis at such length (and have highlighted the credentials of its members) to put to rest any doubts that my understanding of the analysis was faulty or the analysis, itself, ideologically skewed.

To the contrary, the Bush Administration's proposals for reform are a mere excuse to further reduce the safety net, under the guise of fiscal responsibility. Analyses by the Congressional Research Service have estimated that the Administration's retirement and lifetime savings account proposals would ultimately cost $300 billion to $500 billion per decade [241N].

The 2007 Budget includes Social Security reductions which, according to the Center on Budget and Policy Priorities, would save $2.2 billion over five years and $6.3 over ten years [241J]. However, to reiterate, reductions in domestic spending would not be part of an overall plan to reduce the deficit [241K]. The $285 billion in proposed tax cuts over the next five years would exceed these savings by a factor of 100 [214L].

One of my favorite passages in Scripture is at John, Chapter 21. You will recall that the chapter describes the Apostles' fruitless efforts to catch fish until the Lord intervened, after which their net overflowed.

Ministers generally focus on this part of the chapter, from which there are many lessons to be drawn. Not only, however, did the Lord observe the night's toil. He, Himself, made breakfast on the morn.

This is what touches my heart. That the Lord would have been so concerned for the welfare of His followers as to lay a fire and bake bread for them, with His own hands. That even in His resurrected form, even while teaching a spiritual lesson, He would have anticipated their ordinary, physical needs.

> *Then, as soon as they had come to land, they saw a fire of coals there, and fish laid on it, and bread.... Jesus said to them, "Come and eat breakfast."* (John 21: 9, 12).

God realizes we need both physical and spiritual sustenance.

He instructs us to be fishers of men, and promises to bring us safely to shore when our work is done.

OSAMA BIN LADEN: THE APPEAL OF THE VIPER

Do not be overcome by evil, but overcome evil with good. (Romans 12: 20–22)

All that is necessary for the triumph of evil is that good men do nothing. —Edmund Burke

A crucial question the Bush Administration has failed to answer is why the policy of hatred Osama bin Laden espouses has been so attractive to his followers.

It is always been easier for human beings to blame someone else for their troubles, than take responsibility for them. The tendency is a function of what Christians call the "sin nature" of man or the consequences of original sin. (Adam and Eve in the Garden, remember?)

Preferably, the party targeted for blame is an outsider to the group. That way there are fewer loyalties; fewer people to step back and challenge the underlying assumption. It makes things much simpler.

It has always been easier for leaders to find (or fabricate) an enemy, than propose real solutions to difficult problems. When an external enemy cannot be located, an internal enemy will do (so long as sufficient differences exist to distinguish the internal "enemy" from the group as a whole). These differences need not have any significance. They need only *be* differences—whether of race, ethnicity, age, sex, etc.

For leaders, there is an added benefit, in that the presence of an enemy tends to unify the group. If you think this makes human beings terribly sophisticated and complex, I suggest you do some reading on chimpanzee anthropology. Which brings me back to al-Qaeda.

The philosopher, Voltaire said, "Those who can make you believe absurdities, can make you commit atrocities."

Rather than examine (and address) the numerous and convoluted problems arising from despotic rule in the Middle East, Osama bin Laden selected the United States as his external enemy. This allowed him to channel animosity over perceived economic injustice; bypass factional rivalries; and harness what passes for religious fervor in a "pure and holy" cause. To our great sadness, it resulted in the loss of thousands of innocent lives, and is still having repercussions today.

He desires power. There is no other point. His actions have already demonstrated that. His followers have simply elected not to see.

Make no mistake. The terrorism being perpetrated in the name of Islam is a religious war. There are always some who will choose evil and call it "good."

Professor of Law, David Forte of Marshall-Cleveland College of Law, and the John Ashbrook Center for Public Affairs at Ashland University, explains the situation this way:

> ...bin Laden divides the earth into the *dar al-Islam* (the realm of Islam) and the *dar al-harb* (the realm of war)...But for bin Laden, the *dar al-Islam* is no longer...as is sometimes translated, the realm of peace. In common with many Islamic radicals, bin Laden believes that the Islamic world [itself] has fallen into perfidy and apostasy. He makes civil war on Islam as much as he makes international conflict with the United States...Bin Laden and other Islamic radicals claim they represent ancient Islam...but it is a tradition that Islam early on rejected...In the earliest centuries of Islam, a great civil war was fought over who should be the successor to Muhammad...This was the conflict that ultimately led to the division between Sunni and Shi'a Islam... One group was adamantly opposed to...any compromise... The Kharajites withdrew and made war on both factions... [T] hey believed that only they had the true notion of what Islam required. They applied their doctrine with a ferocity

> against both the developing Sunni and Shi'a traditions of Islam…Today, radicals like bin Laden replicate that ancient sect that threatened to destroy Islamic civilization at its inception…a civilization known in its time for…learning, science, openness and toleration [272].

In examining the place of tolerance in (and the possibility for peace with) Islam, Khaled Abou El Fadl, a Distinguished Fellow in Islamic Law at UCLA, writes that fundamentalist sects have been a feature of Islam, until recently checked:

> …[T]he traditional institutions that once sustained and propagated Islamic orthodoxy—and marginalized Islamic extremism—have been dismantled. Traditionally, Islamic epistemology tolerated and even celebrated divergent opinions…The guardians of the Islamic tradition were the jurists (*fuqaha*), whose legitimacy rested largely on their semi-independence from a decentralized political system…But in Muslim countries today, the state…controls the private religious endowments (*awqaf*) that once sustained the juristic class…This…has reduced the clergy's legitimacy, and produced a profound vacuum in religious authority [274A]…
>
> —Abou El Fadl, Khaled; *Islam and the Challenge of Democracy*. Princeton University Press. Reprinted by permission of Princeton University Press.

El Fadl acknowledges that portions of the Koran—at least when stripped of moral and historic context—can be read as encouraging violence toward non-Muslims:

> …Islamic puritans…offer a set of textual references in support of their exclusionary and intolerant theological orientation. For instance, they frequently cite the Qur'anic verse that states: "O you who believe, do not take the Jews and Christians as allies. They are allies of each other, and he amongst you who becomes their ally is one of them"…[T]he

> puritan trend cites the Qur'anic verse commanding Muslims to fight the unbelievers, "until there is no more tumult or oppression, and until faith and all judgment belongs to God [274B]."
>
> —Abou El Fadl, Khaled; *Islam and the Challenge of Democracy.* Princeton University Press. Reprinted by permission of Princeton University Press.

Despite this, El Fadl maintains the Koran can support an ethic of tolerance and diversity:

> The Qur'an not only expects, but even accepts the reality of difference and diversity within human society: "O humankind, God has created you from male and female and made you into diverse nations and tribes so that you may come to know each other. Verily, the most honored of you in the sight of God is he who is the most righteous." Elsewhere, the Qur'an asserts that diversity is part of the Divine intent and purpose in creation: "If thy Lord had willed, He would have made humankind into a single nation, but they will not cease to be diverse...And, for this God created them [humankind]." The classical commentators on the Qur'an did not fully explore the implications of this...[Yet the Qur'an states]: "Those who believe, those who follow Jewish scriptures, the Christians, the Sabians, and any who believe in God and the Final Day, and do good, all shall have their reward with their Lord and they will not come to fear or grief." Significantly, this passage occurs in the same chapter that instructs Muslims not to take the Jews and Christians as allies [274C].
>
> —Abou El Fadl, Khaled; *Islam and the Challenge of Democracy.* Princeton University Press. Reprinted by permission of Princeton University Press.

Professor of Islamic History, Moshe Sharon, of Hebrew University would disagree. During a recent speech to the Herzliya Counter

Terrorism Institute, Sharon warned that Western leaders are gravely mistaken in attempting to distinguish between a peaceful and radical Islam.

Focusing on the aggression-potential of Iran (Iraq's neighbor to the east), Sharon discussed the role of the 12th Imam, known as the Mahdi (in effect, the Shiite messiah) in terrorist activity:

> How will they bring him? Through an apocalypse. He (the Mahdi) needs a war. He cannot come into this world without an Armageddon. He wants an Armageddon. The earlier we understand this the better...The difference between Judaism, Christianity and Islam is as follows: Judaism speaks about national salvation—namely, that at the end of the story, when the world becomes a better place, Israel will be in its own land, ruled by its own king and serving G-d. Christianity speaks about the idea that every single person in the world can be saved from his sins, while Islam speaks about ruling the world...[L]et me quote a verse [from the Koran]..."Allah sent Mohammed with the true religion so that it should rule over all the religions." The idea, then, is not that the whole world would necessarily become Moslem at this time, but that the whole world would be subdued under the rule of Islam [273].

Either way, the issue we face, as Americans, is how best to direct our resources.

Bin Laden has promised to destroy us. He has no other plans for the welfare of the Palestinians (or anyone else) or he could readily have: a) used his great wealth and family connections to persuade Middle Eastern rulers to ease restrictions on their people, and share the oil wealth which supports their regimes; or b) distributed his own vast wealth, on the basis of his supposed dedication to the Palestinian cause.

Admittedly, history in the Middle East is rich and layered. But where is it not? Admittedly, there were mistakes made in the Middle East by the international community—even outright betrayals committed. Was the European colonization of Africa a kindness? Were the Indian Wars in our American West bloodless? I hardly think so.

None of these motives justify a war of vengeance by Radical Islam on civilians who had nothing to do with underlying events. None of these motives justify a systematic program by Radical Islam instructing children in hate [269 and 270].

What drew the focus to us was our astonishing (and shamelessly advertised) material success.

Having been greatly blessed by way of natural resources in this country—and having, alas, made selfish use of the *world's* resources—we forfeited our status as David, and became Goliath. Al-Qaeda members living on far less convinced themselves that equity called for our elimination, by any means possible. Jealousy cemented over any gaps in logic.

Ironically, the Bush Administration seems to have pursued much the same strategy. Crass as this may sound, it was fortuitous for President George W. Bush that the 9/11 attacks took place. He was cast in a heroic pose, and offered an opportunity for greatness. Unfortunately for the country, it was an opportunity he failed to take.

It requires far more strength for a man to stand and take a punch, than strike back blindly. In the judgment of history, 9/11 could have been the President's finest hour. Regrettably, he saw it as an opportunity to appear strong, rather than be strong.

The President convinced the American people (and, very possibly, himself) that Iraq and al-Qaeda were linked. A concrete, external enemy had been identified; serious domestic issues were immediately forced into the background; and off we went.

Ironically, in pursuing the course he did, the President may have fostered the very enemy alliances which did not exist at the start of the Iraqi War.

Even now, the President is having difficulty acknowledging he was in error. Why is that? Does he perhaps feel such an admission would imply he was an unwitting pawn in Vice President Dick Cheney's grand scheme to take over the world? Were this so, there might be some small chance the President would put country before self. After all, former First Lady Barbara Bush raised him.

Given the economic policy President George W. Bush has consistently adopted; the pervasive encroachment on American civil liberties; and the violation of international humanitarian law tolerated at Abu Grabbe; it seems more likely the President has adopted the PNAC Plan as his own, and views the Plan as his legacy.

Meanwhile—like a malignancy—the problem grows:

> Fairfax County, Va.: Dana, What could you tell us about the intelligence community's view of the President's persistent claim that the war in Iraq is not creating more terrorists? It has been my impression that the war was at the very least contributing to radicalization in much of the Arab and Muslim world. Is the president being, at the least, disingenuous in continuing his emphasis only on the potential benefits of the intervention, and not on the costs? Thanks as always.
>
> Dana Priest: It is now a core belief, among every single intelligence person—inside and outside government, both foreign and domestic—that the Iraq war is pouring fuel on the fire, boosting recruitment and giving individuals an anti-American ideology and the commitment to undertake suicide bombings. There is no dispute here [111E].
>
> —Source: *Live Online* interview with Dana Priest, *Washington Post* national security reporter (February 2, 2006).

ABU GRABBE

Born and raised a New Yorker, I wept over 9/11 for months. I watched every clip of news footage; read every news article, until I could watch and read no more. Yet I was speechless when I saw the photographs from Abu Grabbe. I could not believe that Americans would engage in such behavior.

As more information came out, it became clear that this was not a solitary incident, an aberration. It was part of a systematic approach—albeit, poorly conveyed to the lower ranking soldiers expected to carry it out. This is not surprising, since it was entirely inconsistent with

International Humanitarian Law and the very training they had received. *See*, again, the Soldier's Rules, at **Appendix VII.**

I fully expected that there would be an accounting, as far up the chain of command as necessary. Instead, the lowest ranking and smallest possible number of individuals involved were pegged. Oh, and the JAG attorneys who, it seems, must have been designated as potential "fall guys" from the outset. There the inquiry ended.

Former Abu Grabbe Commandant, Brigadier General Janis Karpinski—whom many of us heard initially state knew *every aspect* of what went on at her facility—has safely retired. Donald Rumsfeld, the apparent author of the strategy, retained his job until recently.

Virtually overlooked, insofar as accountability, was our Attorney General, Alberto Gonzales—a man whose proud heritage should have given him a better understanding of how dear we hold our freedoms in this country. Instead, Gonzales opined that the United States could easily re-define torture to exclude any activity not placing the victim at risk of organ failure or death.

By that definition, electrodes to the genitalia at a less than lethal dose could not be classified as torture. Nor would gang rape qualify. What are a few bloodstains on the floor?

By the Gonzales definition, not even castration or, say, incremental amputation would constitute torture (especially if performed under anesthesia). After all, the victim might only end up insane or suffering from Post-Traumatic Stress Disorder for the next 40 years. The Inquisition managed quite well, though clerics were forbidden to shed blood [271].

And, if the victim did survive, all the more proof he had not really been tortured at all, according to Gonzales' reasoning. Ask those of our Vietnam veterans who managed to survive "tiger cages" whether they would agree.

No worries. Gonzales is still gainfully employed—at the nation's expense. And the humanitarian issues continue unabated.

In Guantanamo, we have been retaining prisoners under secretive conditions, without counsel, and for an indeterminate period. The Administration has argued it is America's right to do so, by reason of the fact these are alleged terrorists (not the official soldiers of a recognized nation). Whether torture has been taking place remains unclear, as of this writing.

> *From Karen McLauchlan:*
>
> How can you sign into Law the McCain Amendment while at the same moment provide a "Presidential Signing Statement" that claims your authority to IGNORE that very law? How can the public believe in your assertion NOT to be approving the torture of prisoners under these circumstances? Or have any belief you will obey this law [111F]?
>
> *From Tracy:*
>
> Mr. President, the CIA had described waterboarding, used with administration approval on several al Queda suspects, as the following: "The prisoner is bound to an inclined board, feet raised and head slightly below the feet. Cellophane is wrapped over the prisoner's face and water is poured over him. Unavoidably, the gag reflex kicks in and a terrifying fear of drowning leads to almost instant pleas to bring the treatment to a halt." If this were done to an American soldier, sir, would you consider it torture [111G]?

And we wonder why the worldwide sympathy September 11 generated on our behalf has dissipated. We wonder why the Arab states distrust us.

Do we really want to hold individuals like Bush, Rumsfeld, and Gonzales up as role models for our children?

> ...as soon as they lay down [their arms] and surrender, they cease to be enemies or agents of the enemy, and again become mere men, and it is no longer legitimate to take their lives.
>
> —Jean-Jacques Rousseau.

With this statement, Rousseau voiced a central tenet of International Humanitarian Law [235E].

This Administration can no longer distinguish good from evil. We are making Osama bin Laden's case for him. We are becoming the enemy he made us out to be.

I am not by any means advocating that we submit to al-Qaeda. There is no temporizing with evil. Better ways exist, however, of defeating bin Laden than sending our brave sons and daughters to their deaths in Iraq. One of the best is showing the world America *at her best.*

America's best is not reflected in material success or even military might. There is no denying that material success comprised an integral part of the American Dream from the outset. But material success was never the entire dream. What drew us to these shores originally was the chance to rise, to make a new beginning—though we did not know, and could not begin to calculate, the cost.

What made us extraordinary as a nation was our faith—both in God and the ordinary man. Those truths, so beautifully articulated by Thomas Jefferson, struck a chord in the heart that reverberates still. That is what draws millions of reckless dreamers here to this day. The chance for a future. The dream of what America is—or could be—at her very best.

Today those truths have an opportunity to spread across the globe. That is the real significance of globalization. The same truths in Thai and Arabic, in Swahili and Azer, in Farsi and Burmese, in Tigre and Domari.

We treasure the documents on which they were inscribed, but those precious truths are only empty words, if they are not lived out—again and again—by each succeeding generation. What gave the American Dream substance was sacrifice. What turned those precious truths, on which this country was built—liberty; equality; inalienable rights bestowed by a Creator—from theory into reality was the fact that drawing room oaths were united with bloody footprints in the snow. Both blue-stockinged aristocrat and barefoot farm boy committed their all, to a cause larger than either one.

Before Revolutionary War patriot, Nathan Hale (a 21 year old school teacher) was hanged as a spy by the British, he asked for a Bible, but was refused [268A]. Letters Hale had been given permission to write his mother and a fellow American officer were destroyed by the Provost Marshall on the grounds "the rebels should not know that they had a man in their army who could die with so much firmness [268B]."

Hale's last words—spoken not far from where the Trade Center stood, some two centuries later—were these:

> I only regret that I have but one life to lose for my country [268C].

Is there anyone outside the Bush Administration not moved? Is there anyone outside the Bush Administration delusional enough to think Hale's regret remotely related to lost opportunity for a "killing" on the stock market?

Americans have so much to teach…so much yet to learn, for that matter. Those fundamental truths of ours are the real danger to bin Laden and his ilk. Imperfectly as they have been implemented (and will ever be implemented in an imperfect world), nonetheless, those truths reflect the best of what the human spirit is capable.

And they do so—please, note—not because man is so godlike, as to have deduced these underlying truths. But because the LORD is God (Exodus 20: 2). And it is from His everlasting laws that these fundamental truths derive.

NGOS: MICROCREDIT AND OTHER EFFORTS

Helen Keller said, "I am only one, but still I am one. I cannot do everything, but still I can do something."

Following on this inspiration, we can make use of globalization in combination with non-governmental organizations (NGOs)—charitable organizations which assist in providing physical or emotional support to individuals, families, groups and communities—to benefit the world at large.

> NGOs and governments including the United Nations Development Program, World Bank, USAID and the GTZ invest significant amounts in developing countries

> to build up their knowledge of industry capabilities. This support includes training, market development and the encouragement of corporations to invest in these developing regions...
>
> The most often-utilized benefit of forging relationships with NGOs and governments were the financial incentives, whether to invest in new IT parks, or the reimbursement for development costs. Many governments offer tax incentives and repayment of transfer costs for professionals, as well as waiving visa requirements for workers. However, a secondary benefit often emerged in these relationships, as organizations gained entry into new local markets at a greatly reduced cost.
>
> Many organizations also enjoyed a positive image exposure, and strengthened business prospects from their relationships with NGOs...Experts agree that outsourcing strategies have led to sustained economic growth in many countries by providing employment, creating a service export industry, and contributing positively to the overall standard of living [88].
>
> It has long been claimed that there can be no development without respect for cultural roots and values. This belief has major implications for development cooperation partnerships. It implies that key trends such as social change, democratisation and gender equality cannot be imposed from the outside, but require an endogenous process of cultural change. It means that external partners need to fully understand the cultural dimensions of development, embracing both traditions and ongoing changes [89]...

This will require monitoring and regulation [90]—in part, because human nature is subject to temptation; in part, because corruption is common in many Third World countries. A study by Margaret Gibelman, DSW, and Sheldon R. Gelman, Ph.D., entitled "Very Public Scandals: An Analysis of How and Why Nongovernmental Organizations Get in Trouble—A Working Paper," was presented to the International Society for Third Sector Research on July 7, 2000. It concluded, in relevant part:

> The burgeoning growth and development of NGOs in the last quarter of the 20th Century relates, in part, to the world-wide quest to find alternatives to government in the provision of human services, a quest largely borne out of a disillusionment with government's handling of the welfare state...Our review of instances of wrongdoing on the part of NGOs reveals that all have involved money and are opportunistic in nature. The incidents are motivated by self-interest (greed), perceived entitlement, or sexual fulfillment. Most have occurred over a lengthy period of time, are not precipitous, reflect a lack of board oversight, and have long term impacts on the organization [252].

With care, we could bring about enormous good. For example, microcredit a/k/a village banking has over the past 15–20 years proven highly successful in Latin America, the Caribbean, Africa, Eastern Europe, Central Asia, and the former Soviet Union. This method of banking offers even the poorest of the poor collateral-free working capital (in amounts as little as $50-$500) at a reasonable rate of interest; an opportunity to generate extra income; and a safe place to earn interest on savings.

This might allow a single mother or family to raise chickens or pigs; to start a small grocery or crafts business; to bake bread for market or sell charcoal.

Economic equity may not be the solution to all the world's problems. Still, what you or I spend in a month on latte, could translate into a better way of life for someone.[34]

DISCIPLES OF ALL NATIONS

Allow me to share one last excerpt with you, again from *The Voice of the Martyrs*.[35] Based on the simple idea that love is stronger than hate, it stands in stark contrast—both with the terrorist tactics of

Osama bin Laden, and the policies (and military ambitions) of the Bush Administration:

> Every night on the news, we hear solutions for our physical protection. We can be left with a hole in our soul after turning off the TV. If we are not careful, we can forget that as ambassadors for Christ, safety is not our highest goal…When the disciples were attacked by mobs incited by religious authorities…they didn't compromise to save their skin. Beaten and placed in stocks, they sang about the Solution inside of them, the Victor over hatred, over sin…In the Islamic Republic of Iran…pastors have been murdered…Dozens have been arrested…President of Iran, Mahmud Ahmadinejad, in a speech on July 25, 2005, stated: "Allah willing, Islam will conquer what? It will conquer all the mountaintops of the world." He had been employed as an interrogator and torturer for the Internal Security Department and the Revolutionary Guard…[H]e was, also, an executioner at the notorious Evin Prison in Tehran. Iranian pastor Roubak Hovespian-Mehr was held in this same prison. Pastor Roubak led his own Muslim prison guard to Christ. (Was it worth it? It is up to you whether you choose to be a victim [of terrorism] or a vessel [of grace]). If the president of terrorist Iran wants the mountaintops, he can have them. We support courageous Iranian Christians who go down into the valleys where the lost and hopeless wait for them. More Iranians are turning to Christ now than anytime in history. I have been there. I have met them…The Koran states that those people with whom Allah was angry were cursed and turned into pigs and apes ("The Table," Surah 5, verse 60). Jesus states, "*Love your enemies, do good to those who hate you, bless those who curse you, and pray for those who spitefully use you*" (Luke 6: 27–28)…Do not believe all Muslims are terrorists or even angry…[However, secular reporter] John R. Bradley…[in] *Saudi Arabia Exposed*…writes about Muslims hating Muslims. There is no love. Mosques are burned with gasoline by other Muslim factions. Tribe hates

tribe. Ismaeli high school students are given 800 lashes and four years in prison for expressing different views of Islamic doctrine...[T]he answer to this chaos is very simple. Jesus can save us. We all need the Redeemer...The word "compassion" means "to suffer with." When we as Christians begin to see no difference between working to save the terrorists from harming us and working to save them from themselves, then God will be glorified [110A]...

"*Go therefore and make disciples of all the nations, baptizing them in the name of the Father and of the Son and of the Holy Spirit...and lo, I am with you always, even to the end of the age*" (Matthew 28: 19–20).

APPENDIX I

STATE CONSTITUTIONS (EXCERPTS)

Alabama 1901, Preamble. We the people of the State of Alabama, invoking the favor and guidance of Almighty God, do ordain and establish the following Constitution…

Alaska 1956, Preamble. We, the people of Alaska, grateful to God and to those who founded our nation and pioneered this great land…

Arizona 1911, Preamble. We, the people of the State of Arizona, grateful to Almighty God for our liberties, do ordain this Constitution…

Arkansas 1874, Preamble. We, the people of the State of Arkansas, grateful to Almighty God for the privilege of choosing our own form of government…

California 1879, Preamble. We, the People of the State of California, grateful to Almighty God for our freedom…

Colorado 1876, Preamble. We, the people of Colorado, with profound reverence for the Supreme Ruler of Universe…

Connecticut 1818, Preamble. The People of Connecticut, acknowledging with gratitude the good Providence of God in permitting them to enjoy…

Delaware 1897, Preamble. Through Divine Goodness all men have, by nature, the rights of worshipping and serving their Creator according to the dictates of their consciences.

Florida 1885, Preamble. We, the people of the State of Florida, grateful to Almighty God for our constitutional liberty...establish this Constitution...

Georgia 1777, Preamble. We, the people of Georgia, relying upon protection and guidance of Almighty God, do ordain and establish this Constitution...

Hawaii 1959, Preamble. We, the people of Hawaii, Grateful for Divine Guidance...establish this Constitution...

Idaho 1889, Preamble. We, the people of the State of Idaho, grateful to Almighty God for our freedom, to secure its blessings...

Illinois 1870, Preamble. We, the people of the State of Illinois, grateful to Almighty God for the civil, political and religious liberty which He hath so long permitted us to enjoy and looking to Him for a blessing on our endeavors...

Indiana 1851, Preamble. We, the People of the State of Indiana, grateful to Almighty God for the free exercise of the right to chose our form of government...

Iowa 1857, Preamble. We, the People of the State of Iowa, grateful to the Supreme Being for the blessings hitherto enjoyed, and feeling our dependence on Him for a continuation of these blessings establish this Constitution...

Kansas 1859, Preamble. We, the people of Kansas, grateful to Almighty God for our civil and religious privileges...establish this Constitution...

Kentucky 1891, Preamble. We, the people of the Commonwealth of grateful to Almighty God for the civil, political and religious liberties...

Louisiana 1921, Preamble. We, the people of the State of Louisiana, grateful to Almighty God for the civil, political and religious liberties we enjoy…

Maine 1820, Preamble. We the People of Maine, acknowledging with grateful hearts the goodness of the Sovereign Ruler of the Universe in affording us an opportunity…and imploring His aid and direction…

Maryland 1776, Preamble. We, the people of the state of Maryland, grateful to Almighty God for our civil and religious liberty…

Massachusetts 1780, Preamble. We…the people of Massachusetts, acknowledging with grateful hearts, the goodness of the Great Legislator of the Universe…in the course of His Providence, an opportunity…and devoutly imploring His direction…

Michigan 1908, Preamble. We, the people of the State of Michigan, grateful to Almighty God for the blessings of freedom…establish this Constitution…

Minnesota, 1857, Preamble. We, the people of the State of Minnesota, grateful to God for our civil and religious liberty, and desiring to perpetuate its blessings…

Mississippi 1890, Preamble. We, the people of Mississippi in convention assembled, grateful to Almighty God, and invoking His blessing on our work…

Missouri 1845, Preamble. We, the people of Missouri, with profound reverence for the Supreme Ruler of the Universe, and grateful for His goodness…establish this Constitution…

Montana 1889, Preamble. We, the people of Montana, grateful to Almighty God for the blessings of liberty…establish this Constitution…

Nebraska 1875, Preamble. We, the people, grateful to Almighty God for our freedom…establish this Constitution…

Nevada 1864, Preamble. We the people of the State of Nevada, grateful to Almighty God for our freedom establish this Constitution...

New Hampshire 1792, Part I. Art. I. Sec. V. Every individual has a natural and unalienable right to worship God according to the dictates of his own conscience...

New Jersey 1844, Preamble. We, the people of the State of New Jersey, grateful to Almighty God for civil and religious liberty which He hath so long permitted us to enjoy, and looking to Him for a blessing on our endeavors...

New Mexico 1911, Preamble. We, the People of New Mexico, grateful to Almighty God for the blessings of liberty...

New York 1846, Preamble. We, the people of the State of New York, grateful to Almighty God for our freedom, in order to secure its blessings...

North Carolina 1868, Preamble. We the people of the State of North Carolina, grateful to Almighty God, the Sovereign Ruler of Nations, for our civil, political, and religious liberties, and acknowledging our dependence upon Him for the continuance of those...

North Dakota 1889, Preamble. We, the people of North Dakota, grateful to Almighty God for the blessings of civil and religious liberty, do ordain...

Ohio 1852, Preamble. We the people of the state of Ohio, grateful to Almighty God for our freedom, to secure its blessings and to promote our common...

Oklahoma 1907, Preamble. Invoking the guidance of Almighty God, in order to secure and perpetuate the blessings of liberty...establish this...

Oregon 1857, Bill of Rights, Article I Section 2. All men shall be secure in the Natural right, to worship Almighty God according to the dictates of their consciences...

Pennsylvania 1776, Preamble. We, the people of Pennsylvania, grateful to Almighty God for the blessings of civil and religious liberty, and humbly invoking His guidance...

Rhode Island 1842, Preamble. We the People of the State of Rhode Island grateful to Almighty God for the civil and religious liberty which He hath so long permitted us to enjoy, and looking to Him for a blessing...

South Carolina, 1778, Preamble. We, the people of the State of South Carolina...grateful to God for our liberties, do ordain and establish this Constitution...

South Dakota 1889, Preamble. We, the people of South Dakota , grateful to Almighty God for our civil and religious liberties...establish this

Tennessee 1796, Art. XI.III. That all men have a natural and indefeasible right to worship Almighty God according to the dictates of their conscience...

Texas 1845, Preamble. We the People of the Republic of Texas, acknowledging, with gratitude, the grace and beneficence of God.

Utah 1896, Preamble. Grateful to Almighty God for life and liberty, we establish this Constitution...

Vermont 1777, Preamble. Whereas all government ought to...enable the individuals who compose it to enjoy their natural rights, and other blessings which the Author of Existence has bestowed on man...

Virginia 1776, Bill of Rights, XVI. Religion, or the Duty which we owe our Creator...can be directed only by Reason and that it is the mutual duty of all to practice Christian Forbearance, Love and Charity towards each other...

Washington 1889, Preamble. We the People of the State of Washington, grateful to the Supreme Ruler of the Universe for our liberties, do ordain this Constitution...

West Virginia 1872, Preamble. Since through Divine Providence we enjoy the blessings of civil, political and religious liberty, we, the people of West Virginia reaffirm our faith in and constant reliance upon God...

Wisconsin 1848, Preamble. We, the people of Wisconsin, grateful to Almighty God for our freedom, domestic tranquility...

Wyoming 1890, Preamble. We, the people of the State of Wyoming, grateful to God for our civil, political, and religious liberties...establish this Constitution...

APPENDIX II

ADOPTION INFORMATION**

Waiting Children's Lists

United States Foster Care Adoption Websites
Adopt America Network
AdoptUSKids

International Adoption Agency Websites
Buckner International Adoption
Rainbow Kids

Financial Assistance with Adoption

National Endowment for Financial Education
At http://naic.acf.hhs.gov/pubs/adoption_gip_two.cfm, and http://www.pueblo.gsa.gov/cic_text/family/adoption/adoption.txt. Provides detailed information about the adoption process, the costs related to adoption, and financial assistance.

Federal Adoption Tax Credit
Allows adoptive families a tax credit up to $10,000 for adoption expenses. Publication 968 can be ordered from the IRS online at www.irs.ustreas.gov or by calling 1–800–829–3676.

Adoption from State Foster Care
In many states adoption from the State Foster Care System costs little or nothing. If the child qualifies as having "special needs," he or she may receive up to $500 per month in subsidies.

Special Needs Adoption
Many agencies offer substantial reductions in fees for children with

"special needs." Which conditions qualify will vary from agency to agency. Some are long-term conditions; others are treatable and correctable.

Employee Adoption Benefits

Many corporations assist employees with adoption costs. Human Resource Departments will have this information. Call 1–800-TO-ADOPT for a list of employers offering these benefits.

Military Families

Active duty personnel are eligible to be reimbursed up to $2,000 in adoption expenses by the US military after an adoption has been finalized.

**Courtesy of FamilyLife Ministry

APPENDIX III

FAITH-BASED LEGAL AID: ADDITIONAL READING

Melanie Acevedo, "Client Choices, Community Values: Why Faith-Based Legal Services Providers Are Good for Poverty Law," 70 Fordham Law Review 1491 (2002) © 2002 West

Melanie Acevedo, "Practice What You Preach: Power, Paternalism and the Christian Lawyer for the Poor," 31 Fordham Urban Law Journal 111 (2003)

Joseph Allegretti, *The Lawyer's Calling* (1996)

Joseph Allegretti, "Lawyers, Clients and Covenant: A Religious Perspective on Legal Practice and Ethics," 66 Fordham Law Review 1101 (1998)

Raymond H. Brescia, et al., "Who's In Charge, Anyway? A Proposal for Community Based Legal Services," 25 Fordham Urban Law Journal 831 (1998)

Robert F. Cohran, "Professional and Christian Responsibilities to the Poor," Pepperdine Law (Spring 1999)

Charles W. Colson, *Justice That Restores* (2001)

Jennifer Smodish, "Pepperdine Street Lawyers," Pepperdine Law (Spring 1999)

APPENDIX IV

TEN COMMANDMENTS **

I. *"You shall have no other gods before Me"* (Exodus 20: 3).
II. *"You shall not make for yourself a carved image...you shall not bow down to them nor serve them"* (Exodus 20: 4–5).
III. *"You shall not take the name of the Lord your God in vain..."* (Exodus 20: 7).
IV. *"Remember the Sabbath day, to keep it holy"* (Exodus 20: 8).
V. *"Honor your father and your mother..."* (Exodus 20: 12).
VI. *"You shall not murder" (Exodus 20: 13).*
VII. "You shall not commit adultery" (Exodus 20: 14).
VIII. "You shall not steal" (Exodus 20: 15).
IX. "You shall not bear false witness against your neighbor" (Exodus 20: 16).
*X. "You shall not covet your neighbor's house; you shall not covet your neighbor's wife..."(*Exodus 20: 17).

**There are numerous references to the Ten Commandments throughout Scripture. Not all are given here.

APPENDIX V

EX-OFFENDER RESOURCES AND INFORMATION**

After Prison: Roadblocks to Reentry at http://www.soros.org/initiatives/justice/articles_publications/publications/lac_roadblocks_20040422 . Report by US Justice Dept. grantee, Legal Action Center on legal obstacles faced by those with criminal records attempting to reenter society and become productive, law-abiding citizens.

"Better Life—A Safer Community: Helping Inmates Access Federal Benefits" at www.bazelon.org/issues/criminalization/publications/gains/gains.pdf . Paper from Bazelon Center for Mental Health Law, discussing access to federal benefit programs for adults with serious mental illnesses and juveniles with serious mental or emotional disorders leaving jail, prison, juvenile detention or other correctional institutions.

Christian Association for Prison Aftercare (CAPA) at http://www.capaassociation.org/index.htm. Provides Christian resources and training to professionals and volunteers, serving ex-offenders and their families.

Crisis of the Young African American Male and the Criminal Justice System at http://www.sentencingproject.org/pdfs/5022.pdf by the US Commission on Civil Rights. Examines disproportionate number of Hispanic and African American males incarcerated, and explores potential solutions.

Enterprise Community Partners at http://www.enterprisecommunity.org/index.html. Employment Services, Housing. Provides loans, grants and technical assistance to non-profit organizations rebuilding neighborhoods with goal of providing low-income people with affordable housing, safer streets and access to jobs and child care.

The Ex-Inmate's Complete Guide to Successful Employment (4th Edition), by Errol Craig Sull at The Educational Correction Company, P.O. Box 956, Buffalo, NY 14207 phone:(716) 871–1900, fax (716) 871–1919, email prisonedu@aol.com, website http://www.prisonedu.com/books.html . Includes:

- Developing resumes & cover letters specific for inmates /ex-inmates
- Difficult interview questions (and suggested answers) for ex-inmates
- Developing solid problem-solving, decision making, anger management, and communicative skills
- How to keep and progress on the job

Family Justice at http://www.familyjustice.org/method/ Family-focused ("bodega model"). Partners individuals under justice supervision and their families with community providers.

Forum for Reentry and Community Economic Development (FRCED) at http://www.frced.org/
http://www.frced.org/documents/Housingfora2ndChance.pdf. Provides training to sensitize property managers to re-entry problems faced by ex-offenders, and recommends mutually satisfactory safeguards to make affordable housing available to ex-offenders.

Girl Scouts "Beyond Bars" Life Skills Curriculum (Robert Wood Johnson Foundation) at http://www.girlscouts.org/who_we_are/our_partners/corporations_foundations/robert_wood_johnson_foundation.asp. Self-esteem, self-confidence, and character-building for girls with incarcerated mothers.

Goodwill Industries International at http://www.goodwill.org/. Provides job training and employment services, job placement opportunities and post-employment support.

Housing for a Second Chance: Family, Government and Community Partnerships for Housing People Involved in the Criminal Justice System at http://www.frced.org/documents/Housingfora2ndChance.pdf. Interactive Training Program for successful Reentry Housing, operated jointly by Local Initiatives Support Corporation Community Safety Initiative (LISC CSI), in partnership with Family Justice Inc. and US Department of Justice Community Capacity Development Office. Target audience: Property Managers, Housing Providers, Community Developers, Public Housing Authorities, Police and Corrections Officers.

InnerChange Freedom Initiative® (IFI). Partnership between Texas Department of Criminal Justice and Prison Fellowship with goal of reducing recidivism through a 24-hour-a-day, 7-day-a-week Christian prison program, beginning during incarceration and continuing afterward. Contact (877) 478–0100.

International Network of Prison Ministries at http://prisonministry.net/. Single website allows communication among numerous Christian prison ministries, and access for inmates and their families to those ministries best serving their needs.

Kairos Prison Ministry at http://www.kairosprisonministry.org/. Purpose to establish strong Christian communities within prison population, positively impacting prison environment. Also, reaches out to juvenile offenders. "Kairos Outside" provides loving support to family members who "do time" along with the offender.

Koinonia House at http://koinoniahouse.org/Interface/Public/index.asp, PO Box 1415, Wheaton, IL 60189–1415, (630) 221–9930. Family and home-based ministry for Christians released from prison. Excellent source of information re: operation of Christian halfway houses.

National Fatherhood Initiative (NFI) at http://www.fatherhood.org/. Fathering-skills program with Christian and re-entry versions.

National H.I.R.E. Network at http://www.hirenetwork.org/. Mission to increase number and quality of job opportunities available to people with criminal records by improving public policies and public opinion.

National Institute of Corrections - Transition from Prison to the Community at http://nicic.org/WebPage_222.htm. Initiative to assist states in improving their transition processes, make better use of resources in correctional facilities and communities, increase public safety, reduce recidivism and new victimization.

Office of Justice Programs (Reentry) at http://www.ojp.usdoj.gov/reentry/. Provides resources and funding to develop, implement, enhance, and evaluate reentry strategies for safety of communities and reduction of serious crime.

Reentry Policy Council at http://www.reentrypolicy.org/rp/Main.aspx. Proposed changes to improve inmate re-entry into society.

Road to Redemption by Pat Nolan c/o Prison Fellowship at http://www.pfm.org/AM/Template.cfm?Section=PFM_Site&Template=/CM/HTMLDisplay.cfm&ContentID=12914.

Urban Institute Reentry Mapping Network at http://www.urbanstrategies.org/programs/csj/reentrymapping.html. Initiative to strengthen community strategies for prisoner return. Network focuses on developing neighborhood level data re: incarcertaion and reentry, using GIS technology to analyze and display demographics and signif locations of former inmates in Oakland, CA area. Contact Karen McKenzie (202) 261–5709. *See*, also, *Outside the Walls: A National Snapshot of Community-Based Prisoner Reentry Programs* at http://www.urban.org/publications/410911.html.

**Much of the information here courtesy of Prison Fellowship

APPENDIX VI

Bishop Wilton D. Gregory,
United States Conference of Catholic Bishops, Office of Social Development & World Peace
Letter to President Bush on Iraq, September 13, 2002

The Honorable George W. Bush
The White House
Washington, D.C. 20500

Dear Mr. President:

At its meeting last week, the 60-member Administrative Committee the United States Conference of Catholic Bishops asked me to write you about the situation in Iraq. We welcome your efforts to focus the world's attention on the need to address Iraq's repression and pursuit of weapons of mass destruction in defiance of the United Nations. The Committee met before your speech at the United Nations, but I thought it was important that I express our serious questions about the moral legitimacy of any preemptive, unilateral use of military force to overthrow the government of Iraq.

A year ago, my predecessor Bishop Joseph Fiorenza wrote you about the US response to the horrific attacks we commemorated last week. He told you then that, in our judgment, the use of force against Afghanistan could be justified, if it were carried out in accord with just war norms and as one part of a much broader, mostly non-military effort to deal with terrorism. We believe Iraq is a different case. Given the precedents and risks involved, we find it difficult to justify extending the war on terrorism to Iraq, absent clear and adequate evidence of Iraqi involvement in the attacks of September 11th or of an imminent attack of a grave nature.

The United States and the international community have two

grave moral obligations: to protect the common good against any Iraqi threats to peace and to do so in a way that conforms with fundamental moral norms. We have no illusions about the behavior or intentions of the Iraqi government. The Iraqi leadership must cease its internal repression, end its threats to its neighbors, stop any support for terrorism, abandon its efforts to develop weapons of mass destruction, and comply with UN resolutions. Mobilizing the nations of the world to recognize and address Iraq's threat to peace and stability through new UN action and common commitment to ensure that Iraq abides by its commitments is a legitimate and necessary alternative to the unilateral use of military force. Your decision to seek UN action is welcome, but other questions of ends and means must also be answered.

There are no easy answers. People of good will may apply ethical principles and come to different prudential judgments, depending upon their assessment of the facts at hand and other issues. We conclude, based on the facts that are known to us, that a preemptive, unilateral use of force is difficult to justify at this time. We fear that resort to force, under these circumstances, would not meet the strict conditions in Catholic teaching for overriding the strong presumption against the use of military force. Of particular concern are the traditional just war criteria of just cause, right authority, probability of success, proportionality and noncombatant immunity.

Just cause. What is the *casus belli* for a military attack on Iraq? The Catechism of the Catholic Church, reflecting widely accepted moral and legal limits on why military force may be used, limits just cause to cases in which "the damage inflicted by the aggressor on the nation or community of nations [is] lasting, grave and certain." (#2309). Is there clear and adequate evidence of a direct connection between Iraq and the attacks of September 11th or clear and adequate evidence of an imminent attack of a grave nature? Is it wise to dramatically expand traditional moral and legal limits on just cause to include preventive or preemptive uses of military force to overthrow threatening regimes or to deal with the proliferation of weapons of mass destruction? Should not a distinction be made between efforts to change unacceptable behavior of a government and efforts to end that government's existence?

Legitimate authority. The moral credibility of the use of military force also depends heavily on whether there is legitimate authority for using force to topple the Iraqi government. In our judgment, decisions of such gravity require compliance with US constitutional imperatives, broad consensus within our nation, and some form of international sanction, preferably by the UN Security Council. That is why your decision to seek congressional and United Nations approval is so important. With the Holy See, we would be deeply skeptical about unilateral uses of military force, particularly given the troubling precedents involved.

Probability of success and proportionality. The use of force must have "serious prospects for success" and "must not produce evils and disorders graver than the evil to be eliminated" (Catechism, #2309). War against Iraq could have unpredictable consequences not only for Iraq but for peace and stability elsewhere in the Middle East. Would preventive or preemptive force succeed in thwarting serious threats or, instead, provoke the very kind of attacks that it is intended to prevent? How would another war in Iraq impact the civilian population, in the short- and long-term? How many more innocent people would suffer and die, or be left without homes, without basic necessities, without work? Would the United States and the international community commit to the arduous, long-term task of ensuring a just peace or would a post-Saddam Iraq continue to be plagued by civil conflict and repression, and continue to serve as a destabilizing force in the region? Would the use of military force lead to wider conflict and instability? Would war against Iraq detract from our responsibility to help build a just and stable order in Afghanistan and undermine the broader coalition against terrorism?

Norms governing the conduct of war. While we recognize improved capability and serious efforts to avoid directly targeting civilians in war, the use of massive military force to remove the current government of Iraq could have incalculable consequences for a civilian population that has suffered so much from war, repression, and a debilitating embargo.

We raise these troubling questions to contribute to the vital national debate about ends and means, risks and choices reflecting our responsibilities as pastors and teachers. Our assessment of these questions leads us to urge you to pursue actively alternatives to war. We hope you will persist in the very frustrating and difficult challenges of building broad international support for a new, more constructive and effective approach to press the Iraqi government to live up to its international obligations. This approach could include continued diplomatic efforts aimed, in part, at resuming rigorous, meaningful inspections; effective enforcement of the military embargo; maintenance of political sanctions and much more carefully-focused economic sanctions which do not threaten the lives of innocent Iraqi civilians; non-military support for those in Iraq who offer genuine democratic alternatives; and other legitimate ways to contain and deter aggressive Iraqi actions.

We respectfully urge you to step back from the brink of war and help lead the world to act together to fashion an effective global response to Iraq's threats that conforms with traditional moral limits on the use of military force.

Sincerely yours,
Most Reverend Wilton D. Gregory
Bishop of Belleville
President

Office of Social Development & World Peace
United States Conference of Catholic Bishops
3211 4th Street, N.E., Washington, DC 20017–1194, (202) 541–3000
September 17, 2002

APPENDIX VII

THE SOLDIER'S RULES

Fight only enemy combatants
Treat humanely all who surrender or are captured. Do not harm enemies who surrender—disarm them and turn them over to your superiors.
Do not kill or torture enemy prisoners of war.
Collect and care for the wounded, whether friend or foe.
Treat the dead with respect.
Do not attack medical personnel, facilities, or equipment.
Destroy no more than the mission requires.
Treat all civilians humanely.
Do not steal—respect private property and possessions.
Do your best to prevent violations of the law of war—report all violations to your superiors.

See, also:

Article 52(2) of Protocol I of the 1977 Protocols Additional to the Geneva Conventions, December 12, 1977

Article 22 of the Regulations Respecting the Laws and Customs of War on Land, annexed to the Hague Convention No. IV, October 18, 1907

Article 23e of the Regulations Respecting the Laws and Customs of War on Land, annexed to the Hague Convention No. IV

Department of the Army, Field Manual 27–10, The Law of Land Warfare (July 1956) (change 1) at paragraph 41

Article 51 of Protocol I of the 1977 Protocols Additional to the Geneva Conventions

APPENDIX VIII

PROPHECIES FULFILLED BY JESUS CHRIST (HEBREW: "YESHUA HA'NATSERET—MASHIACH")

The prophecies which follow were made hundreds—sometimes thousands—of years before Jesus Christ was born. Peter Stoner in his work Science Speaks showed that the coincidence of a single man fulfilling even eight of these prophecies is ruled out by the science of probability. (Stoner's analysis concerned the specific eight prophecies marked with asterisks, in the table which follows.)

In Stoner's words, "We find that the chance that any man might have…fulfilled [even these] eight prophecies is 1 in 10^{17}." That would be 1 in 100,000,000,000,000,000. Stoner illustrated this, as follows:

> "…[W]e take 10^{17} silver dollars and lay them on the face of Texas. They will cover all of the state two feet deep. Now mark one of these silver dollars and stir the whole mass thoroughly, all over the state. Blindfold a man and tell him that he can travel as far as he wishes, but he must pick up one silver dollar and say that this is the right one. What chance would he have of getting the right one? Just the same chance that the prophets would have had of writing these eight prophecies and having them all come true in any one man, from their day to the present time, providing they wrote in their own wisdom.
>
> Now these prophecies were either given by inspiration of God or the prophets just wrote them as they thought they should be. In such a case the prophets had just one chance in 10^{17} of having them come true in any man, but they all came true in Christ [Mashiach].
>
> This means that the fulfillment of these eight prophecies alone proves that God inspired the writing of those [eight]

> prophecies to a definiteness which lacks only one chance in 10^{17} of being absolute."
>
> —Original Source: Peter Stoner, Science Speaks (1963).

Stoner then considered 48 prophecies and concluded that the chance of one man fulfilling all 48 prophecies would be 1 in 10^{157}. The notation 10^{157} is represents the number 1 followed by 157 zeros. It looks like this:

> 10,000,000,000,000,000,000,000,000,000,000,000,000,000,00
> 0,000,000,000,000,000,000,000,000,000,000,000,000,000,
> 000,000,000,000,000,000,000,000,000,000,000,000,000,0
> 00,000,000,000,000,000,000,000,000,000,000,000,000.

This is approximately the *total number of electrons in all the mass of the known universe!*

Yet Jesus Christ *fulfilled more than 324 individual prophecies* that the Prophets wrote concerning the Messiah [248].

This should be no real surprise. *"In the beginning was the Word, and the Word was with God, and the Word was God"* (John 1: 1).

FULFILLED MESSIANIC PROPHECIES

Genesis 3:15	He will bruise Satan's head	Hebrews 2:14, 1 John 3:18
Genesis 3:15	Born of the seed of a woman	Matthew 1:18
Genesis 5:24	Bodily ascension to heaven	Mark 6:19
Genesis 9:26, 27	The God of Shem will be the Son of Shem	Luke 3:36
Genesis 12:3	Of the seed of Abraham	Matthew 1:1–16
Genesis 12:3	As Abraham's seed, will bless all nations	Acts. 3:25, 26; Matthew 8:5, 10
Genesis 12:7	The Promise made to Abraham's seed	Galatians 3:16
Genesis 14:18	A priest after Melchizedek	Hebrews 6:20
Genesis 14:18	A King also	Hebrews 7:2
Genesis 14:18	The Last Supper foreshadowed	Matthew 26:26–29
Genesis 17:19	The seed of Isaac	Romans 9:7
Genesis 22:8	The Lamb of God promised	John 1:29
Genesis 22:18	As Isaac's seed, will bless all nations	Galatians 3:16
Genesis 26:2–5	The seed of Isaac promised as the Redeemer	Hebrews 11:18
Genesis 49:10	The time of His coming	Luke 2:1–7; Galatians 4:4
Genesis 49:10	The seed of Judah	Luke 3:33; Matthew 1:1–3
Genesis 49:10	Called Shiloh or One Sent	John 17:3
Genesis 49:10	To come before Judah lost identity	John 11:47–52
Genesis 49:10	To Him shall the obedience of the people be	John 10:16
Exodus 3:13,14	The Great "I Am"	John 4:26
Exodus 12:5	A Lamb without blemish	1 Peter 1:19

Exodus 12:13	The blood of the Lamb saves from wrath	Romans 5:8
Exodus 12:21–27	Christ is our Passover	1 Corinthians 5:7
Exodus 12:46	Not a bone of the Lamb to be broken	John 19:31–36
Exodus 15:2	His exaltation predicted as Yeshua	Acts 7:55,56
Exodus 15:11	His Character—Holiness	Luke 1:35; Acts 4:27
Exodus 17:6	The Spiritual Rock of Israel	1 Corinthians 10:4
Exodus 33:19	His Character—Merciful	Luke 1:72
Leviticus 14:11	Leper cleansed—Sign of priesthood	Luke 5:12–14; Acts 6:7
Leviticus 16:15–17	Prefigures Christ's once-for-all death	Hebrews 9:7–14
Leviticus 16:27	Suffering outside the Camp	Matthew 27:33; Hebrews 13:11,12
Leviticus 17:11	The Blood—life of the flesh	Matthew 26:28; Mark 10:45
Leviticus 17:11	It is the blood that makes atonement	1 John 3:14–18
Leviticus 23:36–37	The Drink-offering:"If any man thirst"	John 19:31–36
Numbers 9:12	Not a bone of Him broken	John 19:31–36
Numbers 21:9	Serpent on a pole—Christ lifted up	John 3:14–18
Numbers 24:17	Time: *"I shall see him, but not now."*	Galatians 4:4
Deuteronomy 18:15	*"This is of a truth that prophet."*	John 6:14; Matthew 2:15
Deuteronomy 18:15–16	*"Had ye believed Moses, ye would believe me."*	John 5:45–47
Deuteronomy 18:18	Sent by the Father to speak His word	John 8:28, 29
Deuteronomy 18:19	Whoever will not hear must bear his sin	John 12:15
Deuteronomy 21:23	Cursed is he that hangs on a tree	Galatians 3:10–13
Judges 13:5; Amos 2:11; Lamentations 4:7	A Nazarene	Matthew 2:23
Ruth 4:4–9	Christ, our kinsman, has redeemed us	Ephesians 1:3–7
1 Samuel 2:10	Shall be an anointed King to the Lord	Matthew 28:18; John. 12:15
2 Samuel 7:12	David's Seed	Matthew 1:1
2 Samuel 7:14a	The Son of God	Luke 1:32

2 Samuel 7:16	David's house established forever	Luke 3:31; Revelation 22:16
2 Samuel 22:44–45; Psalm 2:7–8; Isaiah 55:5,60:3, 65:1; Malachi 1:11	Gentiles flock to him	Matthew 8:10
2 Kings 2:11	Bodily ascension to heaven	Luke 24:51
1 Chronicles 17:11	David's Seed	Matthew 1:1; 9:27
1 Chronicles 17:12, 13a	To reign on David's throne forever	Luke 1:32, 33
1 Chronicles 17:13a	*"I will be His Father, He... my Son."*	Hebrews 1:5
Job 19:23–27	The Resurrection predicted	John. 5:24–29
Psalm 2:1–3	The enmity of kings foreordained	Acts 4:25–28
Psalm 2:2	To own the title, Anointed (Christ)	Acts 2:36
Psalm 2:6	His Character—Holiness	John 8:46; Revelation 3:7
Psalm 2:6	To own the title King	Matthew 2:2
Psalm 2:7	Declared the Beloved Son	Matthew 3:17
Psalm 2:7, 8	The Crucifixion and Resurrection intimated	Acts 13:29–33
Psalm 2:12	Life comes through faith in Him	John 20:31
Psalm 8:2	The mouths of babes perfect His praise	Matthew 21:16
Psalm 8:5, 6	His humiliation and exaltation	Luke 24:50–53; 1 Corinthians 15:27
Psalm 16:10	Was not to see corruption	Acts 2:31
Psalm 16:9–11	Was to arise from the dead	John 20:9
Psalm 17:15; 49:15	The resurrection predicted	Luke 24:6
Psalm 22:1	Forsaken because of sins of others	2 Corinthians 5:21
Psalm 22:1	Words spoken from Calvary, "*My God...*"	Mark 15:34; Matthew 27:46
Psalm 22:2	Darkness upon Calvary	Matthew 27:45
Psalm 22:7	They shoot out the lip and shake the head	Matthew 27:39
Psalm 22:8	*"He trusted in God, let Him deliver Him."*	Matthew 27:43
Psalm 22:9	Born the Savior	Luke 2:7
Psalm 22:14	Died of a broken (ruptured) heart	John 19:34
Psalm 22:14,15	Suffered agony on Calvary	Mark 15:34–37
Psalm 22:15	He thirsted	John 19:28
Psalm 22:16**	They pierced His hands and His feet	John 19:34, 37; 20:27

Psalm 22:17,18	Stripped Him before the stares of men	Luke 23:34,35; Matthew 27:36
Psalm 22:18	They parted His garments	Matthew 27:35; John 19:23, 24
Psalm 22:20,21	He committed Himself to God	Luke 23:46
Psalm 22:20,21	Satanic power bruising the Redeemer's heel	Hebrews 2:14
Psalm 22:22	His Resurrection declared	John 20:17; Mark 16:6
Psalm 22:27	He shall be the governor of the nations	Colossians 1:16
Psalm 22:31	*"It is finished."*	John 19:30
Psalm 23:1	*"I am the Good Shepherd."*	John 10:11
Psalm 24:3	His exaltation predicted	Acts 1:11; Philippians 2:9
Psalm 30:3	His resurrection predicted	Acts 2:32
Psalm 31:5	*"Into thy hands I commit my spirit."*	Luke 23:46
Psalm 31:11	His acquaintances fled from Him	Mark 14:50
Psalm 31:13	They took counsel to put Him to death	John 11:53
Psalm 31:14, 15	*"He trusted in God, let Him deliver him."*	Matthew 27:43
Psalm 34:20; Numbers 9:12	Not a bone of Him broken	John 19:31–36,
Psalm 35:11	False witnesses rose up against Him	Mathew 26:59–60
Psalm 35:19	He was hated without a cause	John 15:25; Matthew 27:23
Psalm 38:11	His friends stood afar off	Luke 23:49
Psalm 40:2–5	The joy of His resurrection predicted	John 20:20
Psalm 40:6–8	His delight-the will of the Father	John 4:34
Psalm 40:9	He was to preach the Righteousness in Israel	Matthew 4:17
Psalm 40:14	Confronted by adversaries in the Garde	John 18:4–6
Psalm 41:9**	Betrayed by a familiar friend	John 13:18, 21
Psalm 45:2	Words of Grace come from His lips	Luke 4:22
Psalm 45:6	To own the title, God or Elohim	Hebrews 1:8
Psalm 45:7	A special anointing by the Holy Spirit	Matthew 3:16; Hebrews1:9
Psalm 45:7,8	Called the Christ (Messiah or Anointed)	Luke 2:11
Psalm 53:7	Silent to accusations	Matthew 27:14
Psalm 55:12–14	Betrayed by a friend, not an enemy	John 13:18

Psalm 55:15	Unrepentant death of the Betrayer	Matthew 27:3–5; Acts 1:16–19
Psalm 68:18	To give gifts to men	Ephesians 4:7–16
Psalms 68:18	Ascended into Heaven	Luke 24:51
Psalm 69:4	Hated without a cause	John 15:25
Psalm 69:8	A stranger to own brethren	Luke 8:20,21
Psalm 69:9	Zealous for the Lord's House	John 2:17
Psalm 69:14–20	Messiah's anguish of soul before crucifixion	Matthew 26:36–45
Psalm 69:20	*"My soul is exceeding sorrowful."*	Matthew 26:38
Psalm 69:21	Given vinegar in thirst	Matthew 27:34
Psalm 69:26	The Savior given and smitten by God	John. 17:4; 18:11
Psalm 72:10,11	Great persons were to visit Him	Matthew 2:1–11
Psalm 72:10,11	Presented with gifts	Matthew 2:1, 11
Psalm 72:16	The corn of wheat to fall into the Ground	John 12:24
Psalm 72:17	His name, Yinon, will produce offspring	John 1:12,13
Psalm 72:17	All nations shall be blessed by Him	Acts 2:11,12, 41
Psalm 78:1,2	He would teach in parables	Matthew 13:34–35
Psalm 78:2b	To speak the Wisdom of God with authority	Matthew 7:29
Psalm 88:8	They stood afar off and watched	Luke 23:49
Psalm 89:27	Emmanuel to be higher than earthly kings	Luke 1:32,33
Psalm 89:35–37	David's Seed, throne, kingdom endure forever	Luke 1:32,33
Psalm 89:36–37	His character:Faithfulness	Revelation 1:5
Psalm 90:2; Micah 5:2	He is from everlasting	John 1:1
Psalm 91:11,12	Identified as Messianic; used to tempt Christ	Luke 4; 10,11
Psalm 97:9	His exaltation predicted	Acts 1:11; Ephesians 1:20
Psalm 100:5	His character—Goodness	Matthew 19:16,17
Psalm 102:1–11	The Suffering and Reproach of Calvary	John 21:16–30
Psalm 102:25–27	Messiah is the Preexistent Son	Heb. 1:10–12
Psalm 109:25	Ridiculed	Matthew 27:39
Psalm 110:1	Son of David	Matthew 22:43

Psalm 110:1	To ascend to the right hand of the Father	Matthew 22:44; Mark 12:36;16:19; Luke 20:42–43; Acts 2:34–35; Hebrews 1:13
Psalm 110:1	David's son called Lord	Matthew 22:44,45
Psalm 110:4	A priest after Melchizedek's order	Hebrews 5:5–6; 6:20; 7:15–17
Psalm 112:4	His character—Compassionate, Gracious	Matthew 9:36
Psalm 118:17,18	His Resurrection assured	Luke 24:5–7; 1 Corinthians 15:20
Psalm 118:22,23	The rejected stone is Head of the corner	Matthew 21:42,43; 1 Peter 2:7
Psalm 118:26a	The Blessed One presented to Israel	Matthew 21:9
Psalm 118:26b	To come while Temple standing	Matthew 21:12–15
Psalm 132:11	The Seed of David (the fruit of His Body)	Luke 1:32
Psalm 138:1–6	The supremacy of David's Seed amazes kings	Matthew. 2:2–6
Psalm 147:3,6	The earthly ministry of Christ described	Luke 4:18
Psalm 1:23	He will send the Spirit of God	John 16:7
Song of Solomon 5:16	The altogether lovely One	John 1:17
Isaiah 6:1	When Isaiah saw His glory	John 12:40–41
Isaiah 6:9–10	Parables fall on deaf ears	Matthew 13:13–15
Isaiah 6:9–12	Blinded to Christ and deaf to His words	Acts. 28:23–29
Isaiah 7:14	To be born of a virgin	Luke 1:35
Isaiah 7:14	To be Emmanuel—God with us	Matthew 1:18–23
Isaiah 8:8	Called Emmanuel	Matthew 28:20
Isaiah 8:14	A stone of stumbling, a Rock of offense	1 Peter 2:8
Isaiah 9:1,2	His ministry to begin in Galilee	Matthew 4:12–17
Isaiah 9:6	A child born—Humanity	Luke 1:31
Isaiah 9:6	A Son given—Deity	Luke 1:32; John. 1:14; 1 Timothy 3:16
Isaiah 9:6	Declared to be the Son of God with power	Romans 1:3,4
Isaiah 9:6	The Wonderful One, Peleh	Luke 4:22
Isaiah 9:6	The Counsellor, Yaatz	Matthew 13:54
Isaiah 9:6	The Mighty God, El Gibor	Matthew 11:20

Isaiah 9:6	The Everlasting Father, Avi Adth	John 8:58, Matthew 1:23
Isaiah 9:6	The Prince of Peace, Sar Shalom	John 16:33
Isaiah 9:7	To establish an everlasting kingdom	Luke 1:32–33
Isaiah 9:7	His Character:Just	John 5:30
Isaiah 9:7	No end to his Government, Throne, and Peace	Luke 1:32–33
Isaiah 11:1	Called a Nazarene—the Branch, Netzer	Matthew 2:23
Isaiah 11:1	A rod out of Jesse—Son of Jesse	Luke 3:23,32
Isaiah 11:2	The anointed One by the Spirit	Matthew 3:16,17
Isaiah 11:2	His Character:Wisdom, Understanding, et al	John 4:4–26
Isaiah 11:4	His Character:Truth	John 14:6
Isaiah 11:10	The Gentiles seek Him	John 12:18–21
Isaiah 12:2	Called Jesus—Yeshua	Matthew 1:21
Isaiah 25:8	The Resurrection predicted	1 Corinthians 15:54
Isaiah 26:19	His power of Resurrection predicted	John 11:43, 44
Isaiah 28:16	The Messiah is the precious corner stone	Acts 4:11,12
Isaiah 29:13	People trust in traditions of men	Matthew 15:9
Isaiah 29:13	People give God lip service	Matthew 15:8
Isaiah 29:14	The wise are confounded by the Word	1 Corinthians 1:18–31
Isaiah 29:18	Heal blind/deaf/lame/dumb	Matthew 11:5
Isaiah 32:2	A Refuge—A man shall be a hiding place	Matthew 23:37
Isaiah 35:4	He will come and save you	Matthew 1:21
Isaiah 35:5	To have a ministry of miracles	Matthew 11:4–6
Isaiah 40:3, 4**	Preceded by forerunner	John 1:23; Matthew 3:3
Isaiah 40:9	*"Behold your God."*	John 1:36; 19:14
Isaiah 40:11	A shepherd, compassionate life-giver	John 10:10–18
Isaiah 42:1	God delights in Him	Matthew 3:17, 17:5
Isaiah 42:1–4	The Servant—a faithful, patient Redeemer	Matthew 12:18–21
Isaiah 42:2	Meek and lowly	Matthew 11:28–30
Isaiah 42:3	He brings hope for the hopeless	John 4
Isaiah 42:4	The nations shall wait on His teachings	John 12:20–26
Isaiah 42:6	The Light (salvation) of the Gentiles	Luke 2:32
Isaiah 42:1,6	His is a Worldwide compassion	Matthew 28:19,20

Isaiah 42:7	Blind eyes opened	John 9:25–38
Isaiah 43:11	He is the only Savior	Acts. 4:12
Isaiah 44:3	He will send the Spirit of God	John 16:7,13
Isaiah 45:23	He will be the Judge John 5:22;	Romans 14:11
Isaiah 48:12	The First and the Last	John 1:30; Revelation 1:8,17
Isaiah 48:17	He came as a Teacher	John 3:2
Isaiah 49:1	Called from the womb—His humanity	Matthew 1:18
Isaiah 49:5	A Servant from the womb	Luke 1:31; Philippians 2:7
Isaiah 49:6	He is Salvation for Israel	Luke 2:29–32
Isaiah 49:6	He is the Light of the Gentiles	Acts 13:47
Isaiah 49:6	He is Salvation unto the ends of the earth	Acts 15:7–18
Isaiah 49:7	He is despised of the Nation	John 8:48–49
Isaiah 50:3	Heaven is clothed in black at His humiliation	Luke 23:44,45
Isaiah 50:4	He is a learned counselor for the weary	Matthew 11:28,29
Isaiah 50:5	The Servant bound willingly to obedience	Matthew 26:39
Isaiah 50:6a	*"I gave my back to the smiters."*	Matthew 27:26
Isaiah 50:6b	He was smitten on the cheeks	Matthew 26:67
Isaiah 50:6c	He was spat upon	Matthew 27:30
Isaiah 52:7	To publish good tidings of peace	Luke 4:14,15
Isaiah 52:13	The Servant exalted	Acts 1:8–11; Ephesians 1:19–22
Isaiah 52:13	*"Behold, My Servant"*	Matthew 17:5; Philippians 2:5–8
Isaiah 52:14	The Servant shockingly abused	Luke 18:31–34; Matthew 26:67,68
Isaiah 52:15	Nations startled by message of the Servant	Romans 15:18–21
Isaiah 52:15	His blood shed to make atonement for all	Revelations 1:5
Isaiah 53:1	His people would not believe Him	John 12:37–38
Isaiah 53:2a	He would grow up in a poor family	Luke 2:7
Isaiah 53:2b	Appearance of an ordinary man	Philippians. 2:7–8
Isaiah 53:3	Despised	Luke 4:28–29
Isaiah 53:3a	Rejected	Matthew 27:21–23

Isaiah 53:3b	Rejected by His own	Matthew 21:42; Mark 8:31, 12:10; Luke 9:22, 17:25
Isaiah 53:3c	Great sorrow and grief	Luke 19:41–42
Isaiah 53:3d	Men hide from being associated with Him	Mark 14:50–52
Isaiah 53:4	He would have a healing ministry	Luke 6:17–19
Isaiah 53:4a	He would bear the sins of the world	1 Peter 2:24
Isaiah 53:4b	He bore our sickness	Matthew 8:16–17
Isaiah 53:4c	Thought to be cursed by God	Matthew. 27:41–43
Isaiah 53:5a	Bears penalty for mankind's transgressions	Luke 23:33; John 6:51
Isaiah 53:5b	His sacrifice...peace between man and God	Colossians 1:20
Isaiah 53:5c	His back would be whipped	Matthew 27:26
Isaiah 53:6a	He would be the sin-bearer for all mankind	Galatians 1:4
Isaiah 53:6b	God's will that He bear sin for all mankind	1 John. 4:10
Isaiah 53:7a	Oppressed and afflicted	Matthew 27:27–31
Isaiah 53:7b**	Silent before his accusers	Matthew 27:12–14
Isaiah 53:7c	Sacrificial lamb	John 1:29
Isaiah 53:8a	Confined and persecuted	Matthew 26:47–27:31
Isaiah 53:8b	He would be judged	John 18:13–22
Isaiah 53:8c	Killed	Matthew 27:35
Isaiah 53:8d	Dies for the sins of the world	1 John 2:2
Isaiah 53:9a	Buried in a rich man's grave	Matthew 27:57, 60
Isaiah 53:9b	Innocent and had done no violence	Mark 15:3
Isaiah 53:9c	No deceit in his mouth	John 18:38
Isaiah 53:10a	God's will that He die for mankind	John 18:11
Isaiah 53:10b.	An offering for sin	Matthew.20:28; Mark 10:45
Isaiah 53:10c	Resurrected and live forever	Mark 16:16
Isaiah 53:10d	He would prosper	John 17:1–5
Isaiah 53:11a	God fully satisfied with His suffering	John 12:27
Isaiah 53:11b	God's servant	Romans 5:18–19
Isaiah 53:11c	He would justify man before God	Romans 5:8–9
Isaiah 53:11d	The sin-bearer for all mankind	Hebrews 9:28
Isaiah 53:12a	Exalted by God because of his sacrifice	Matthew 28:18

Isaiah 53:12	He would give up his life to save mankind	Luke 23:46
Isaiah 53:12c	Grouped with criminals	Matthew 27:35; Luke 23:32
Isaiah 53:12d	Sin-bearer for all mankind	2 Corinthians 5:21
Isaiah 53:12e	Intercede to God in behalf of mankind	Luke 23:34
Isaiah 55:3	Resurrected by God	Acts 13:34
Isaiah 55:4	A witness	John. 18:37
Isaiah 59:15–16a	He would come to provide salvation	John 6:40
Isaiah 59:15–16b	Intercessor between man and God	Matthew 10:32
Isaiah 59:20	He would come to Zion as their Redeemer	Luke 2:38
Isaiah 61:1	Preached to the poor/brokenhearted/captives	Matthew 11:5
Isaiah 61:1–2a	The Spirit of God upon him	Matthew 3:16–17
Isaiah 61:1–2b	The Messiah would preach the good news	Luke 4:17–21
Isaiah 61:1–2c	Provide freedom from the bondage of sin and death	John 8:31–32
Isaiah 61:1–2d	Proclaim a period of grace	John 5:24
Jeremiah 23:5–6a	Descendant of David	Luke 3:23–31
Jeremiah 23:5–6b	The Messiah would be God.	John 13:13
Jeremiah 23:5–6c	The Messiah would be both God and Man	1 Timothy 3:16
Jeremiah 31:15	Slaughter of the children	Matthew 2:18
Jeremiah 31:22	Born of a virgin	Matthew 1:18–20
Jeremiah 31:31–34	The Messiah would be the new covenant	Matthew 26:28; Romans 11:27; Galatians 3:17, 4:24; Hebrew 8:6, 8,10; 10:16, 29; 12:24; 13:20
Jeremiah 33:14–15; Ezekiel 17:22–24, 34:23–24	Descendant of David	Luke 3:23–31; Matthew 1:1
Daniel 7:13–14a	He would ascend into heaven	Acts 1:9–11
Daniel 7:13–14b	Highly exalted	Ephesians 1:20–22
Daniel 7:13–14c	His dominion would be everlasting	Luke 1:31–33
Daniel 9:24a	To make an end to sins	Galatians 1:3–5
Daniel 9:24b	He would be holy	Luke 1:35
Daniel 9:25	Announced to his people 483 years *to the exact day*, after the decree to rebuild the city of Jerusalem	John 12:12–13
Daniel 9:26a	Killed	Matthew 27:35

Daniel 9:26b	Die for the sins of the world	Matthew 20:28; Hebrews 2:9
Daniel 9:26c	Killed before the destruction of the temple	Matthew 27:50–51
Daniel 10:5–6	Messiah in a glorified state	Revelations 1:13–16
Hosea 11:1	Called out of Egypt	Matthew 2:15
Hosea 13:14	He would defeat death	1 Corinthians 15:55–57
Joel 2:32	Offer salvation to all mankind	Romans 10:12–13
Amos 8:9	Darkness over the land	Matthew 27:45
Micah 5:2	His pre-existence	John 1:1, 14
Micah 5:2a**	Born in Bethlehem	Matthew 2:1–2
Micah 5:2b	God's servant	John 15:10
Micah 5:2c	From everlasting	John 8:58
Micah 7:6	Came to bring a sword, not peace	Matthew 10:34–35
Haggai 2:6–9	He would visit the second Temple	Luke 2:27–32
Haggai 2:23	Descendant of Zerubbabel	Luke 3:23–27
Zechariah 3:8	God's servant	John 17:4
Zechariah 6:12–13	Priest and King	Hebrew 8:1
Zechariah 9:9a	Greeted with rejoicing in Jerusalem	Matthew 21:8–10
Zechariah 9:9b	Beheld as King	John 12:12–13
Zechariah 9:9c	The Messiah would be just	John 5:30
Zechariah 9:9d	The Messiah would bring salvation	Luke 19:10
Zechariah 9:9e	The Messiah would be humble	Matthew 11:29
Zechariah 9:9f**	Presented to Jerusalem riding on a donkey	Matthew 21:6–9
Zechariah 10:4	The cornerstone	Ephesians 2:20
Zechariah 11:4–6a	At His coming, Israel to have unfit leaders	Matthew. 23:1–4
Zechariah 11:4–6b	Rejection causes God to remove His protection	Luke 19:41–44
Zechariah 11:4 6c	Rejected in favor of another king	John 19:13–15
Zechariah 11:7	Ministry to "poor," the believing remnant	Matthew 9:35–36
Zechariah 11:8a	Unbelief forces Messiah to reject them	Matthew 23:33
Zechariah 11:8b	Despised	Matthew 27:20
Zechariah 11:9	Stops ministering to the those who rejected Him	Matthew 13:10–11
Zechariah 11:10–11a	Rejection causes God to remove protection	Luke 19:41–44

Zechariah 11:10–11b	The Messiah would be God	John 14:7
Zechariah 11:11–12**	Betrayed for thirty pieces of silver	Matt. 26:14–15; Luke 22:5
Zechariah 11:12–13a	Rejected	Matthew 26:14–15
Zechariah 11:12–13b**	Thirty pieces of silver given for the potter's field thrown into the temple	Matthew 27:3–5, 9–10
Zechariah 11:12–13c	The Messiah would be God	John 12:45
Zechariah 12:10a	The Messiah's body would be pierced	John 19:34–37; John 20:25, 27
Zechariah 12:10b	The Messiah would be both God and man	John 10:30
Zechariah 12:10c	The Messiah would be rejected	John 1:11
Zechariah 13:7a	God's will He die for mankind	John 18:11
Zechariah 13:7b	A violent death	Matthew 27:35
Zechariah 13:7c	Both God and man	John 14:9
Zechariah 13:7d	Forsaken by His disciples	Matthew 26:56
Zechariah 13:7e	Israel scattered as a result of rejecting Him	Matthew 26:31–56
Malachi 3:1a	Messenger to prepare the way for Messiah	Matthew 11:10
Malachi 3:1b	Sudden appearance at the temple	Mark 11:15–16
Malachi 3:1c	Messenger of the new covenant	Luke 4:43
Malachi 3:2–3	His coming glory	Luke 3:17
Malachi 4:5	Forerunner in the spirit of Elijah	Matthew 3:1–2
Malachi 4:6	Forerunner would turn many to righteousness	Luke 1:16–17

REFERENCES

1A http://www.nypl.org/research/chss/jws/jewes, *The New York Public Library*, Research Libraries, Humanities and Social Sciences Library, Collections & Reading Rooms, Dorot Jewish Division, Jewes in America: "Conquistadors, Knickerbockers, Pilgrims, and the Hope of Israel" (Exhibition Guide), Source: Philipp van Limborch, *Historia Inquisitionis* [History of the Inquisition] (Amsterdam: H. Wetsteen, 1692), Dorot Jewish Division © 1995–2004 The New York Public Library, Astor, Lenox and Tilden Foundations.

1B Ibid.

1C http://www.nypl.org/research/chss/jws/jewes, *The New York Public Library*, Research Libraries, Humanities and Social Sciences Library, Collections & Reading Rooms, Dorot Jewish Division, Jewes in America: "Conquistadors, Knickerbockers, Pilgrims, and the Hope of Israel" (Exhibition Guide), Source: Christopher Columbus, *De Insula Inventis* [Regarding the Newfound Islands] (Basel: 1493), Rare Books Division © 1995–2004 The New York Public Library, Astor, Lenox and Tilden Foundations.

2 http://www.nypl.org/research/chss/jws/jewes, *The New York Public Library*, Research Libraries, Humanities and Social Sciences Library, Collections & Reading Rooms, Dorot Jewish Division, Jewes in America: "Conquistadors, Knickerbockers, Pilgrims, and the Hope of Israel" (Exhibition Guide), Source: Christopher Columbus, *Letter to Luis de Santangel*, Chancellor of Aragon (Barcelona: 1493), Rare Books Division, from Lenox Library © 1995–2004 The New York Public Library, Astor, Lenox and Tilden Foundations.

2 A http://www.nypl.org/research/chss/jws/jewes, *The New York Public Library*, Research Libraries, Humanities and Social Sciences Library, Collections & Reading Rooms, Dorot Jewish Division, Jewes in America: "Conquistadors, Knickerbockers, Pilgrims, and the Hope of Israel" (Exhibition Guide), Source: George Carleton, *A Thankfull Remembrance of God's Mercie (*London: Printed by Aug. Math[ewes] for Robert Mylbourne and Humphrey Robinson,1630), Rare Books Division © 1995–2004 The New York Public Library, Astor, Lenox and Tilden Foundations.

2B Ibid.

2C Ibid.

2D Ibid.

2E Shakespeare, Willliam, "Merchant of Venice," 1597 (New York: Penguin Putnam Inc., 2000) © 1959, Revised 1970 Penguin Books Inc. © 2000 Penguin Putnam Inc.

3 http://www.nypl.org/research/chss/jws/jewes, *The New York Public Library*, Research Libraries, Humanities and Social Sciences Library, Collections & Reading Rooms, Dorot Jewish Division, Jewes in America: "Conquistadors, Knickerbockers, Pilgrims, and the Hope of Israel" (Exhibition Guide), Source: *Genealogia of Captains Gaspar and Pardo Calderon de Mendoza* (Oaxaca: 1615), Manuscripts and Archives Division, HW Poole Collection © 1995–2004 The New York Public Library, Astor, Lenox and Tilden Foundations.

3A http://www.nypl.org/research/chss/jws/jewes, *The New York Public Library*, Research Libraries, Humanities and Social Sciences Library, Collections & Reading Rooms, Dorot Jewish Division, Jewes in America: "Conquistadors, Knickerbockers, Pilgrims, and the Hope of Israel" (Exhibition Guide), Source: Mathias de Bocanegra, *Auto General de la Fee* [Public Demonstration of Faith] (Mexico City: Antonio Calderon, 1649), Rare Books Division, from the Astor Library © 1995–2004 The New York Public Library, Astor, Lenox and Tilden Foundations.

4 http://www.nypl.org/research/chss/jws/jewes, *The New York Pub-*

lic Library, Research Libraries, Humanities and Social Sciences Library, Collections & Reading Rooms, Dorot Jewish Division, Jewes in America: "Conquistadors, Knickerbockers, Pilgrims, and the Hope of Israel" (Exhibition Guide), Source: Saul Levi Mortera, *Providencia de Dios con Ysrael, Verdad y Eternidad de la Ley de Moseh y Nulidad de las Demas Leies* [God's Providential Care for Israel, the Truth and Permanence of the Law of Moses, and the Nullity of Other Religions], Translated from the Portuguese by Moses Raphael d'Aguilar (rabbi in Recife, 1642–8) and copied by Solomon the Salonikan, Amsterdam, 1689, Dorot Jewish Division, Jack and Helen Nash Fund © 1995–2004 The New York Public Library, Astor, Lenox and Tilden Foundations.

5 Ibid.

6 http://www.nypl.org/research/chss/jws/jewes, *The New York Public Library*, Research Libraries, Humanities and Social Sciences Library, Collections & Reading Rooms, Dorot Jewish Division, Jewes in America: "Conquistadors, Knickerbockers, Pilgrims, and the Hope of Israel" (Exhibition Guide), Source: *Minutes of the Burgomasters and Schepens* (New Amsterdam: 1654), Municipal Archives of the City of New York © 1995–2004 The New York Public Library, Astor, Lenox and Tilden Foundations.

7 http://www.nypl.org/research/chss/jws/jewes, *The New York Public Library*, Research Libraries, Humanities and Social Sciences Library, Collections & Reading Rooms, Dorot Jewish Division, Jewes in America: "Conquistadors, Knickerbockers, Pilgrims, and the Hope of Israel" (Exhibition Guide), Source: Peter Stuyvesant, *Letter to West India Company Directors* (October 30, 1655), Manuscripts and Archives Division, Bontemantel Collection, New Netherland Papers © 1995–2004 The New York Public Library, Astor, Lenox and Tilden Foundations.

7A http://www.nypl.org/research/chss/jws/jewes, *The New York Public Library*, Research Libraries, Humanities and Social Sciences Library, Collections & Reading Rooms, Dorot Jewish Division, Jewes in America: "Conquistadors, Knickerbockers, Pilgrims, and the Hope of Israel" (Exhibition Guide), Source: Minutes of the Burgomasters and Schepens (New Amsterdam: 1656), Municipal Archives of the City of New York © 1995–2004 The New York Public Library, Astor, Lenox and Tilden Foundations.

8 http://www.nypl.org/research/chss/jws/jewes, *The New York Public Library*, Research Libraries, Humanities and Social Sciences Library, Collections & Reading Rooms, Dorot Jewish Division, Jewes in America: "Conquistadors, Knickerbockers, Pilgrims, and the Hope of Israel" (Exhibition Guide), Source: *Promulgation of the City of New Amsterdam* (1653, Copied by Jacob Kip, New Amsterdam, 1656), Manuscripts and Archives Division, Bontemantel Collection, New Netherland Papers © 1995–2004 The New York Public Library, Astor, Lenox and Tilden Foundations.

8A http://www.indians.org/welker/blackelk.htm, *Indians.org*, Indigenous People's Literature, Glenn Welker, "Black Elk: Holy Man of the Oglala Sioux (1863–1950)," Sources including: Greene, Carol, *Black Elk: A Man with a Vision* (Chicago: Children's Press, 1990); Neihardt, John G., *Black Elk Speaks, the life story of a beloved Holy Man of the Oglala Sioux* (1989); Turtle, Eagle Walking, *Keepers of the Fire, Journey to the Tree of Life, based on Black Elk's Vision* (1987).

8B http://www.sacred-texts.com/nam/iro/parker/coh1003.htm, *Sacred Texts*, Native American, Iroquois, Introduction: "Handsome Lake."

9 http://www.nypl.org/research/chss/jws/jewes, *The New York Public Library*, Research Libraries, Humanities and Social Sciences Library, Collections & Reading Rooms, Dorot Jewish Division, Jewes in America: "Conquistadors, Knickerbockers, Pilgrims, and the Hope of Israel" (Exhibition Guide), Source: Peter Stuyvesant, *Letter to West India Company Directors* (June 10, 1656), Manuscripts and Archives Division, Bontemantel Collection, New Netherland Papers © 1995–2004 The New York Public Library, Astor, Lenox and Tilden Foundations.

10 http://www.nypl.org/research/chss/jws/jewes, *The New York Public Library*, Research Libraries, Humanities and Social Sciences Library, Collections & Reading Rooms, Dorot Jewish Division, Jewes in America: "Conquistadors, Knickerbockers, Pilgrims, and the

Hope of Israel" (Exhibition Guide), Source: *New Netherland Council Report to West India Company Directors* (1657–8, July 23, 1658), Manuscripts and Archives Division, Bontemantel Collection, New Netherland Papers © 1995–2004 The New York Public Library, Astor, Lenox and Tilden Foundations.

11A http://www.nypl.org/research/chss/jws/jewes, *The New York Public Library*, Research Libraries, Humanities and Social Sciences Library, Collections & Reading Rooms, Dorot Jewish Division, Jewes in America: "Conquistadors, Knickerbockers, Pilgrims, and the Hope of Israel" (Exhibition Guide), Source: John Udall, *Mafteah Leshon Ha-kodesh, That is, The Key of the Holy Tongue (*Leiden: Frans van Ravelingen, 1593) © 1995–2004 The New York Public Library, Astor, Lenox and Tilden Foundations.

11B Ibid.

12 http://www.nypl.org/research/chss/jws/jewes, *The New York Public Library*, Research Libraries, Humanities and Social Sciences Library, Collections & Reading Rooms, Dorot Jewish Division, Jewes in America: "Conquistadors, Knickerbockers, Pilgrims, and the Hope of Israel" (Exhibition Guide), Source: John Cotton, *Abstract of the Lawes of New England As They are Now Established* (London: Printed for F. Coules and W. Ley, 1641), Rare Books Division © 1995–2004 The New York Public Library, Astor, Lenox and Tilden Foundations.

13 Ibid.

14 Ibid.

15 Ibid.

16 Ibid.

17A http://www.nypl.org/research/chss/jws/jewes, *The New York Public Library*, Research Libraries, Humanities and Social Sciences Library, Collections & Reading Rooms, Dorot Jewish Division, Jewes in America: "Conquistadors, Knickerbockers, Pilgrims, and the Hope of Israel" (Exhibition Guide), Source: Roger Williams, *The Bloudy Tenent of Persecution for Cause of Conscience* (London, 1644),

Rare Books Division, from the Lenox Library © 1995–2004 The New York Public Library, Astor, Lenox and Tilden Foundations.

17B Ibid.

18 Ibid.

19 http://www.nypl.org/research/chss/jws/jewes, *The New York Public Library*, Research Libraries, Humanities and Social Sciences Library, Collections & Reading Rooms, Dorot Jewish Division, Jewes in America: "Conquistadors, Knickerbockers, Pilgrims, and the Hope of Israel" (Exhibition Guide), Source: George Keith, *Truth Advanced in the Correction of Many Gross & Hurtful Errors,* (New York: William Bradford, 1694), Rare Books Division © 1995–2004 The New York Public Library, Astor, Lenox and Tilden Foundations.

20 Ibid.

21 http://www.nypl.org/research/chss/jws/jewes, *The New York Public Library*, Research Libraries, Humanities and Social Sciences Library, Collections & Reading Rooms, Dorot Jewish Division, Jewes in America: "Conquistadors, Knickerbockers, Pilgrims, and the Hope of Israel" (Exhibition Guide) re: *Benedictus de Spinoza, Iudeus et Atheista* [Benedict de Spinoza, Jew and Atheist] Etching, ca. 1700, Miriam and Ira D. Wallach Division of Art, Prints and Photographs, Print Collection © 1995–2004 The New York Public Library, Astor, Lenox and Tilden Foundations.

22 http://www.bartleby.com/cambridge, The Cambridge History of English and American Literature in 18 Volumes (1907–21), Volume III. Renascence and Reformation, XVIII, "Of the Laws of Ecclesiastical Polity." § 1. The Elizabethan settlement.

22A Ibid.

23 http://www.nypl.org/research/chss/jws/jewes, *The New York Public Library*, Research Libraries, Humanities and Social Sciences Library, Collections & Reading Rooms, Dorot Jewish Division, Jewes in America: "Conquistadors, Knickerbockers, Pilgrims, and the Hope of Israel" (Exhibition Guide) re: *IV Dollars* (Charleston: Printed by P[eter] Timothy, 1777), Rare Books Division ©

1995–2004 The New York Public Library, Astor, Lenox and Tilden Foundations.

24A http://www.nypl.org/research/chss/jws/jewes, *The New York Public Library*, Research Libraries, Humanities and Social Sciences Library, Collections & Reading Rooms, Dorot Jewish Division, Jewes in America: "Conquistadors, Knickerbockers, Pilgrims, and the Hope of Israel" (Exhibition Guide), Source: John Dury, *A Case of Conscience, Whether it be Lawful to Admit Jews into a Christian Common-wealth?* (London: Printed for Richard Wodenothe, 1656), Rare Books Division, Jacob Schiff Fund © 1995–2004 The New York Public Library, Astor, Lenox and Tilden Foundations.

24B Ibid.

25 http://www.nypl.org/research/chss/jws/jewes, *The New York Public Library*, Research Libraries, Humanities and Social Sciences Library, Collections & Reading Rooms, Dorot Jewish Division, Jewes in America: "Conquistadors, Knickerbockers, Pilgrims, and the Hope of Israel" (Exhibition Guide), Source: Samuel Hayne, *An Abstract of All the Statutes Made Concerning Aliens Trading in England*, (London: Printed by N.T. for the author, 1685), Rare Books Division © 1995–2004 The New York Public Library, Astor, Lenox and Tilden Foundations.

26A http://www.nypl.org/research/chss/jws/jewes, *The New York Public Library*, Research Libraries, Humanities and Social Sciences Library, Collections & Reading Rooms, Dorot Jewish Division, Jewes in America: "Conquistadors, Knickerbockers, Pilgrims, and the Hope of Israel" (Exhibition Guide), Source: William Penn, *The Frame of the Government of the Province of Pennsilvania in America,* (London: [William Bradford], 1682, First impression of the first edition), Rare Books Division, from the library of E. Dwight Church, Brooklyn © 1995–2004 The New York Public Library, Astor, Lenox and Tilden Foundations.

26B Ibid.

26C Ibid.

27A http://www.geocities.com/peterroberts.geo/Relig-Politics/USRelig.html, *God & Country—Religion and Politics in the US*, "Religious Views of the Founding Fathers, Presidents, and Vice-Presidents."

27B Ibid.

27C Ibid.

27D Ibid.

27E Ibid.

27F Ibid.

27G Ibid.

27H Ibid.

28A http://www.nypl.org/research/chss/jws/jewes, *The New York Public Library*, Research Libraries, Humanities and Social Sciences Library, Collections & Reading Rooms, Dorot Jewish Division, Jewes in America: "Conquistadors, Knickerbockers, Pilgrims, and the Hope of Israel" (Exhibition Guide), Source: *The Constitution of the State of New-York, (*Fishkill, NY: Printed by Samuel Loudon, 1777 First impression of the first edition), Rare Books Division © 1995–2004 The New York Public Library, Astor, Lenox and Tilden Foundations.

28B Ibid.

28C Ibid.

28D Ibid.

28E http://www.nypl.org/research/chss/jws/jewes, *The New York Public Library*, Research Libraries, Humanities and Social Sciences Library, Collections & Reading Rooms, Dorot Jewish Division, Jewes in America: "Conquistadors, Knickerbockers, Pilgrims, and the Hope of Israel" (Exhibition Guide), Source: George Bush, *The Valley of Vision, or, The Dry Bones of Israel Revived (*New York: Saxton & Miles, 1844), Dorot Jewish Division © 1995–2004 The New York Public Library, Astor, Lenox and Tilden Foundations.

28F Ibid.

28G http://www.nypl.org/research/chss/jws/jewes, *The New York Public Library*, Research Libraries, Humanities and Social Sciences Library, Collections & Reading Rooms, Dorot Jewish Division, Jewes in America: "Conquistadors, Knickerbockers, Pilgrims, and the Hope of Israel" (Exhibition Guide), Source: *The Constitution of the State of New-York (*Fishkill, NY: Printed by Samuel Loudon, 1777 First impression of the first edition), Rare Books Division © 1995–2004 The New York Public Library, Astor, Lenox and Tilden Foundations.

29 http://www.nypl.org/research/chss/jws/jewes, *The New York Public Library*, Research Libraries, Humanities and Social Sciences Library, Collections & Reading Rooms, Dorot Jewish Division, Jewes in America: "Conquistadors, Knickerbockers, Pilgrims, and the Hope of Israel" (Exhibition Guide), Source: *An Act to Permit Persons Professing the Jewish Religion, to be Naturalized by Parliament (*Edinburgh: John Basket, 1753), Dorot Jewish Division, Jack and Helen Nash Fund © 1995–2004 The New York Public Library, Astor, Lenox and Tilden Foundations.

30 http://www.nypl.org/research/chss/jws/jewes, *The New York Public Library*, Research Libraries, Humanities and Social Sciences Library, Collections & Reading Rooms, Dorot Jewish Division, Jewes in America: "Conquistadors, Knickerbockers, Pilgrims, and the Hope of Israel" (Exhibition Guide), Source: *Lista das Pessoas* [List of Names] (Lisbon, 1747), Dorot Jewish Division, Jack and Helen Nash Fund © 1995–2004 The New York Public Library, Astor, Lenox and Tilden Foundations.

31A http://www.sims.berkeley.edu:8000/courses/is182/s02/first13.html, George Keith, "New-England's spirit of persecution" (New York: 1693).

31B http://www.nypl.org/research/chss/jws/jewes, *The New York Public Library*, Research Libraries, Humanities and Social Sciences Library, Collections & Reading Rooms, Dorot Jewish Division, Jewes in America: "Conquistadors, Knickerbockers, Pilgrims, and the

Hope of Israel" (Exhibition Guide), Source: George Keith, *Truth Advanced in the Correction of Many Gross & Hurtful Errors (*New York: William Bradford, 1694), Rare Books Division © 1995–2004 by The New York Public Library, Astor, Lenox and Tilden Foundations.

31C http://www.answers.com/topic/william-bradford-1663–1752, *Answers.com*, William Bradford, Source: *Wikipedia Encyclopedia,* William Bradford, GNU Free Documentation License.

32A http://www.nypl.org/research/chss/jws/jewes, *The New York Public Library*, Research Libraries, Humanities and Social Sciences Library, Collections & Reading Rooms, Dorot Jewish Division, Jewes in America: "Conquistadors, Knickerbockers, Pilgrims, and the Hope of Israel" (Exhibition Guide), Source: *An Act to Permit Persons Professing the Jewish Religion, to be Naturalized by Parliament, (*Edinburgh: John Basket, 1753), Dorot Jewish Division, Jack and Helen Nash Fund © 1995–2004 The New York Public Library, Astor, Lenox and Tilden Foundations.

32B Ibid.

32C Ibid.

33 http://www.nypl.org/research/chss/jws/jewes, *The New York Public Library*, Research Libraries, Humanities and Social Sciences Library, Collections & Reading Rooms, Dorot Jewish Division, Jewes in America: "Conquistadors, Knickerbockers, Pilgrims, and the Hope of Israel" (Exhibition Guide), Source: *An Earnest and Serious Address to the Freeholders and Electors of Great-Britain, on the Occasion of the Clamor Raised Against the Bill to Permit Persons to Apply for Naturalization, Professing the Jewish Religion (*London: Printed for R. Baldwin, 1753), Dorot Jewish Division, Jack and Helen Nash Fund © 1995–2004 The New York Public Library, Astor, Lenox and Tilden Foundations.

34 http://www.nypl.org/research/chss/jws/jewes, *The New York Public Library*, Research Libraries, Humanities and Social Sciences Library, Collections & Reading Rooms, Dorot Jewish Division, Jewes in America: "Conquistadors, Knickerbockers, Pilgrims, and the

Hope of Israel" (Exhibition Guide), Source: Joseph I, King of Portugal, *Dom José* [Proclamation of King Joseph] (Lisbon, 1774), Dorot Jewish Division, Gift of Jack and Helen Nash © 1995–2004 The New York Public Library, Astor, Lenox and Tilden Foundations.

35A http://www.nypl.org/research/chss/jws/jewes, *The New York Public Library*, Research Libraries, Humanities and Social Sciences Library, Collections & Reading Rooms, Dorot Jewish Division, Jewes in America: "Conquistadors, Knickerbockers, Pilgrims, and the Hope of Israel" (Exhibition Guide), Source: Arnold Fischel, *Letter to Joshua Cohen* (New York: October 29, 1860), Dorot Jewish Division, Jack and Helen Fund © 1995–2004 The New York Public Library, Astor, Lenox and Tilden Foundations.

35B Ibid.

35C Ibid.

36 http://www.nypl.org/research/chss/jws/jewes, *The New York Public Library*, Research Libraries, Humanities and Social Sciences Library, Collections & Reading Rooms, Dorot Jewish Division, Jewes in America: "Conquistadors, Knickerbockers, Pilgrims, and the Hope of Israel" (Exhibition Guide), Source: Leicester Stanhope, Earl of Harrington, *Jews Bill as Amended on Report* (London, 1858), Dorot Jewish Division, Jack and Helen Nash Fund © 1995–2004 The New York Public Library, Astor, Lenox and Tilden Foundations.

37A http://www.nypl.org/research/chss/jws/jewes, *The New York Public Library*, Research Libraries, Humanities and Social Sciences Library, Collections & Reading Rooms, Dorot Jewish Division, Jewes in America: "Conquistadors, Knickerbockers, Pilgrims, and the Hope of Israel" (Exhibition Guide), Source: James Monroe, "Notes on a Constitution for France" (Paris, 1795), Manuscripts and Archives Division, Monroe Papers © 1995–2004 The New York Public Library, Astor, Lenox and Tilden Foundations.

37B Ibid.

37C http://www.nypl.org/research/chss/jws/jewes, *The New York Public Library*, Research Libraries, Humanities and Social Sciences Library, Collections & Reading Rooms, Dorot Jewish Division, Jewes in America: "Conquistadors, Knickerbockers, Pilgrims, and the Hope of Israel" (Exhibition Guide) re: M.M. Noah, Drawn by J.R. Smith and engraved by Thomas Gimbrede for Noah's *Travels,* (New York: Kirk and Mercein, 1819), Dorot Jewish Division, Jack and Helen Nash Fund © 1995–2004 The New York Public Library, Astor, Lenox and Tilden Foundations.

38 http://www.nypl.org/research/chss/jws/jewes, *The New York Public Library*, Research Libraries, Humanities and Social Sciences Library, Collections & Reading Rooms, Dorot Jewish Division, Jewes in America: "Conquistadors, Knickerbockers, Pilgrims, and the Hope of Israel" (Exhibition Guide), Source: Judah P. Benjamin, *Letter to Thomas O. Moore* (Richmond, October 13, 1861), Dorot Jewish Division, Jack and Helen Nash Fund © 1995–2004 The New York Public Library, Astor, Lenox and Tilden Foundations.

39A http://www.liu.edu/cwis/cwp/library/period/~sylvest.htm, Long Island University, C.W. Post Campus, B. Davis Schwartz Memorial Library, Sources including: *The African American: A Journey from Slavery to Freedom; African American Freedom Fighters: Soldiers For Liberty; African Americans and the Old West; African Americans: Books and Personalities; African Americans in Motion Pictures: The Past and the Present; African Americans in the Sports Arena; African Americans in the Twentieth Century: Historical Events, Personalities, and Milestones, 1900–2000; African Americans in the Visual Arts: A Historical Perspective; Langston Hughes: Understanding the Man, His Works, and His Legacy; Lynchings in America: A History Not Known by Many; Negro Periodicals in the United States: 1827–1960; A Tribute to Dr. Martin Luther King, Jr.*

39B Ibid.

40A http://www.mamiwata.com/history.html, Mami Wata Yeveh Vodoun: Celebrating the Resurrected Spiritual Heritage of the Diaspora, Vodoun ("Voodoo"), The Religious Practices of Southern Slaves in America, Mamaissii "Zogbe" Vivian Hunter-Hindrew, Hounon Amengansie, M. Ed., "A History of Persecution and Suppression" © 2000–2005 Mamaissii "Zogbe" Vivian Hunter-Hindrew, Hounon Amengansie.

40B Ibid.

41A http://www.mamiwata.com/slavery2.html, *Mami Wata Yeveh Vodoun: Celebrating the Resurrected Spiritual Heritage of the Diaspora,* Prof. Terry Matthews, Adjunct Asst. Prof. Wake Forrest University, "The Religion of the Slaves" © 2000–2005 Mamaissii "Zogbe" Vivian Hunter-Hindrew, Hounon Amengansie.

41B Ibid.

41C Ibid.

42 http://www.bartleby.com/66/63/26563.html, *Columbia World of Quotations*: Hamer, Fannie Lou, 1996.

43A http://www.simpletoremember.com/vitals/HistoryJewishPersecution.htm, *SimpleToRemember.com*, Jewish Persecution, Timeline of Judaism, History of AntiSemitism, " Lesser Known Highlights of Jewish International Relations In The Common Era (an Abbreviated sampling)," Source: P.E. Grosser & E.G. Halperin, Anti-Semitism: Causes and Effects. (New York: Philosophical Library, 1978).

43B http://www.aish.com/tishaBavOverview/tishaBavOverviewDefault/Destruction_on_the_Tenth_of_Av.asp, *Aish.com*, Tisha B'Av & the Three Weeks, Overview & Laws, Larry Domnitch, "Destruction on the 10 of Av" © 1995–2007 Aish HaTorah.

43C http://www.aish.com/tishaBavAntisemitism/tishaBavAntisemitismDefault/The_Final_Solution_on_Tisha_Bav.asp, *Aish.com*, Tisha B'Av & the Three Weeks, Antisemitism and Suffering, Yaakov Astor, "The Final Solution on Tisha B'Av" © 1995–2007 Aish HaTorah.

43D http://www.aish.com/literacy/jewishhistory/Crash_Course_in_Jewish_History_Part_46_-_Blood_Libel.asp, *Aish.com*, Jewish Literacy, Jewish History, Rabbi Ken Spiro, "Crash Course in Jewish History #46: Blood Libel," September 30, 2001 © 1995–2007 Aish HaTorah.

43E http://www.ou.org/about/judaism/bhyom/nov.htm, *Orthodox Union (OU)*, This Day in Jewish History, "November 1 [1210]" © 2007 Orthodox Union.

43F http://www.heretical.com/British/jews1290.html, *Heretical.co.uk*, Geoffrey H. Smith and Arnold S. Leese, "The Edict of Expulsion of 1290."

43G Ibid.

43H Ibid.

43I http://www.british-history.ac.uk/report.asp?compid=45055, *British History Online*, Old Jewry; Source: Old and New London: Volume 1, Chapter XXXVII, pp. 423–435, "Old Jewry" (1878) © 2003–2007 University of London & History of Parliament Trust.

44 http://academic.csuohio.edu/perloffr/lynching/, *The Press and Lynchings of African Americans,* Richard M. Perloff, Professor of Communications, Cleveland University, (Summary of "The Press and Lynchings of African Americans" from *Journal of Black Studies,* pp. 315–330, January 2000).

45A http://users.erols.com/mwhite28/warstat0.htm#20worst . *Twentieth Century Atlas - Historical Body Count.* "Selected Death Tolls for Wars, Massacres and Atrocities Before the 20th Century: Crusades (1095–1291)."

45B Ibid.

45C Ibid.

46 http://www.trestlegroup.com, *Trestle Group*, "Trestle Group Hosts 2nd Financial Services Outsourcing Roundtable in London, UK."

47 http://www.gprep.org/music/musikbok/chap18.html, Gary Daum, "Music: A User's Guide for the Beginner."

48 http://www.150.si.edu/150trav/remember/amerinv.htm, *American Inventors and Inventions.*

49 Ibid.

50 Ibid.

51 Ibid.

52 http://www.enchantedlearning.com/inventors/black.shtml, *African American Inventors.*

53 http://www.singermemories.com/singer-empire.html, *Singer Memor*ies.

54 http://library.thinkquest.org/CR0215480/skyscraper1.htm, *ORACLE ThinkQuest Education Foundation*, Chicago History: "The First Skyscraper" © 2002 ThinkQuest USA.

55 http://www.angelfire.com/ga2/Andersonvilleprison, *Andersonville Civil War Prison.*

56 http://www.censusdiggins.com/civil_war_prisons.html, *Civil War Prison Camps.*

57 http://www.lib.utah.edu/spc/photo/9066/9066.htm , *Japanese-Americans Internment Camps During World War II.*

58 http://www.achievement.org/autodoc/page/sa10bio-1, *Academy of Achievement*, Jonas Salk, MD Biography.

59 http://nfo.net/usa/etymol.html, The Great American Big Bands: Jazz Etymology.

60 http://www.cbmr.org/styles/jazz.htm, *Center for Black Music Research.*

61 http://en.wikipedia.org/wiki/Roots_of_hip_hop_music, *Wikipedia Encyclopedia,* "Roots of Hip Hop," GNU Free Documentation License.

62A http://www.now.org/issues/economic/welfare/072604tanf.html, *NOW*, Rachel Weisshaar, Truth-Telling About Welfare: "As Senate Votes to Temporarily Extend TANF, Expert Panel Advises Lawmakers to Address Challenges that Face Low-Income Women and Children," July 26, 2004.

62B Ibid.

63 Ibid.

64 Ibid.

65 www.thetruthaboutgeorge.com/economy/index.html, *National Organization for Women (NOW)*, The Truth About George, Source: www.nwlc.org/pdf/womentax2.pdf, National Women's Law Center, "Women and Children Last: The Bush Tax Cut Plan," March 5, 2001.

66 www.thetruthaboutgeorge.com/economy/index.html, *National Organization for Women (NOW)*, The Truth About George, Source: Center on Budget and Policy Priorities, Joel Friedman, Robert Greenstein, and Richard Kogan, "The Administration's Proposal to Make the Tax Cut Permanent," February 4, 2002 © 2002–2005.

67 http://pqasb.pqarchiver.com/washingtonpost/access/341257801.html?dids-341257801:3412, *Washington Post*, Dana Milbank, "Bush Signs $350 Billion Tax Cut Measure," May 29, 2003 © The Washington Post Company.

68 www.thetruthaboutgeorge.com/economy/index.html, *National Organization for Women (NOW)*, The Truth About George, Sources: Center on Budget and Policy Priorities, "Administration Budget Includes Additional Health Tax Cuts That Primarily Benefit Higher-Income Individuals," and Edwin Park, "Health Proposals in Administration's Budget Could Weaken the Employer-Based Health Insurance System," February 5, 2002 © 2002–2005.

69 http://pqasb.pqarchiver.com/washingtonpost/access/238997341.html?dids=238997341:2389, *Washington Post*, Dana Milbank, "This Time a Bush Embraces 'Voodoo Economics' Theory," November 14, 2002 © The Washington Post Company.

70 http://www.afscme.org/action/fy2006.htm, *LEGISLATIVE ACTION*, Homepage of American Federation of State, County and Municipal Employees (AFSCME), February 8, 2005.

71 Ibid.

72A Ibid.

72B Ibid.

73 Ibid.

74 Ibid.

75 Ibid.

76 Ibid.

77 Ibid.

78 Ibid.

79A Ibid.

79B Ibid.

80A http://www.nypl.org/research/chss/jws/jewes, *The New York Public Library*, Research Libraries, Humanities and Social Sciences Library, Collections & Reading Rooms, Dorot Jewish Division, Jewes in America: "Conquistadors, Knickerbockers, Pilgrims, and the Hope of Israel" (Exhibition Guide), Source: John Locke, *The Fundamental Constitutions of Carolina* (London, 1682, 1669 edition reprinted in 1682, with manuscript revisions in Locke's hand for the revised constitution promulgated that year), Rare Books Division © 1995–2004 The New York Public Library, Astor, Lenox and Tilden Foundations.

80B http://www.afscme.org/action/fy2006.htm, *LEGISLATIVE ACTION,* Homepage of American Federation of State, County and Municipal Employees (AFSCME), February 8, 2005.

81 http://www.nypl.org/research/chss/jws/jewes, *The New York Public Library*, Research Libraries, Humanities and Social Sciences Library, Collections & Reading Rooms, Dorot Jewish Division, Jewes in America: "Conquistadors, Knickerbockers, Pilgrims, and the Hope of Israel" (Exhibition Guide) re: Samuel Sewall ae[tate] 77, 1728 [Samuel Sewall, aged 77, 1728], Drawn by H. Emmons; steel engraving by Oliver Pelton, Boston, 19th century, Miriam and Ira D. Wallach Division of Art, Prints and Photographs, Print Collec-

tion © 1995–2004 The New York Public Library, Astor, Lenox and Tilden Foundations.

82 http://www.nypl.org/research/chss/jws/jewes, *The New York Public Library*, Research Libraries, Humanities and Social Sciences Library, Collections & Reading Rooms, Dorot Jewish Division, Jewes in America: "Conquistadors, Knickerbockers, Pilgrims, and the Hope of Israel" (Exhibition Guide), Source: *Lista das Pessoas* [List of Names] (Lisbon: 1747), Dorot Jewish Division, Jack and Helen Nash Fund © 1995–2004 The New York Public Library, Astor, Lenox and Tilden Foundations.

83 http://www.personal.psu.edu/users/a/m/amw288, Andrew M. Wrzosek, "The '*Auto de Fe*' of Madrid in 1680" © 1995–2004 The New York Public Library, Astor, Lenox and Tilden Foundations.

84 http://pqasb.pqarchiver.com/washington post/access/737253991.html?dids=737253991:7372, Editorial Board, *Washington Post*, "Soaring Ceilings," November 17, 2004 © The Washington Post Company.

85 http://www.thetruthaboutgeorge.com/economy/index.html?printable=yes, The Truth About George: Economy, "Bush Attempts to Give Tax Breaks Worth Hundreds of Millions to Corporatioons," Source: Citizens For Tax Justice, Corporate Annual Reports © 1995–2006 National Organization for Women.

86 www.thetruthaboutgeorge.com/economy/index.html, *National Organization for Women (NOW)*, The Truth About George, "The Administration Refuses to Support Unemployed Workers and Their Families," Source: *Gannett News Service*, Brian Tumulty, "Senate Panel Considers Renewal of Extended Jobless Benefits," September 12, 2002 © 1995–2006 National Organization for Women.

87 Rogers, Will, "Breaking into the Writing Game," *Illiterate Digest* (1924).

88 www.trestlegroup.com, *Trestle Group*, Trestle Group Hosts 2nd Financial Services Outsourcing Roundtable in London, UK.

89 www.ecdpm.org, *ECDPM 2004*, InfoCotonou No. 6: Taking culture seriously, Maastricht.

90 www.etherzone.com, *Ether Zone*, Ted Lang, "Another United Way Scandal—Disillusionment with the Welfare State"

91 http://www.thetruthaboutgeorge.com/economy/index.html, *National Organization for Women (NOW)*, The Truth About George, "Bush Administration Fails to Jumpstart Economy," Source: Jenna Churchman, *Center for American Progress*, Economic Policy Weekly, June 6, 2005 © 1995–2006 National Organization for Women.

92 www.the truthaboutgeorge.com/economy/index.html, *National Organization for Women (NOW)*, The Truth About George, Source: *Boston Globe*, "Boom and Bust," November 9, 2003 © 1995–2006 National Organization for Women.

93 "Poverty, Gender and Human Trafficking in Sub-Saharan Africa: Rethinking Best Practices in Migration Management" by Thanh-Dam Truong © UNESCO 2006.

94A http://www.globalchange.umich.edu/globalchange2/current/lectures/dev_pov/dev_pov.html, *Development and Poverty*, January 4, 2006.

94B Ibid.

95 http://www.monitor.upeace.org/archive.cfm?id_article=313, University for Peace, *Peace & Conflict Monitor*, Benjamin Hess, Measuring Poverty, October 21, 2005.

96 http://www.5clir.org/Slavery.htm, *SLAVERY AND ITS LEGACY—A Series of Symposia Focusing on Black Slavery and Its Consequences for Our Times*, "The Residue of Slavery and Jim Crow In the Black Family: the Bad and the Good"; Moderator: Henry Thomas III, CEO, Springfield Urban League; Speakers Mary Hall, Smith College School for Social Work, Rev. Dr. Howard-John Wesley, St. John's Congregational Church, and Peter Brandon, Sociology, UMass.; March 30, 2005.

97 http://www.5clir.org/Slavery.htm, *SLAVERY AND ITS LEGA-*

CY—A Series of Symposia Focusing on Black Slavery and Its Consequences for Our Times, "Challenges of Black Economic Development: Discrimination and Access Issues; Moderator: Henry Thomas III, CEO, Springfield Urban League; Speakers: Joyce Everett, Smith College School for Social Work, Glenn Davis, Springfield Urban League, Dean Robinson, Political Science, UMass Amherst; March 23, 2005.

98 http://www.5clir.org/Slavery.htm, *SLAVERY AND ITS LEGACY—A Series of Symposia Focusing on Black Slavery and Its Consequences for Our Times*, "Slavery's Legacy: The Permanence of Racism in American Life;" Speaker Derrick Bell, NYU Law School; April 7, 2005.

99 Patrick Henry, Speech at Virginia Convention, March 1775.

100 http://news.nationalgeographic.com/news/2003/01/0131_030203_jubilee2.html, *National Geographic News*, Howard Dodson, "How Slavery Helped Build a World Economy," second in a series of five excerpts from *Jubilee: The Emergence of African American Culture* by the Schomburg Center for Research in Black Culture of the New York Public Library (National Geographic Books 2003), January 31, 2003.

101 http://news.nationalgeographic.com/news/2003/02/0205_030205_jubilee4_2.html, *National Geographic News*, Howard Dodson, "America's Cultural Roots Traced to Enslaved African Ancestors," fourth in a series of five excerpts from *Jubilee: The Emergence of African American Culture* by the Schomburg Center for Research in Black Culture of the New York Public Library (National Geographic Books 2003), February 5, 2003.

102 http://www.siecus.org/policy/PUpdates/pdate0100.html, *Sexuality Information & Education Council of the United States (SIECUS)*, "Policy & Advocacy–Update April 2004," Sources including: President's Emergency Plan for AIDS Relief: The U.S. Five-Year Strategy to Fight Global HIV/AIDS, pages 9, 23–24; "Uganda Reverses the Tide of HIV/AIDS," World Health Organization; "Senate Foreign Relations Subcommittee 'Praises' Uganda's 'ABC' HIV/AIDS

Prevention Method at Hearing," Kaiser Daily HIV/AIDS Report, May 21, 2003.

103 http://en.wikipedia.org/wiki/Situational_ethics, *Wikipedia Encyclopedia,* Situational Ethics, GNU Free Documentation License.

104 Ibid.

105 McBride, James, *The Color of Water: A Black Man's Tribute To His White Mother* (Riverhead: The Berkeley Publishing Group, 1996) © James McBride.

106 Makinson, Larry, *Speaking Freely: Washington Insiders Talk About Money in Politics,* February 20, 2003.

107A http://www.opensecrets.org/orgs/index.asp, *Center for Responsive Politics.*

107B http://www.opensecrets.org/orgs/list.asp?order=A, *Center for Responsive Politics,* Top All-Time Donor Profiles.

108A http://www.concordcoalition.org/issues/socsec/index.html, The Concord Coalition, Social Security, "Social Security's Longterm Imbalance."

108B http://www.concordcoalition.org/issues/socsec/issue-briefs/SS-Brief1-CantWaitForACrisis.htm, *Concord Coalition*, Social Security Reform, Issue #1, "Reform Should Not Wait for a Crisis" (March 4, 2005).

108C http://www.concordcoalition.org/issues/socsec/issue-briefs/SS-Brief2-TrustFundCan'tMaskProblem.htm, *The Concord Coalition,* Social Security Reform, Issue #2,"Social Security's Trust Funds Mask the Problem" (March 11, 2005).

108D http://www.concordcoalition.org/issues/socsec/issue-briefs/SS-Brief5—IncreaseNationalSavings.htm, *Concord Coalition*, Social Security Reform, Issue #5, "A Real Fix for Social Security Requires an Increase in National Saving" (April 13, 2005).

108E Ibid.

108F Ibid.

108G http://www.concordcoalition.org/facing-facts/FacingFactsQuarterly1–1.pdf, *Concord Coalition*, Facing Facts Quarterly, Vol. 1, #1, pp.2–3, A Report About Entitlements & the Budget from the Concord Coalition, "The Real Problem with the President's Social Security Plan," March 2005.

109A www.prisonfellowship.org, *Prison Fellowship.*

109B Ibid.

109C Ibid.

109D Ibid.

109E Nolan, Pat, Foreword by Colson, Chuck, *When Prisoners Return* © 2004 Prison Fellowship.

110A White, Dr. Tom, "The Gospel—Winning the War on Terror," *The Voice of the Martyrs*, Special Issue 2006.

110B *The Voice of the Martyrs,* Country Summaries, Special Issue 2006; February 2006; and December 2005.

110 C http://www.nationalreview.com/comment/shea_rayis200501060730.asp, *National Review Online*, Nina Shea and James Y. Rayis, Christian Crisis: "ChaldoAssyrian Christians may soon leave Iraq en masse," January 6, 2005.

111A http://www.washingtonpost.com/wp-dyn/content/linkset/2005/04/11/LI2005041100879.html, *WashingtonPost.com–White House Briefing*, Dan Froomkin, "Questions of Credibility," February 10, 2006.

111B Ibid.

111C Ibid.

111D Ibid.

111E Ibid.

111F Ibid.

111G Ibid.

111H Ibid.

111I Ibid.

111J Ibid.

111K Ibid.

111L Ibid.

111M Ibid.

111N Ibid.

111O Ibid.

111P Ibid.

112A http://www.firstamendmentcenter.org/rel_liberty/establishment/topic.aspx?topic=public_displays, *First Amendment Center*, Hon. Avern L. Cohn, Senior District Judge and Bryan J. Anderson, Contributing Writer, "Ten Commandments, Other Displays & Mottos," January 17, 2006.

112B Ibid.

112C Ibid.

112D Ibid.

112E Ibid.

112F Ibid.

112G Ibid.

112H Ibid.

112I Ibid.

112J http://www.firstamendmentcenter.org/analysis.aspx?id=15483, *First Amendment Center*, Tony Mauro, "Context is key to sorting out Commandments rulings," June 28, 2005.

113 http://www.mnsu.edu/emuseum/information/biography/klmno/mendel_gregor.html, Gregor Mendel.

114 http://www-groups.dcs.st-and.ac.uk/~history/Mathematicians/Pascal.html, Blaise Pascal.

115 http://www.iep.utm.edu/a/aquinas.htm, The Internet Encyclopedia of Philosophy, "Thomas Aquinas."

116 http://www.newton.cam.ac.uk/newtlife.html, *Isaac Newton Institute for Mathematical Sciences,* "Isaac Newton's Life."

117 http://en.wikipedia.org/wiki/James_Clerk_Maxwell, *Wikipedia Encyclopedia*, "James Maxwell," GNU Free Documentation License.

118 http://en.wikipedia.org/wiki/William_Thomson%2C_1st_Baron_Kelvin, *Wikipedia Encyclopedia,* "William Thomson, 1st Baron Kelvin," GNU Free Documentation License.

119 http://en.wikipedia.org/wiki/Roger_Bacon, *Wikipedia Encyclopedia,* "Roger Bacon," GNU Free Documentation License.

120 http://en.wikipedia.org/wiki/Johannes_Kepler, *Wikipedia Encyclopedia,* "Johannes Kepler," GNU Free Documentation License.

121 http://en.wikipedia.org/wiki/Robert_Boyle, *Wikipedia Encyclopedia,* "Robert Boyle," GNU Free Documentation License

122 http://en.wikipedia.org/wiki/George_Washington_Carver, *Wikipedia Encyclopedia,* "George Washington Carver," GNU Free Documentation License.

123 http://en.wikipedia.org/wiki/Georges_Lemaitre, *Wikipedia Encyclopedia,* "Georges Lemaitre," GNU Free Documentation License.

124 http://galileo.rice.edu/sci/instruments/telescope.html, *The Galileo Project*, *Rice University*, "The Telescope."

125 http://galileo.rice.edu/sci/theories/ptolemaic_system.html, *The Galileo Project*, *Rice University*, "The Ptolemaic System."

126 http://galileo.rice.edu/bio/tov.html#inquisition, *The Galileo Project*, *Rice University*, "The Inquisition."

127A http://www.sciencemag.org/cgi/content/full/282/5396/1985, *Science,* Vol. 282. no. 5396, pp. 1985–1986; DOI: 10.1126/science.282.5396.1985; Essays On Science and Society, John Brooke, former Professor of History, Lancaster University, now Andreas Idreos Professor Emeritus of Science & Religion, Oxford University, "Science and Religion: Lessons from History?" December 11, 1998.

127B Ibid.

128A http://www.talkorigins.org/faqs/dover/kitzmiller_v_dover_decision.html, Kitzmiller, et al. v. Dover Area School District, Decision of the Court.

128B Ibid.

128C Ibid.

128D Ibid.

128E Ibid.

128F Ibid.

128G Ibid.

129 http://www.intelligentdesignnetwork.org/Press%20Release%20122105%20final%20.pdf, *ID Net, Intelligent Design network, inc.,* News Release: "Dover Court Establishes State Materialism," December 20, 2005.

130 http://www.geocities.com/Heartland/2964/darwin-trial.html, *Darwin on Trial* , Phillip E. Johnson (1991, Regnery Gateway, Washington, D.C.).

131 http://www.geocities.com/Heartland/2964/sagan.html, *Simple Catholicism*, Fr. Phil Bloom, Pastor, Holy Family Church, Seattle, Washington, "The Moral Law: A Response to Carl Sagan."

132A Ibid.

132B http://www.geocities.com/Heartland/2964/sagan.html, *Simple Catholicism*, Fr. Phil Bloom, Pastor, Holy Family Church, Seattle, Washington, "The Moral Law: A Response to Carl Sagan," Source: William Shakespeare, "Hamlet."

133A http://en.wikipedia.org/wiki/Institut_f%C3%BCr_Sexualwissenschaft, *Wikipedia Free Encyclopedia*, "Institut für Sexualwissenschaft—Nazi Era," March 13, 2007 © GNU.

133B http://radio.weblogs.com/0110001/2003/05/10.html, Captain NEMO's Radio Weblog, May 10, 2003 © 2003 Captain NEMO.

134 http://fcit.usf.edu/HOLOCAUST/gallery/01622.htm, *A Teacher's Guide to the Holocaust,* "Book Burning."

135A http://www.ronaldbrucemeyer.com/rants/0510almanac.htm, *Stop Censorship*, Ronald Bruce Meyer, "Nazi Book-Burning (1933): Churches and Censorship."

135B Ibid.

136A http://www.familylife.com/hopefororphans/church_orphans.asp, *FamilyLife*, "Hope for Orphans" Ministry.

136B Ibid.

137A http://www.infopt.demon.co.uk/nazi.htm, *Gay History & Literature: Essays by Rictor Norton*, "One Day They Were Simply Gone—The Nazi Persecution of Homosexuals" © 1975, 1998.

137B Ibid.

138 http://www.harvestusa.org, *Harvest USA.*

139A http://www.religioustolerance.org/hom_news_03c.htm, *Religious Tolerance - Gay and Lesbian News: For 2003–July to September.*

139B http://www.christianadvice.net/homosexuality_and_the_bible_wink.htm, *Christian Advice,* Dr. Walter Wink, "Homosexuality and the Bible" © 2001 Christian Advice.net.

139C http://www.christianadvice.net/homosexuality_and_the_bible_Mauser.htm, *Christian Advice*, Dr. Ulrich W. Mauser, "Homosexuality and the Bible" © 2001 Christian Advice.net.

140 http://www.harvestusa.org/articles/lev18&20.htm, *Harvest USA,* Jonathan D. Inman, Homosexuality and the Scriptures: A Survey of the Central Texts (A Four-Part Series)–Part Two, Leviticus 18: 22

& 20: 13: "Homosexuality and Old Testament Law" © 1999–2005 Harvest USA.

141A "Street Gangs: A Secret History" (English Visual) by Greg DeHart, D. Paul Thomas, and Roger Mudd, History Channel (Television network), Arts and Entertainment Network, New Video Group; Termite Art Productions © 2000.

141B Ibid.

141C Ibid.

141D Ibid.

141E Ibid.

141F Ibid.

141G Ibid.

141H Ibid.

141I Ibid.

141J Ibid.

141K Ibid.

141L Ibid.

141M Ibid.

141N Ibid.

141O Ibid.

141P Ibid.

141Q Ibid.

141R Ibid.

141S Ibid.

141T Ibid.

141U Ibid.

141V Ibid.

141W Ibid.

141X Ibid.

141Y Ibid.

141Z Ibid.

141AA Ibid.

141BB Ibid.

141CC Ibid.

141DD Ibid.

141EE Ibid.

141FF Ibid.

141GG Ibid.

141HH Ibid.

141II Ibid.

141JJ Ibid.

141KK Ibid.

141LL Ibid.

141MM Ibid.

142 http://www.citivu.com/ktla/sc-ch1.html, *Stan Chambers; News at 10*; Stan Chambers, "Rodney King and The Los Angeles Riots," February 17, 2005 © 1995–97, 2005.

143 http://www.fightcrime.org/legupdate.php, *Fight Crime: Invest in Kids—Legislative Update*, Federal Policy Update, Juvenile Justice, December 14, 2005.

144A http://thomas.loc.gov/cgi-bin/bdquery/z?d109:hr1704:, *Library of Congress*, THOMAS, Second Chance Act of 2004: Community Safety Through Recidivism Prevention (H.R. 1704; S. 1934), Sponsors including Rep. Rob Portman, Introduced April 19, 2005, Subcommittee Hearings Held February 8, 2006.

144B http://www.hrw.org/english/docs/2004/06/24/usdom8947.htm, *Defending Human Rights Worldwide*, Human Rights News, "Summary of H.R. 4676 the Second Chance Act of 2004" © 2004.

145 http://www.transitionaljobs.net/Policy/SupportForHR4676.pdf, Organizations that Support the Second Chance Act of 2004, H.R. 4676 (sic).

146A www.clla.org/press_releases.cfm?release=8, Adobe Reader—[LawProfsLetter [1][1].pdf], Letter to Senators Arlen Specter and Patrick Leahy from 90 Law Professors re: The Bankruptcy Abuse Prevention and Consumer Protection Act of 2005 (S. 256), February 16, 2005.

146B http://nacba.com/legislation/debate.asp, *National Association of Consumer Bankruptcy Attorneys (NACBA),* Legislation, Robert Gordon, "Bankruptcy Reform Hurts Struggling Families," Source: Baltimore Sun, March 4, 2005.

147 http://www.house.gov/davis/offender2.htm, *Congressman Danny K. Davis—Ex -Offender Info Page*, "The 2nd Chance Bill," October 24, 2005.

148 http://www.reformed.org/webfiles/antithesis/v1n1/ant_v1n1_racism.html, Douglas M. Jones III, "The Biblical Offense of Racism" © Covenant Community Church 1990.

149A http://www.emedicine.com/ped/topic2784.htm, *eMedicine*, KN Siva Subramanian, MD, "Extremely Low Birth Weight Infant," October 31, 2002.

149B Ibid.

149C Ibid.

149D Ibid.

149E Ibid.

149F Ibid.

149G Ibid.

150A http://apa.org/releases/preterm.html, *APA Online*, APA Press Release, "Preterm Infants Found to Be at Risk for Cognitive and Behavioral Problems after Ten Years" © 2007 American Psychological Association.

150B http://www.fhs.mcmaster.ca/pubrel/saigal.htm, *McMaster University*, Faculty of Health Sciences, "Preemies Defy Odds and Overcome Difficulties by Adulthood: Study," February 7, 2006, Sources: www.jama.com, *Journal of the American Medical Association*, Vol. 295, No. 6675, Saroj Saigal, et al, "Transition of Extremely Low Birth Weight Infants from Adolescence to Young Adulthood—Comparison with Normal Birth Weight Controls," February 8, 2006 © 2006 JAMA and www.pediatrics.org/cgi/content/full/118/3/1140, *Pediatrics*, Saroj Saigal, et al, "Perceived Quality of Life of Former Extremely Low Birth Weight Infants at Young Adulthood," September 18, 2006 © 2006 The American Academy of Pediatrics.

150C Ibid.

150D Ibid.

150E http://www.comeunity.com/premature/research/helen-followup.html, *ComeUnity*, Premature Baby/Premature Child, Helen Harrison, "The Need for Better Followup Studies on Prematurity."

150F http://www.fhs.mcmaster.ca/pubrel/saigal.htm, *McMaster University*, Faculty of Health Sciences, "Preemies Defy Odds and Overcome Difficulties by Adulthood: Study," February 7, 2006, Sources: www.jama.com, *Journal of the American Medical Association*, Vol. 295, No. 6675, Saroj Saigal, et al, "Transition of Extremely Low Birth Weight Infants from Adolescence to Young Adulthood—Comparison with Normal Birth Weight Controls," February 8, 2006 © 2006 JAMA and www.pediatrics.org/cgi/content/full/118/3/1140, *Pediatrics*, Saroj Saigal, et al, "Perceived Quality of Life of Former Extremely Low Birth Weight Infants at Young Adulthood," September 18, 2006 © 2006 The American Academy of Pediatrics.

150G http://www.sciencedaily.com/releases/1997/06/970606122249.htm,

ScienceDaily, "Very Low Birth Weight Children Have Long-Term Behavioral and Psychological Consequences," June 6, 1997 © 1995–2007 Science Daily.

150H http://www.upi.com/ConsumerHealthDaily/view.php?StoryID=20061002–030808–3375r, *United Press International*, Consumer Health Daily, Aaron Rupar, "Study: Low Birth Weight Babies May Have Lower IQs," October 2, 2006 © 2007 United Press International, Inc.

151A http://www.timesonline.co.uk/article/0,,2087–1641429,00.html, *Times Online*, The Sunday Times–Britain, Sarah-Kate Templeton, "Expert tells doctors: let youngest premature babies die," June 5, 2005.

151B Ibid.

152 http://www.sfgate.com/cgi-bin/article.cgi?file=/c/a/2004/10/07/MNGII94D931.DTL, *San Francisco Chronicle*, Erin McCormick and Reynolds Holding, Too Young To Die—Part 5: "Saving Babies," October 7, 2004.

153A http://grants.nih.gov/grants/guide/pa-files/PA-99–045.html, *NIH Guide*, "Low Birth Rate in Minority Populations," January 22, 1999.

153B Ibid.

154 http://www.sailing.org/disabled/world_disabled_sailor_03_00.pdf, *WORLD DISABLED SAILOR: Newsletter of the International Foundation for Disabled Sailing*, Edition No. 6, March 2000.

155 http://cybermessageboard.bizland.com/amputee/viewtopic.php?t=496, *Amputee Online Forum*, Viewer Comment, Posted December 18, 2005.

157 http://www.angelfire.com/ne/cre8vityunltd/xepshunl.html, *Exceptional/Extraordinary Individuals.*

158 http://courses.washington.edu/conj690/print/rehab_manual.pdf, Clinical Practice of Physical Medicine & Rehabilitation, Universi-

ty of Washington, School of Medicine, Medical Student Syllabus, Mark A. Harrast, M.D.

159 Eereckson Tada, Joni, *Diamonds in the Dust* (Zondervan Publishing House © 1993 by Joni Eareckson Tada).

160 Sheen, Archbishop Fulton J., *Cross-Ways* (originally published in 1967 under the title *Lenten and Easter Inspirations*). Also, appearing in Sheen, Archbishop Fulton J., *Our Grounds for Hope* (Resurrection Press, February 2000).

161 Ibid.

162A Wacker, Grant. "The Christian Right," essay in *Divining America: Religion and the National Culture*, in *TeacherServ* ® from the National Humanities Center, 1997: http://www.nhc.rtp.nc.us/tserve/twenty/tkeyinfo/chr_rght.htm.

162B Ibid.

162C Ibid.

162D Ibid.

162E Ibid.

162F Ibid.

162G Ibid.

162H Ibid.

162I Ibid.

162J Ibid.

162K Ibid.

162L Ibid.

162M Ibid.

163A Lienesch, Martin, *Redeeming Politics* (1993).

163B Ibid.

163C Ibid.

163D Ibid.

164 Martin, William, *With God on Our Side: The Rise of the Religious Right in America* (Lumiere Productions Inc.) © 1996 William Martin and Lumiere Productions, Inc.

165A http://www.religion-online.org/showarticle.asp?title=1658, *Religion Online*, William Martin Chavanne, "With God on Our Side: Reflections on the Religious Right," Presentation at Center for Progressive Christianity (1997).

165B Ibid.

165C Ibid.

165D Ibid.

165E Ibid.

166A http://www.cbmw.org/news/ram150404.php, *Council on Biblical Manhood and Womanhood (CBMW)*, R. Albert, Mohler, "Is Homosexuality in the Genes?" April 15, 2004.

166B Ibid.

166C Ibid.

166D Ibid.

166E Ibid.

166F Ibid.

167 http://cas.bellarmine.edu/tietjen/RootWeb/npr_letters_on_the_biological_ba.htm, *NPR Letters on the Biological Basis of Homosexuality.*

168A http://www.geocities.com/southbeach/boardwalk/7151/biobasis.html, *MY WACKY PAGE O'CRAZED STUFF*, "Sylvia," "The Biological Basis of Homosexuality" (1997), Sources including: http://www.psych.org/public_info/HOMOSE~1.HTM *American Psychological Association*, "Statement on Homosexuality," November 4, 1997;

Burr, Chandler, *A Separate Creation* (New York: Hyperion, 1996); http://www.theatlantic.com/atlantic/issues/97jun/burr2.htm, *Atlantic Monthly Online,* Chandler Burr, "Homosexuality and Biology," (March 1993), November 4, 1997; Hall, J. A. Y. and D. Kimura, *Behavioral Neuroscience*, Vol.108, "Dermatoglyphic Asymmetry and Sexual Orientation in Men," p. 1203–1206 (1994); Hamer, Dean and Peter Copeland, *The Science of Desire* (New York: Simon and Schuster, 1994); and LeVay, Simon, *The Sexual Brain* (Cambridge: MIT Press, 1993).

168B Ibid.

168C Ibid.

168D Ibid.

168E Ibid.

168F Ibid.

169 http://members.aol.com/qbchoice/TWINS.html, *TWINS*, "Why Ask Why? The Research on Homosexuality and Biology."

170A http://www.freerepublic.com/focus/f-religion/1338373/posts, *Free Republic*, The Catholic Church in England and Wales, Catholic Bishop Conference of England and Wales, "UK Bishops did NOT ban 'discrimination' against homosexuals, fornicators," February 2, 2005, Source: Diversity and Equality Guidelines, prepared by Department for Christian Responsibility and Citizenship, approved by Catholic Bishops' Conference of England & Wales © 2005 CBCEW.

170B Ibid.

170C Ibid.

171 http://www.rmnetwork.org/, *Reconciling Ministries Network.*

172 http://www.herewestandumc.org/, *HereWeStand*, "Calling the United Methodist Church to Embody God's Love and Justice," Adopted December 1, 2005.

173A http://www.democratandchronicle.com/apps/pbcs.dll/

article?AID=/20050912/OPINION02/509120312/1039/OPINION, *Rochester Democrat and Chronicle*, Amy Campbell, "Help women find better options than abortion," September 12, 2005.

173B Ibid.

173C Ibid.

173D Ibid.

173E Ibid.

174A http://www.pbs.org/wgbh/nova/miracle/stemcells.html, *PBS NOVA Online*, Ronald M. Green, "Life's Greatest Miracle: The Stem Cell Debate," November 2001 © WGBH.

174B Ibid.

174C Ibid.

174D Ibid.

174E Ibid.

174F Ibid.

174G Ibid.

174H Ibid.

174I Ibid.

174J Ibid.

174K Ibid.

174L Ibid.

174M Ibid.

174N Ibid.

175A Green, Dr. Ronald, *The Human Embryo Research Debates: Bioethics in the Vortex of Controversy*, (Oxford University Press, 2001).

175B Ibid.

175C Ibid.

175D Ibid.

175E Ibid.

176 http://www.newscientist.com/article.ns?id=dn1826, *New Scientist*, Sylvia Pagan Westphal, Breaking News: "Ultimate stem cell discovered," January 23, 2002.

177 http://www.bio.org/bioethics/background/ethics0117.asp, *BIO*, "Stem Cell Research," January 17, 2001 © Biotechnology Industry Organization.

178A http://mednews.stanford.edu/stanmed/2004fall/stem-main.html, *Stanford School of Medicine, Stanford Medicine Magazine*, "The great stem cell divide," Fall 2004.

178B Ibid.

178C Ibid.

178D Ibid.

178E Ibid.

178F Ibid.

178G Ibid.

179A http://www.democratsforlife.org/index.php?option=com_content&task=view&id=124&Itemid=2, *Democrats for Life of America*, Steven Ertelt of *LifeNews.com*, "Adult Stem Cell Research Scientists Find New Stem Cell in Umbilical Cord Blood," February 14, 2006.

179B Ibid.

180A http://www.findarticles.com/p/articles/mi_m1272/is_2658_128/ai_60868324/pg_3, *USA Today (Society for the Advancement for Education)*, Holly Wagner, "Umbilical Cord Blood Banking: Insurance Against Future Disease?" March 2000 © Society for the Advancement of Education, Gale Group.

180B Ibid.

181 http://www.nationalreview.com/interrogatory/george200506290814.asp, *National Review Online,* Responses by Robert P. George to Questions by Kathryn Jean Lopez, Scientific Breakthroughs: "Getting Beyond Stem Cell Obstacles," Q&A , June 29, 2005.

182A http://www.lifeissues.net/writers/smit/smit_06adultstemcell.html, *Lifeissues.net: Clear Thinking About Crucial Issues,* Wesley J. Smith, "Why Adult Stem Cell Research Successes Get Downplayed by the Media" © 2001–2002 Wesley J. Smith.

182B Ibid.

182C Ibid.

183 http://www.stemcellresearch.org/facts/miscupdate1.htm, *Do No-Harm—Coalition of Americans for Research Ethics,* "Adult Stem Cell Advances Continue to Challenge the 'Need' for Destructive Embryonic Research," Sources including: *The Washington Post,* Rick Weiss, "Studies Raise Hopes of Cardiac Rejuvenation," March 31, 2001.

184 https://www3.nationalgeographic.com/genographic/population.html, *National Geographic,* The Genographic Project, Population Genetics © 1996–2005 National Geographic Society.

185A http://www.wi.mit.edu/news/archives/2005/rj_1016.html, *Whitehead Institute,* David Cameron, "Researchers Offer Proof-of-Concept for Altered Nuclear Transfer," October 17, 2005.

185B Ibid.

185C Ibid.

185D Ibid.

186 http://www.quotationspage.com/quote/38045.htmlbid, *The Quotations Page,* Quote Details: Aesop, "United we stand, divided we fall."

187A *In Touch Magazine*, Allen Harris, "Unlikely Allies," February 2006.

187B Ibid.

187C Ibid.

187D Ibid.

188 http://www.quotationspage.com/search.php3?homesearch=lincoln&page=2, *The Quotations Page*, Quote Search: Abraham Lincoln.

189A http://academic.udayton.edu/race/06hrights/WaronTerrorism/Homeland01.htm, *University of Dayton School of Law*; *Race, Racism and the Law: Speaking Truth to Power!* Vernellia R. Randall, Professor of Law, Web Editor, "Take the Homeland Security Quiz," Source: William Rivers Pitt "Truthout/Perspective Sunday," December 1, 2002 © 1997, 1998, 1999, 2001.

189B Ibid.

189C Ibid.

189D Ibid.

189E Idid.

189F Ibid.

189G Ibid.

189H Ibid.

189I Ibid.

189J Ibid.

190A http://www.firstamendmentcenter.org/speech/internet/topic.aspx?topic=internet_hate_speech, *First Amendment Center*, Jarrod F. Reich, Internet & First Amendment in Speech: "Hate Speech Online," May 12, 2005.

190B Ibid.

190C Ibid.

190D Ibid.

190E Ibid.

190F Ibid.

190G Ibid.

190H Ibid.

190I Ibid.

190J Ibid.

190K Ibid.

190L Ibid.

190M Ibid.

190N Ibid.

190O Ibid.

190P Ibid.

191A http://academic.udayton.edu/race/06hrights/WaronTerrorism/racia103.htm, *University of Dayton School of Law*; *Race, Racism and the Law: Speaking Truth to Power!* Vernellia R. Randall, Professor of Law, Web Editor, "Right-wing and Racial Terrorism," Source: The *Norwegian Institute of International Affairs*, Tore Bjorgo, "Right-wing and Racist Terrorism" © 1997, 1998, 1999, 2001.

191B Ibid.

191C Ibid.

191D Ibid.

191E Ibid.

191F Ibid.

191G Ibid.

191H Ibid.

191I Ibid.

191J Ibid.

191K Ibid.

191L Ibid.

191M Ibid.

191N Ibid.

191O Ibid.

192 http://www.policyreview.org/jun04/bar.html, *Policy Review Online* (Published by Hoover Institution), Issue No. 125, Shmuel Bar, "The Religious Sources of Islamic Terrorism."

193 http://academic.udayton.edu/race/06hrights/WaronTerrorism/terrorism08.htm, *University of Dayton School of Law*; Race, Racism and the Law: Speaking Truth to Power! Vernellia R. Randall, Professor of Law, Web Editor, "Ahmed's Secret Incarceration," Source: *Amerasia Journal,* Eric K. Yamamoto and Susan Kiyomi Serrano, "The Loaded Weapon," Vol. 27: Chapter 3 (2001) pp. 51–52/ Vol 28: Chapter 1(2002): pp. 51–53.

194A http://www.epic.org/privacy/profiling/tia/, *Electronic Privacy Information Center*, Terrorism (Total) Information Awareness Page, "Study Finds Extensive Data Mining in Federal Agencies," May 27, 2004.

194B Ibid.

195A http://akaka.senate.gov/~akaka/releases/04/05/2004527449.html, *News from Daniel Kahikina Akaka*, "GAO Report Discloses Widespread Data Mining by Federal Agencies," May 27, 2004.

195B Ibid.

196 http://www.epic.org/privacy/budget/fy2006/, *Electronic Privacy Information Center*, U.S. Domestic Surveillance Budget Fiscal Year 2006, April 2005.

197A http://www.epic.org/privacy/terrorism/fisa/crs_analysis.pdf, *Congressional Research Service*, Elizabeth B. Bazan and Jennifer K. Elsea, Legislative Attorneys, American Law Division, "Memorandum re: Presidential Authority to Conduct Warrantless Electronic Surveillance to Gather Foreign Intelligence Information."

197B Ibid.

197C Ibid.

197D Ibid.

197E Ibid.

197F I bid.

197G Ibid.

197H Ibid.

198A http://www.law.umkc.edu/faculty/projects/ftrials/salem/SALEM.HTM, *Famous American Trials*, Douglas Linder, The Salem Witchcraft Trials of 1692: "An Account of Events in Salem," January 2006

198B http://www.law.umkc.edu/faculty/projects/ftrials/salem/salem-causes.html, *Famous American Trials,* Causes of the Salem Witchcraft Trials: "Causes for the Outbreak of Witchcraft Hysteria in Salem."

198C Ibid.

198D Ibid.

198E http://www.law.umkc.edu/faculty/projects/ftrials/salem/salemmap.HTM, *Famous American Trials,* Map of Salem Village in 1692 (WP Upham), Map of Witchcraft Accusations, University of Virginia.

199 http://www.nationalgeographic.com/salem/, *National Geographic: Salem Witch-Hunt* (Interactive).

200 http://www.femalepatient.com/html/arc/edi/pc/pc_1201.asp, *The Female Patient,* Dennis J. Butler, PhD., Gregory L. Brotzman, MD, "Bioterrorism and Anthrax Anxiety," December 2001 © 2000–2006 Quadrant HealthCom Inc.

201 http://www.hbci.com/~wenonah/history/ergot.htm, *PBS Secrets of the Dead II—Witches' Curse*, "Ergot Poisoning - the cause of the Salem Witch Trials."

202A http://www.pbs.org/wnet/americanmasters/database/mccarthyism.html, *PBS, American Masters,* McCarthyism: "The Loss of Nameless Things."

202B Ibid.

202C Ibid.

202D Ibid.

203 http://en.wikipedia.org/wiki/McCarthyism, *Wikipedia Encyclopedia*, McCarthyism, GNU Free Documentation License.

204A http://www.sentencingproject.org/pdfs/5022.pdf, *US Commission on Civil Rights*, Sentencing Project, Marc Mauer, Assistant Director, "The Crisis of the Young African American Male and the Criminal Justice System," April 15–16, 1999.

204B Ibid.

205 http://etext.virginia.edu/jefferson/quotations/jeff0100.htm, *Thomas Jefferson: On Politics & Government,* Compiled and Edited by Eyler Robert Coates, Sr., 1. Inalienable Rights, December 21, 1995 © 1995–2001 Eyler Robert Coates, Sr.

206A http://www.firstamendmentcenter.org/rel_liberty/history/overview.aspx, *FIRST AMENDMENT CENTER: History of Religious Liberty in America*, Charles Haynes, written for *Civitas: A Framework for Civic Education* © 1991 Council for the Advancement of Citizenship and the Center for Civic Education.

206B Ibid.

206C Ibid.

206D Ibid.

206E Ibid.

206F Ibid.

206G Ibid.

206H Ibid.

206I Ibid.

206J Ibid.

206K Ibid.

206L Ibid.

206M Ibid.

206N Ibid.

2060 Ibid.

206P Ibid.

206Q Ibid.

206R Ibid.

206S Ibid.

206T Ibid.

206U Ibid.

207 http://www.pbs.org/wnet/aalives/science_race.html, *PBS: African American Lives (4-Part Series)*, The Science and the Investigators, Henry Louis Gates, Jr. (film), Shebana Coehlo and Kelly Quinn (website), "Race and Science" © 2006 Educational Broadcasting Corporation.

208A http://www.upi.com/inc/view.php?StoryID=15042002–084051–5356r, *United Press International (UPI)*, Washington Politics & Policy, Steve Shriver, "Analysis: White prof finds he's not," May 8, 2002 © 2006 United Press International Inc.

208B Ibid.

208C Ibid.

209A http://academic.udayton.edu/race/06hrights/WaronTerrorism/crisis01.htm, *University of Dayton School of Law*; Race, Racism and the Law: Speaking Truth to Power! Vernellia R. Randall, Professor of Law, Web Editor, "Social Justice Organizing in a Time of Crisis,"

Source: Bill Quigley, Loyola Law School, New Orleans, Louisiana, "Ten Ideas for Social Justice Organizing in a Time of Crisis," December 9, 2001.

209B Ibid.

209C Ibid.

209D Ibid.

210A http://www.cnn.com/2006/US/02/23/ports.timeline/index.html, CNN.com, *Lou Dobbs Tonight*, Lou Dobbs, "Timeline of controversial ports deal," February 24, 2006 © 2006 Cable News Network.

210B Ibid.

211A http://transcripts.cnn.com/TRANSCRIPTS/0602/23/ldt.01.html, CNN.com, Transcripts, *Lou Dobbs Tonight*, February 23, 2006 © 2006 Cable News Network.

211B Ibid.

211C Ibid.

211D Ibid.

211E Ibid.

211F http://transcripts.cnn.com/TRANSCRIPTS/0602/24/ldt.01.html, CNN.com, Transcripts, *Lou Dobbs Tonight*, February 24, 2006 © 2006 Cable News Network.

212 http://transcripts.cnn.com/TRANSCRIPTS/0602/13/ldt.01.html, CNN.com, Transcripts, *Lou Dobbs Tonight*, February 13, 2006 © 2006 Cable News Network.

213 http://www.radioink.com/listingsEntry.asp?ID=381178&PT=industryqa, *Radio Ink*, Industry Q&A, Reed Bunzel, "Lou Dobbs: The Truth Is Not Always Fair Or Balanced" (October 3, 2005), February 24, 2006 © 2006 Streamline Media Inc.

214A http://www.washingtonpost.com/wp-dyn/content/article/2005/10/13/AR2005101301729.html *Washington Post*, Michael A. Fletcher and Spencer S. Hsu, "Storms Alter Louisiana Politics—Population Loss Likely to Reduce Influence of Black Voters, " October 14, 2005, page A07 © 1996–2006 Washington Post Company.

214B Ibid.

215A http://www.racismagainstindians.org/Perspectives/Essays/IndianSlaves.htm, *STAR—Students and Teachers Against Racism,* Indian 101, "Indian Slaves," Source: Orcutt, Samuel, *Indian of the Housatonic and Naugatuck Valleys* (1882).

215B Ibid.

215C Ibid.

215D Ibid.

215E Ibid.

215F Ibid.

215G Ibid.

216 http://www.ioa.com/~shermis/socjus/socdar.html, *Introduction to Social Justice*, S. Samuel Shermis, PhD, "Social Darwinism."

217A http://www.nhgazette.com/shop/uploads/latest_issue.pdf, *New Hampshire Gazette*, Fortnightly Rant, Editor Steven Fowle, "State of *What* Union?" January 27, 2006.

217B Ibid.

217C http://www.nhgazette.com/shop/uploads/latest_issue.pdf, *New Hampshire Gazette*, Fortnightly Rant, Editor Steven Fowle, "The War on Troops & Veterans" January 27, 2006.

217D Ibid.

218A http://www.williambowles.info/gispecial/gi-2.31/gi-2–31.html, *G.I. Special #2.31: Some Home Truth*, February, 23, 2004, Source: *The Guardian*, Jonathan Franklin, "Soldiers Are Fighting—To Get Out of the Military," February 21, 2004.

218B http://www.williambowles.info/gispecial/gi-2.31/gi-2–31.html, *G.I. Special #2.31: Some Home Truth*, February, 23, 2004, Source: *The Hightower Lowdown*, Troop News, Jim Hightower and Philip Frazer, "Bushites' Betrayal of Our Troops and Vets," February 2004.

218C Ibid.

218D Ibid.

218E http://www.williambowles.info/gispecial/gi-2.31/gi-2–31.html, *G.I. Special #2.31: Some Home Truth*, February, 23, 2004, Source: *Now*, Bill Moyers, 2003.

218F http://www.williambowles.info/gispecial/gi-2.31/gi-2–31.html, *G.I. Special #2.31: Some Home Truth*, February, 23, 2004.

218G Ibid.

218H http://alacarte.lexisnexis.com/partners/int/lexisnews/viewdoc.asp?mtid=0&doc=75666&skey={BA0FF23F-A253–46D7–86B7–7F2EF8034D0F}, *Newhouse News Service (archived at Lexis/Nexis),* Washington, David Wood, "Army's Humvees In Iraq Lack Critical Armor Protection," February 18, 2004 © Newhouse News Service.

218I as at 218B http://www.williambowles.info/gispecial/gi-2.31/gi-2–31.html, *G.I. Special #2.31: Some Home Truth*, February, 23, 2004, Source: *The Hightower Lowdown*, Troop News, Jim Hightower and Philip Frazer, "Bushites' Betrayal of Our Troops and Vets," February 2004.

219 http://www.informationclearinghouse.info/article1544.htm, *Harper's Magazine,* Vol. 305, Issue 1829, David Armstrong, "Dick Cheney's Song of America," October 2002 © 2002 by *Harper's Magazine.*

220A http://www.informationclearinghouse.info/article1665.htm, *Information Clearing House*, William Rivers Pitt, "The Project for the New American Century," February 25, 2003.

220B Ibid.

221A http://www.informationclearinghouse.info/article10186.htm, *In-*

formation Clearing House, "The Independent" News, Paul Vallely, UN report: "Parts of America are as poor as Third World," September 8, 2005, Source: Kevin Watkins, UN Development Report.

221B Ibid.

221C Ibid.

221D Ibid.

221E Ibid.

222A http://www.informationclearinghouse.info/article5754.htm, *Information Clearing House*, Los Angeles Times, Judy Foreman, "In Health, Canada tops US," February 23, 2004.

222B Ibid.

222C Ibid.

222D Ibid.

222E Ibid.

222F Ibid.

222G Ibid.

223A http://www.informationclearinghouse.info/article10109.htm, *Information Clearing House*, ICH, Stephen Crocket, co-host of Democratic Talk Radio, "Killing Americans by Health Care Policy," September 4, 2005.

223B Ibid.

223C Ibid.

224A http://www.commondreams.org/views05/0915–27.htm, *Common Dreams News Center*, February 25, 2006, Sources: *Dissent Magazine,* Peter Dreier, Katrina in Perspective: "The Hurricane Raises Key Questions About the Role of Government in Society," September 15, 2005; and *Chicago Tribune* © 2005 Foundation for Study of Independent Ideas, Inc.

224B Ibid.

224C Ibid.

224D Ibid.

224E Ibid.

224F Ibid.

224G Ibid.

224H http://www.commondreams.org/views05/0915-27.htm, *Common Dreams News Center*, Sources: *Dissent Magazine,* Peter Dreier, Katrina in Perspective: "The Hurricane Raises Key Questions About the Role of Government in Society" (September 15, 2005), February 25, 2006; and *New York Times*, September 10, 2005 © 2005 Foundation for Study of Independent Ideas, Inc.

224I Ibid.

224J Ibid.

224K Ibid.

224L Ibid.

224M Ibid.

224N Ibid.

225 http://www.tgwu.org.uk/Templates/News.asp?NodeID=90772&int1stParentNodeID=42438&int2ndParentNodeID=89396&Action=Display, *T&G News*, Proven dangers of construction industry prompt renewed calls for killing law, May 13, 2004 © 2003 onwards, Transport and General Workers' Union.

226 Baker-Smith, Machiavelli, Niccolo, Marriott, WK, *The Prince*, Chapter XVIII "Concerning the Way in Which Princes Should Keep Faith," (New York: Alfred A. Knopf, a division of Random House), Introduction, Bibliography, and Chronology © 1992 David Campbell Publishers, Ltd.

227A http://www.gsnmagazine.com/aug_05/dod_lawyers.html, *GSN Magazine: Government Security News*, Jacob Goodwin, "Did DoD

Lawyers blow the chance to nab Atta?" Sources including: *Times Herald* of Norristown, PA, Keith Phucas, June 19, 2005.

227B Ibid.

227C Ibid.

227D Ibid.

227E Ibid.

227F Ibid.

227G Ibid.

227H Ibid.

228A http://en.wikipedia.org/wiki/Able_Danger, *Wikipedia Encyclopedia*, Able Danger, February 24, 2006, Sources including: *GSN Magazine: Government Security News*, Jacob Goodwin, "Did DoD Lawyers blow the chance to nab Atta?"; and *Times Herald* of Norristown, PA, Keith Phucas, June 19, 2005, GNU Free Documentation License.

228B Ibid.

229 A http://web.nexis.com/research/, *Newhouse News Service* (archived at Lexis/Nexis), National Security, David Wood, "Army Amputees Face Struggle in Returning to Duty," November 30, 2004 © Newhouse News Service.

229B http://web.nexis.com/research/, *Newhouse News Service* (archived at Lexis/Nexis), National Security, David Wood, "Military Acknowledges Massive Supply Problems in Iraq War," January 22, 2004 © Newhouse News Service.

230A http://www.washingtonpost.com/wp-dyn/content/linkset/2005/04/11/LI2005041100879.html, *WashingtonPost.com—White House Briefing*, Dan Froomkin, "Questions of Credibility," February 10, 2006.

230B Ibid.

230C Ibid.

231A http://www.usccb.org, Bishop Wilton D. Gregory, United States Conference of Catholic Bishops, Office of Social Development & World Peace, *Letter to President Bush on Iraq*, September 13, 2002 © September 17, 2002 Unites States Conference of Catholic Bishops.

213B Ibid.

231C Ibid.

231D Ibid.

231E Ibid.

231F Ibid.

231G Ibid.

231H Ibid.

231I Ibid.

231J Ibid.

232A http://www.iep.utm.edu/j/justwar.htm, *Internet Encyclopedia of Philosophy*, Alexander Mosele, "Just War Theory" © 2006.

232B Ibid.

232C Ibid.

232D Ibid.

232E Ibid.

232F Ibid.

232G Ibid.

232H Ibid.

232I Ibid.

232J Ibid.

232K Ibid.

232L Ibid.

232M Ibid.

232N Ibid.

232O Ibid.

232P Ibid.

232Q Ibid.

233A http://www.mtholyoke.edu/acad/intrel/feros-pg.htm, *Resources for the Study of International Relations and Foreign Policy*, Vincent Ferraro, "Principles of the Just War," April 18, 2005.

233B Ibid.

233C Ibid.

233D Ibid.

233E Ibid.

234 *Public Papers of the Presidents of the United States 1953* (US Government Printing Office, 1960), p. 182.

235A *What Are the Origins of International Humanitarian Law? Answers to Your Questions* © October 2002 International Committee of the Red Cross (ICRC*)*, second edition December 2004.

235B Ibid.

235C Ibid.

235D Ibid.

235E Ibid.

235F Ibid.

236 http://www.icrc.org/Web/Eng/siteeng0.nsf/iwpList304/114E245DA2286D1BC1256B66005E8ACC, *International Committee of the Red Cross (ICRC),* International Review of the Red Cross No. 838, Howard S. Levie, "History of the law of war on land," March 6, 2000, pp. 339–350 © 2006 International Committee of the Red Cross.

237A http://www.icrc.org/Web/Eng/siteeng0.nsf/iwpList304/D9DAD4EE8533DAEFC1256B66005AFFEF, *International Committee of the Red Cross (ICRC),* International Review of the Red Cross No. 320, Robert Kolb, "Origin of the twin terms *jus ad bellum/jus in bello,*" October 31, 1997, pp. 553–562 © 2006 International Committee of the Red Cross.

237B Ibid.

237C Ibid.

237D Ibid.

237E Ibid.

237F Ibid.

237G Ibid.

237H Ibid.

237I Ibid.

237J Ibid.

238A Article 52(2) of Protocol I of the 1977 Protocols Additional to the Geneva Conventions, December 12, 1977; Article 22 of the Regulations Respecting the Laws and Customs of War on Land, annexed to the Hague Convention No. IV, October 18, 1907; Article 23e of the Regulations Respecting the Laws and Customs of War on Land, annexed to the Hague Convention No IV; Department of the Army, Field Manual 27–10, The Law of Land Warfare (July 1956) (change 1) at paragraph 41; and Article 51 of Protocol I of the 1977 Protocols Additional to the Geneva Conventions.

238B Ibid.

238C Ibid.

238D Ibid.

238E Email From: DA Washington DC//DAMO-AOC//; To: DCSG3 collectivetraining@HQDA-DMS.ARMY.MIL; Subject: Law of War Training; Text: Unclassified; Date: August 23, 2005.

238F Ibid.

238G Ibid.

239A http://www.rbc.org/ds/q0402/q0402.html#top#top, *RBC Ministries*, "Can I Really Trust the Bible?" Managing Editor: David Sper © 2000 RBC Ministries.

239B Ibid.

239C Ibid.

239D Ibid.

240A http://www.turkishodyssey.com/places/marmara/marmara8.htm, *Turkish Odyssey*, Part 8 Istanbul–Troy–Assos, Destination: Canakkale Bogazi [The Dardanelles], "Archeological Evidence," February 2, 2000 © 1997 Serif Yenen.

240B Ibid.

241A http://www.cbpp.org/2-6-06bud.htm, *Center on Budget and Policy Priorities*, "The President's 2007 Budget: A Preliminary Analysis," Revised February 10, 2006.

241B Ibid.

241C Ibid.

241D Ibid.

241E Ibid.

241F Ibid.

241G Ibid.

241H Ibid.

214I Ibid.

241J Ibid.

241K Ibid.

241L Ibid.

241M Ibid.

241N Ibid.

242 http://www2.gol.com/users/quakers/quaker_declaration_of_pacifism.htm, *Tokyo Quakers Monthly Meeting of the Religious Society of Friends*, "Quaker Declaration of Pacifism" to Charles II, 1660.

243A Brock, Peter, *The Quaker Peace Testimony 1660 to 1914,* (York, England: Sessions Book Trust, 1990), p. 27, Source: Isaac Penington, "Somewhat spoken to a Weighty Question, concerning the Magistrate's Protection of the Innocent" (1661).

243B Brock, Peter, *The Quaker Peace Testimony 1660 to 1914*, (York, England: Sessions Book Trust, 1990), p. 95.

244 http://www.bobdylan.com/songs/believeinyou.html, *Bob Dylan*, "I Believe In You," First Release: Slow Train Coming, 1979 © 1979 Special Rider Music © COLUMBIA Records, Sony BMG Entertainment.

245 http://aolsearch.aol.com/aol/search?encquery=9732204b12bf36c4ff60518d26ebfdd0&invocationType=keyword_rollover&ie=UTF-845, *Wikipedia Encyclopedia*, Predestination: "Various Views on Christian Predestination," March 1, 2006 GNU Free Documentation License.

246 http://www.msnbc.msn.com/id/11627394/, *MSNBC*, Katrina—The Long Road Back, "Video Shows Bush Got Explicit Katrina Warning," March 2, 2006, Source: Associated Press, Margaret Ebrahim and John Solomon, "Bush, Chernoff Warned Before Katrina Hit, Video Shows" © Associated Press.

247 http://pqasb.pqarchiver.com/washingtonpost/access/796199461.html?dids=796199461:7961, *Washington Post*, "Bush's '06 Budget Would Scrap or Reduce 154 Programs," Judy Sarasohn, February 22, 2005 © The Washington Post Company.

248 McDowell, Josh, "Mathematical Probabilities of Fulfilled Prophecies," adapted from: McDowell, Josh, *Evidence that Demands a Ver-*

dict (1979 edition) pp. 166, 167, Source: Stoner, Peter, *Science Speaks* (Chicago: Moody Press, 1963) pp. 100–110.

249 Baker-Smith, Dominic, Machiavelli, Niccolo, Marriott, WK, *The Prince*, Chapter XVII "Concerning Cruelty And Clemency, And Whether It Is Better To Be Loved Than Feared," (New York: Alfred A. Knopf, a division of Random House), Introduction, Bibliography, and Chronology © 1992 David Campbell Publishers, Ltd.

250 http://en.wikipedia.org/wiki/United_States_Democratic_Party, *Wikipedia Encyclopedia*, Democratic Party (United States) GNU Free Documentation License.

251 http://en.wikipedia.org/wiki/United_States_Republican_Party, *Wikipedia Encyclopedia*, Republican Party (United States) GNU Free Documentation License.

252 Gibelman, Margaret, DSW, and Gelman, Sheldon R., PhD, "Very Public Scandals: An Analysis of How and Why Nongovernmental Organizations Get in Trouble—A Working Paper;" presented to International Society for Third Sector Research July 7, 2000; published, without revision, as "Very Public Scandals: Nongovernmental Organizations in Trouble" in *Voluntas: International Journal of Voluntary and Nonprofit Organizations*, 12(1), pp. 49–66 (2001).

253 http://www.prospect.org/print/V14/2/reich-r.html, *The American Prospect,* Robert B. Reich, "The Rove Machine Rolls On," vol. 14 no. 2, February 1, 2003 © 2003 The American Prospect Online.

254 http://www.alternet.org/story/16080/, BuzzFlash *(AlterNet),* Mark Karlin, "Bad Brains," Posted June 5, 2003 © 2006 Independent Media Institute.

255 http://www.usnews.com/usnews/news/articles/041115/15faith.htm, *US News & World Report*, Reporter Dan Gilgoff, "The morals and values crowd—Evangelicals turned out for Bush. Now they expect his support," November 15, 2004.

256 http://www.usatoday.com/news/politicselections/2004–11–04-religion_x.htm, *USA Today.com*, The Associated Press, "Election rein-

forces USA's religious schism," Posted November 4, 2004, Updated November 8, 2004 © 2005 The Associated Press.

257 http://www.georgetown.edu/faculty/bassr/heath/syllabuild/iguide/sewall.html, Georgetown University, Samuel Sewell (1652–1730), Source: Sewel, Samuel, "The Selling of Joseph" (1701).

258A http://www.historynow.org/09_2005/historian2.html, *History Now: American History Online*, Sylvia R. Frey, "Antislavery Before the Revolutionary War," Issue 5.

258B http://www.historynow.org/09_2005/historian2.html, *History Now: American History Online*, Sylvia R. Frey, "Antislavery Before the Revolutionary War," Issue 5, September 2005, Source: Sewel, Samuel, "The Selling of Joseph" (1701).

259 Rhode, Deborah L., *Access to Justice*, (New York: Oxford University Press, 2004).

260 Patterson, Ben, *Waiting: Finding Hope When God Seems Silent* (Downers Grove: InterVarsity Press, 1989) © 1973, 1978 International Bible Society © 1989 Ben Patterson.

261 http://www.abanet.org/cpr/e2k-redline.html, *American Bar Association (ABA), Center for Professional Responsibility*, Model Rules of Professional Conduct as Adopted by ABA House of Delegates, February 2002 (Ethics 2000).

262 http://www.ushistory.org/Paine/crisis/c-01.htm, *USHistory.org*, Thomas Paine, "The Crisis" (December 23, 1776) © 1999–2006 Independence Hall Association.

263 http://sglyrics.myrmid.com/bridge.htm#track02, *Simon and Garfunkel Lyrics Archive*, Bridge Over Troubled Water, J. Milchberg/D. A. Robles, 1933, English Lyrics, Paul Simon/Music, Art Garfunkel, 1970, "*El Condor Pasa*" [If I Could] (Released 1970).

264 http://www.risa.co.uk/sla/song.php?songid=17193, *Risa Song Lyrics Archive*, Neil Diamond: His Twelve Greatest Hits, Neil Diamond, "Done Too Soon" © 1970 Prophet Music Inc.

265 http://www.online-literature.com/shakespeare/macbeth/, *The Literature Network*, William Shakespeare, "Macbeth."

266 http://www.msnbc.msn.com/id/5953508, *MSNBC.com*, NBC, China Begins to Face Sex-Ratio Imbalance, Eric Baculinao, "China Grapples With Legacy of Its Missing Girls," September 14, 2004 © 2006 Microsoft.

267A Wade, Nicholas, *New York Times*, "Stem Cells May Be Key to Cancer, Scientists Say," February 21, 2006.

267B Ibid.

267C Ibid.

268A http://www.ctssar.org/patriots/nathan_hale.htm, *The Connecticut Society of the Sons of the American Revolution*, Rev. Edward Everett Hale, "Captain Nathan Hale (1755 - 1776)," December 21, 1996 © 1996–2002 CTSSAR.

268B Ibid.

268C Ibid.

269 http://www.memri.org/bin/articles.cgi?&ID=SP81904, *The Middle East Media Research Institute (MEMRI),* Special Dispatch Series - No. 819, MEMRI TV Project: "Mothers of Hizbullah Martyrs: We are Very Happy and Want to Sacrifice More Children," November 25, 2004 © MEMRI.

270 http://www.memritv.org/Search.asp?ACT=S5&P1=165, *The Middle East Media Research Institute (MEMRI), TV Monitor Project;* Inciting Children:

#1185 "Egyptian Cleric Sheik Muhammad Nassar Tells a Group of Children about Child Martyrdom in the Early Days of Islam," Al-Nas TV (Egypt), June 15, 2006;

#1184 "Egyptian Cleric Sheik Muhammad Sharaf Al-Din on a Children Show: The Jews Are the People of Treachery, Betrayal, and Vileness," Al-Nas TV (Egypt), June 21, 2006;

#1183 "Egyptian Cleric Sheik Muhammad Nassar on a Children Show:

The Infidels Invent Nuclear Missiles but The Lord Sends Earthquakes That Swallow Them Up," Al-Nas TV (Egypt), June 22, 2006;

#1066 "Palestinian Legislative Council Member 'Umm Nidal' Farhat: 'If Someone Is Destined to Die, He Will Die Even If He Hides in a Crate, But Why Shouldn't We Take the Initiative and Die as Martyrs?'" Iraq TV (Saudi Arabia), February 19, 2006;

#968 "Iraq TV Interviews Young Child: We Don't Want Peace with the Jews," Iraq TV (Saudi Arabia), December 7, 2005;

#964 "Jews Turn into Apes and Pigs in an Clay-mation Film for Children on Hizbullah TV," Al-Manar TV (Lebanon), December 7, 2005;

#908 "Palestinian Children Clash with an Israeli Soldier in an Iranian Animated Movie," IRIB/Jaam-E-Jam1 (Iran), October 28, 2005;

#906 "Iranian Animated Film for Children Promotes Suicide Bombings," IRIB/Jaam-E-Jam3 (Iran), October 28, 2005;

#907 "Children Drive Cruel Israeli Soldiers Away Using Eggplant Grenades in an Iranian Animated Movie," IRIB/Jaam-E-Jam1 (Iran), October 28, 2005;

#807 "Al-Arabiya TV Special on the Culture of Martyrdom and Suicide Bombers," Al-Arabiya TV (Dubai), July 22, 2005;

#551 "Footage from the 26th Anniversary of the Iranian Revolution Demonstrations," Iran Ch.1, Iran Ch.2, IRINN (Iran), Iran Ch.3, February 10, 2005;

#371 "Mothers of Hizbullah 'Martyrs': We Are Very Happy And Want to Sacrifice More Children," Al-Manar TV (Lebanon), November 11, 2004;

#364 "Tehran Children on 'Jerusalem Day': We Came to Say Death to Israel, Death to America," November 12, 2004;

#363 "Children's Song on Iranian TV: The Palestinian Child is Willing to Shed His Blood for His Country," Iran Ch. 2; and

#362 "Tehran Children on 'Jerusalem Day': We Came To Do the 'Death to America' Thing," Iran Ch. 3 © MEMRI.

271 http://www.thenazareneway.com/inquisition.htm, *The Nazarene Way*, "The Inquisition," Sources: George G. Coulton, *The Inquisition* (1929; reprinted 1974); Paul J. Hauben, ed., *The Spanish Inquisition* (1969); Henry A. Kamen, *The Spanish Inquisition and Society in Spain in the Sixteenth and Seventeenth Centuries* (1985); John Langdon-Davies, *The Spanish Inquisition* (1938; reprinted 1964); Henry C. Lea, *A History of the Inquisition in the Middle Ages*, 3 vols. (1888; reprinted 1988); Emmanuel Le Roy Ladruie, *Montaillou: The Promised Land of Error*, translated by Barbara Bray (1978); William Monter, *Frontiers of Heresy* (1990); John A. O'Brien, *The Inquisition* (1973); Edward Peters, *Inquisition* (1988; reprinted 1989); Cecil Roth, *The Spanish Inquisition* (1938; reprinted 1987); Walter L. Wakefield, *Heresy, Crusade, and Inquisition in Southern France, 1100–1250* (1974).

272 http://www.ashbrook.org/publicat/oped/forte/01/islam.html, *Ashbrook Center for Public Affairs at Ashland University*, David Forte, "Radical Islam v. Islam," September 2001.

273 http://www.israelnn.com/news.php3?id=112066, *Arutz Sheva—IsraelNationalNews.com*, Ezra HaLevi, 'Islamic History Expert: Moslem Peace with Israel? Never!" September 15, 2006 © Israel National News.

274 A http://bostonreview.net/BR26.6/elfadl.html, *Boston Review*, Khaled Abou El Fadl, "The Place of Tolerance in Islam," © 1993–2005 Boston Review.

274B Ibid.

274C Ibid.

275 http://www.unmuseum.org/piltdown.htm, *The Unnatural Museum*, Piltdown: The Man that Never Was © 1996 Lee Krystek.

ENDNOTES

1. This is subject to the biblical prohibition against Christians suing one another where both are members in good standing and their church(es) faithful to Scriptures (1 Corinthians 6: 1–8). There has been substantial confusion over this passage (perhaps, also, the source of judicial distrust). Where both church and state have jurisdiction, it is entirely appropriate to pursue legal remedies simultaneously with church remedies, e.g. in cases of child abuse, or where other irreparable harm could occur in the event of delay. In civil matters, the applicable Statute of Limitations would have bearing. A professing Christian who refuses to obey the directives of a church obeying Scriptures, can readily be taken to court.

2. Christian theologians vary in their interpretation of the term "predestination." As understood by St. Augustine of Hippo, human will is enslaved to sin. The individual does not lack knowledge of good, but lacks the desire for it. God's grace cures this, setting the will free to choose what is good [245].

3. According to the Center on Budget and Policy Priorities, the Bush Administration's *2007 Budget* would increase the deficit over both the short and long run. The budget again proposes significant reductions in a broad array of domestic programs. However, these would not be used to reduce the deficit [241A].

4. Again according to the Center on Budget and Policy Priorities, the *2007 Budget* proposes $285 billion in tax cuts over 5 years and $1.7 trillion in cuts over 10 years. These figures "significantly understate" the cost of the cuts, since they fail to include the cost

of continuing relief from the cost of continuing the Alternative Minimum Tax post-2006. Proposals re: health savings accounts, retirement and lifetime savings accounts are designed so their costs in the first 5–10 years would be substantially less than those in later decades, when huge amounts of revenue will be lost. The Health Savings Accounts proposal is projected to cost $156 billion over the first ten years alone. Past analyses by the Congressional Research Service have indicated the Administration's retirement and lifetime savings account proposals would ultimately cost $300-$500 per decade (in today's dollars). As previously, proposed 2007 tax cuts would favor the wealthy; program cuts would impact low- and middle-income Americans [241B]."

5. This same pattern is repeated in the Administration's *2007 Budget* proposals. According to the Center on Budget and Policy Priorities, apart from Homeland Security, non-defense discretionary spending is to be cut by $125 billion over 5 years or an average of 10% per program. Among other things, deep cuts are proposed to Section 202 housing for low income elderly and Section 811 housing for low income individuals with disabilities [241C].

6. New York University (NYU), subsequently founded in 1830, viewed itself as the democratic alternative to more elitist and Episcopalian, Columbia University. Ironically, New York City's first secular college deemed it impossible to permit a Jew to teach Hebrew. Consequently, a renowned Hebrew scholar was passed over, in favor of the pedestrian (but Christian) George Bush. The President is the descendant of that NYU professor's uncle, Timothy [28F].

7. Legal citations for the cases in this Chapter are as follows: *Bradfield v. Roberts*, 175 U.S. 291 (1899); *Capital Square Review and Advisory Board v. Pinette*, 114 S. Ct. 2481 (1995) ; *Church of Holy Trinity v. US* (1892); *Edwards v. Arkansas*, 482 U.S. 578 (1987); *Epperson v. Arkansas*, 393 U.S. 97 (1968); *Everson v. Board of Education*, 330 U.S. 1 (1947); *Kitzmiller, et al. v. Dover Area School District* (Docket No. 04–2688) US District Ct., Middle District of PA (2005); *Lee v. Wessman*, 505 U.S. 577 (1992); *Lemon v.*

Kurtzman, 403 U.S. 602 (1971); *Marsh v. Chambers*; 463 U.S. 783 (1983); *North Carolina Civil Liberties Union Legal Foundation v. Constangy*, 947 F.2d 1145 (4th Cir. 1991), cert. denied, 505 U.S. 1219 (1992); *Van Orden v. Perry* 351 F.3d 173, affirmed; *Vidal v. Girard's Executors* (1844).

8. A great deal of ignorance and confusion have developed over the distinction between a) teaching religious tenets (for the purpose of conversion); and b) teaching *about* religion and freedom of religion, e.g. about the impact of religion on America's immigration policy. In an attempt to help clarify matters, the US Dept. of Education in 2000 distributed to public schools across the country guidelines on the freedom of religion rights of students, the relationship between public schools and religious minded-communities, and the role of religion in the public school curriculum [206T].

9. For reference purposes, the Ten Commandments may found at **Appendix IV**.

10. A detailed list of the hundreds of individual Messianic prophecies fulfilled by Jesus Christ is *attached* at **Appendix VIII**. Also, provided is a discussion of the mathematic probability of any one man fulfilling all these prophecies.

11. Only 5–7% of women commonly seek abortions for rape, incest, or to save their own lives [173D].

12. There are Christian organizations which do offer practical help and hope to women contemplating abortion. I do not mean to overlook or disparage these.

13. "[Left unaltered] Bush's [2006] budget [would have shifted] at least $60 billion in Medicaid costs to the states over 10 years. This level of cuts . . . [would] almost certainly [have] push[ed] hard-pressed states to eliminate coverage for a substantial number of low-income people, increasing the ranks of the uninsured and underinsured. The magnitude of the [proposed] cuts . . . [would] also [have] increase[d] the already heavy uncompensated care burdens for hospitals and other providers [71] . . ."

14. This is *not*, by the way, to imply that women must cease employment outside the home or take up abusive relationships—in physical danger and dependent for their exclusive support and survival upon men (many of whom may never, themselves, have experienced genuine love and commitment). The Bible does not condone abuse, by either sex.

15. This applies to the support provided by Christian law students and paralegals, also.

16. This Initiative was actually launched while President George W. Bush was still governor.

17. Cotton Mather overlooked Moses' second marriage (Numbers 12: 1–10). This was inter-racial, to a Black woman. We are told that Moses' siblings, Miriam and Aaron, "*spoke against Moses because of the Ethiopian woman whom he had married.*" Their rebelliousness stemmed from the fact the woman was a foreigner and of another race. However, in view of God's statement that Moses was "*faithful in all My house*," the Ethiopian woman had been made part of the covenant. The consequence was that "*the anger of the Lord burned against*" Miriam and Aaron. In what seems a particularly fitting judgment, the Lord punished Miriam with leprosy which made her "*as white as snow* [148]."

18. Legal citations for the cases in this Chapter are as follows: *Brown v. Board of Education*, 347 US 483 (1954); *Dred Scott v. Sandford*, 19 How. 393 (1857); *Plessy v. Ferguson*, 163 US 537 (1896).

19. The Christian attorney providing legal aid, in this context, must be prepared to face hostility. Because racism is a reality in our society, some clients will have experienced years of rejection and may attempt to "test" the legal professional by presenting in a hostile manner. Others will feign indifference to the process or their own welfare. Still others may have been so often defeated, it is very nearly an overwhelming challenge for them to reach out for assistance at all. This "testing" should not provoke the Christian professional to anger, but rather be recognized for what

it is, i.e. a mask for fear either of the legal process or of further rejection.

20. Theory (developed by Episcopal priest, Joseph Fletcher based on "agape" love) that the morality of an act is a function of the state of the system at the time it was performed [103].

21. Theory that there is no universal moral truth [104].

22. This is a weak approach, even with teens.

23. Authorization for Use of Military Force (Pub. L. 107–40, 115 Stat. 224 (2001).

24. Legal citations for the cases in this Chapter are as follows: *Korematsu v. US,* 323 U.S. 214 (1944) ; *NLRB v. Robbins Tire Co.* 437 US 214 (1978); and *Youngstown Sheet and Tube Co. v. Sawyer* 343 US 579 (1952).

25. Samuel Sewall, English-born Harvard graduate when appointed in 1692 to Massachusetts' new Court of Oyer and Terminer, that year achieved celebrity status with the nineteen death sentences of the witches of Salem. In 1697, Sewall made further news with an act of public contrition for those convictions [81].

26. Legal citations for the cases in this Chapter are as follows: *Brandenburg v. Ohio*, 395 US 444 (1969); *Chaplinsky v. New Hampshire*, 315 U.S. 568 (1942); *National Socialist Party v. Skokie*, 432 U.S. 43 (1977); *Planned Parenthood of the Columbia/Willamette, Inc. v. American Coalition of Life Activists,* 244 F.3d 1007 (9th Cir. 2001); *RAV v. City of St. Paul* 505 U.S. 307 (1992); and *Wisconsin v. Mitchell*, 508 U.S. 476 (1993).

27. *See*, Department of Defense Directive 5100.77, DoD Law of War Program, 9 December 1998 at paragraph 5.3.1.

28. The civilian deaths at Haditha on November 19, 2005 (still under investigation, as of this writing) bear out the need for the Soldier's Rules.

29. The full text of Bishop Gregory's letter may be found at http://

www.mtholyoke.edu/acad/intrel/bush/bishops.htm. For convenience, a copy is *attached* at **Appendix VI**.

30. According to Jari A. Villanueva (curator for the "Taps Bugle Exhibit" at Arlington National Cemetery from 1999–2002, and foremost authority on the subject) at jvmusic@erols.com the bugle call "Taps" was adapted from an older tune by Gen. Daniel Butterfield for the men of the Third Brigade, First Division, Fifth Army Corps, Army of the Potomac, in 1862. It soon spread to both Union and Confederate units. There are no official words to "Taps." The verse here is among the most popular. Butterfield later received the Medal of Honor for service beyond the call of duty at the Battle of Gaines Mill.

31. The full text of "Rebuilding America's Defenses—A Report of the Project for the New American Century" can be located at http://www.informationclearinghouse.info/pdf/RebuildingAmericasDefenses.pdf .

32. A detailed analysis by Bette Stockbauer entitled, "Rebuilding America's Defenses—A Summary" can be located on *Information Clearing House* at http://www.informationclearinghouse.info/article3249.htm.

33. The Concord Coalition is jointly chaired by Republican Warren Rudman and Democrat Bob Kerrey. Senator Rudman, in addition to many other accomplishments, co-authored the Gramm-Rudman-Hollings Deficit Reduction Law, a critical step toward imposing structure on the federal budget process for the purpose of reducing the deficit. Former Senator Kerrey, also well-accomplished, served on the Finance and Appropriations Committees, as well as on the Kerrey-Danforth Bipartisan Commission on Entitlement and Tax Reform and the Breaux-Thomas National Bipartisan Commission on the Future of Medicare. Former Secretary of Commerce, Peter Peterson (a previous Chairman of Lehman Brothers and of the Federal Reserve Bank of New York) serves as President of the Coalition.

34. Though this has been used extensively overseas, it has not been

tried to any large extent in the US. With accountability built into the program, it might be an approach worth exploring. Difficulties with credit are endemic among our poor (and growing among the lower middle-class). However, given that the cost of living here is much higher than in the Third World, larger amounts by way of working capital would have to be extended in the US than overseas.

35. For those who may be interested, donations to *The Voice of the Martyrs* can be made online at http://www.persecution.com or mailed to *The Voice of the Martyrs*, PO Box 443 Bartlesville, OK 74005